STUDY GUIDE TO ACCOMPANY

ADVANCED ACCOUNTING

Concepts and Practice

FIFTH EDITION

ARNOLD J. PAHLER

San Jose Stae Universtiy

The Dryden Press
Harcourt Brace College Publishers

Fort Worth   Philadelphia   San Diego   New York   Orlando   Austin   San Antonio
Toronto   Montreal   London   Sydney   Tokyo

Address for Editorial Correspondence
The Dryden Press, 301 Commerce Street, Suite 3700, Fort Worth, TX 76102

Address for Orders
The Dryden Press, 6277 Sea Harbor Drive, Orlando, FL 32887
1-800-782-4479, or 1-800-433-0001 (in Florida)

ISBN: 0-03-003593-7

Printed in the United States of America

4 5 6 7 8 9 0 1 2 3   095   9 8 7 6 5 4 3 2 1

The Dryden Press
Harcourt Brace College Publishers

TO THE STUDENT

This Study Guide was prepared to assist you as you work through *Advanced Accounting: Concepts and Practice,* Fifth Edition. Each of its 29 chapters corresponds to the textbook chapter and contains approximately 65 study items that are grouped into the following sections:

> Chapter Highlights
> Completion Statements
> True-or-False Statements
> Conceptual Multiple-Choice Questions
> Application Multiple-Choice Questions
> Problems (for Chapters 4–6 only)

Chapter Highlights. These highlights (about 25 per chapter) are an expanded summary of the major points of each chapter. (They supplement the textbook's Summary of Key Points contained in the End-of-Chapter Review section of each chapter.)

Completion Statements. The completion statements assess your knowledge of key terms and concepts. (A Glossary of new terms is contained in each End-of-Chapter Review section.)

True-or-False Statements and Multiple-Choice Questions. These questions test your ability to recall material and also give you practice in taking tests. Many of the multiple-choice questions included are reflective of the type of multiple-choice questions that appear on the CPA examination. (The multiple-choice questions supplement the Self-Study Questions contained in each End-of-Chapter Review section.)

Problems (for Chapters 4–6). The purpose of these comprehensive problems is to allow you to work with fresh data as you apply the conceptual issues of the chapter. (These problems are similar to the comprehensive Demonstration Problems contained in the End-of-Chapter Review sections of Chapters 4–6.)

Recommended Approach. Before using this Study Guide, you should thoroughly read the applicable chapter in the textbook. Then work through all the End-of-Chapter Review material. If you miss any of the Self-Study Questions, refer to the textbook to determine the correct answer. After you have satisfied yourself that you have demonstrated a basic understanding of the chapter, proceed with the Study Guide. For completion statements, true-or-false statements, and multiple-choice questions that you answer incorrectly, again refer to the relevant discussion in the textbook. As a final test of your mastery of the material, we suggest you write out the major points of the chapter. Afterwards, compare your summary to the Chapter Highlights listed in the Study Guide. We highly recommend this last step as it has been shown that active writing is also beneficial in retaining new subject material.

Arnold J. Pahler

CONTENTS

CHAPTER 1

INTERNAL EXPANSION: ACCOUNTING FOR WHOLLY OWNED CREATED SUBSIDIARIES AT DATE OF CREATION

CHAPTER HIGHLIGHTS

1. A business may expand or diversify through **internal expansion** or **external expansion.**

2. A new operation being created by internal expansion may be organized as a **subsidiary** (a separate legal entity) or a **branch** or **division** (an extension of the existing legal entity).

3. External expansion is when a company combines with another existing business (called a **business combination**).

4. To limit the existing operation's **potential loss exposure** to the amount it has invested in the new operation, an internally expanding company may choose the subsidiary form of organization.

5. **Income tax considerations** generally favor the subsidiary form of organization over the branch form of organization when expanding overseas.

6. A foreign subsidiary's income is taxed by the Internal Revenue Service **when the parent receives dividends,** whereas a foreign branch's earnings are taxed **when earned.**

7. To **retain patent or copyright protection** being transferred to an overseas operation, the **branch form of organization** is used for the overseas operation (often a branch of a newly created U.S. subsidiary).

8. A **parent-subsidiary relationship** exists whenever one company owns **more than 50%** of the outstanding common stock of another company.

9. **Consolidated financial statements** are the financial statements of a parent and its subsidiary that have been added together in a manner that portrays the resulting financial statements **as if they were the financial statements of a single company.**

10. Consolidated statements are **pro forma statements.** The separate legal entity status of the parent and the subsidiary is disregarded.

11. Consolidated statements constitute the **general-purpose financial statements** of companies having one or more subsidiaries, that is, statements to be furnished to a parent's stockholders when a parent-subsidiary relationship exists.

12. Two manners of presenting consolidated statements are (A) a **disaggregated** "layered" reporting approach and (B) an **aggregated** "unlayered" reporting approach.

13. In the **disaggregated format,** the subsidiary's assets and liabilities are **shown separately** from the parent's assets and liabilities in a **layered** (tiered, stacked, or pancake) manner. (This format makes most sense when the parent and subsidiary are in different lines of business.)

14. In the **aggregated format**, the subsidiary's assets and liabilities are **summed,** thus presenting only one amount for each asset, liability, and income statement account. (This format makes most sense when the parent and subsidiary are in the same line of business.)

15. A **consolidation worksheet** is necessary to prepare consolidated statements because **a general ledger is not kept for the consolidated reporting entity.**

16. **Consolidation worksheets** are just as much a part of the **books and records** of the parent company as its general ledger.

17. **Consolidation worksheet entries** (usually called elimination entries) are **never** posted to a general ledger.

18. The Investment in Subsidiary account and the subsidiary's equity accounts (Common Stock and Additional Paid-in Capital) have a **reciprocal balance relationship.**

19. Under *SFAS No. 94,* **all** subsidiaries are consolidated unless (A) **control is lacking** or (B) **control is expected to be temporary**.

20. *SFAS No. 94* (issued in 1987) eliminated the **nonhomogeneity exception** previously allowed.

21. Under the rules of the Securities and Exchange Commission, a publicly owned company may be deemed to have control over an entity by means **other than majority ownership** of the voting interest.

22. In preparing consolidated statements, all **intercompany transactions** are eliminated (undone) just as if none of the intercompany transactions had occurred.

23. Because of the limitation of consolidated statements, *SFAS No. 14* requires specified information on **industry segments** and **foreign operations**.

24. When a subsidiary **cannot distribute some or all of its earnings** to its parent (such as a result of borrowing arrangements, regulatory restraints, or foreign government actions), disclosures of the restrictions may be needed depending on the extent of the restrictions.

COMPLETION STATEMENTS

1. The process of **combining** the financial statements of a parent and a subsidiary is called _____ .

2. A parent **cannot** consolidate a subsidiary when the parent does not have _____ _____ .

3. A parent **need not** consolidate a subsidiary if control is expected to be _____ _____ .

4. The two manners of reporting a subsidiary's financial statements in the consolidated statements are the _____ format and the _____ _____ format.

5. Consolidated statements constitute the _____ financial statements for reporting to the parent's stockholders.

6. Consolidated statements are prepared using a(n) _____ _____ .

7. The entries made in consolidation are commonly called _____ _____ .

8. The parent's Investment in Subsidiary account has a(n) _____ _____ relationship to the subsidiary's equity accounts.

9. In parent-subsidiary relationships, accounts having a debit balance on one set of books and a credit balance on the other set of books are commonly referred to as the _____ accounts.

10. Consolidation is essentially a(n) _____ process.

TRUE-OR-FALSE STATEMENTS

1. T F It is **inappropriate** to consolidate a foreign subsidiary.

2. T F It is **appropriate** to consolidate a subsidiary in a different line of business from the parent and its other subsidiaries.

3. T F When a subsidiary is consolidated, the separate financial statements of the subsidiary **must** also be presented as supplemental information to the consolidated statements.

4. T F It is **inappropriate** to consolidate a subsidiary that is in such severe financial difficulty that it has filed for bankruptcy reorganization.

5. T F It **may** be necessary to consolidate a company in which the investor company does **not** own a majority voting interest.

6. T   F   The only way to determine if control exists is by determining if a majority of the voting common stock is owned.

7. T   F   The consolidation rules of the SEC do not apply to **nonpublicly owned** companies.

8. T   F   **All** intercompany transactions must be eliminated in consolidation.

9. T   F   Elimination entries are **never** posted to a general ledger.

10. T   F   A general ledger is **not** maintained for the consolidated entity.

11. T   F   When a subsidiary is in a **different line of business** than the parent and its other subsidiaries, the **disaggregated reporting format** must be used in presenting the consolidated statements.

12. T   F   A foreign subsidiary that **cannot pay dividends** because of restraints imposed by the foreign government would still be consolidated in most cases.

13. T   F   It would be **inappropriate** to consolidate a subsidiary that has **not** yet become profitable.

14. T   F   It would be inappropriate to consolidate a subsidiary that is prohibited by law from making loans to its parent.

15. T   F   A subsidiary can be consolidated only if it has the **same year-end** as its parent company.

MULTIPLE-CHOICE QUESTIONS

Conceptual Questions

1. A reason for using the branch form of organization instead of the subsidiary form of organization is
   a. It better insulates legally the existing operation from the new operation.
   b. It better limits the ability of foreign taxing authorities to examine the books and records of the domestic operation.
   c. A foreign unit's earnings are not taxed in the United States until remitted to the domestic unit.
   d. Patent protection can better be maintained when establishing a new operation in a foreign country that has no protection laws.
   e. None of the above.

2. Which of the following is the rationale for preparing consolidated statements of a parent company and its subsidiary?
   a. In form and substance, the companies are one company.
   b. In form and substance, the companies are separate companies.
   c. In form, the companies are one company. In substance, they are separate.
   d. In form, the companies are separate. In substance they are one company.
   e. None of the above.

3. Which of the following is an allowable reason for **not consolidating** a subsidiary?
    a. The subsidiary is not under the control of the parent company.
    b. The subsidiary is in a separate line of business from that of the parent.
    c. The subsidiary is a foreign subsidiary.
    d. Applicable state law prohibits the subsidiary from making loans to its parent company.
    e. None of the above.

4. Each of the following is a valid explanation for a subsidiary **not being under the control** of the parent company **except**
    a. The subsidiary has filed for bankruptcy protection.
    b. The subsidiary is located in a foreign country that has imposed severe currency transfer restrictions.
    c. Applicable state laws prohibit the subsidiary from making loans to the parent company.
    d. The subsidiary is effectively managed by a foreign government.
    e. None of the above.

5. Which of the following is a valid reason for **not consolidating** a subsidiary?
    a. The subsidiary has not yet become profitable.
    b. The subsidiary's liabilities equal its assets.
    c. Under federal regulatory rules, the subsidiary is restricted from distributing more than 25% of its retained earnings as dividends.
    d. A significant percentage of the subsidiary's profits result from intercompany inventory sales to the parent company.
    e. None of the above.

6. Which of the following is a valid reason for **not consolidating** a subsidiary?
    a. The parent (publicly owned) controls the subsidiary by means other than a majority ownership in the voting interest.
    b. The parent is taking steps to sell the subsidiary.
    c. The parent has established a policy of having the subsidiary reinvest all of its earnings for expansion purposes.
    d. The subsidiary is consistently losing money.
    e. None of the above.

7. The **disaggregated reporting format** makes the most sense when the subsidiary is
    a. In a different line of business than the parent.
    b. Restricted from paying dividends to the parent by regulatory authorities.
    c. Located in a foreign country.
    d. Losing money.
    e. None of the above.

8. From a **consolidated perspective,** the subsidiary's outstanding common stock is viewed as
    a. Potentially dilutive shares.
    b. Treasury stock.
    c. Restricted securities.
    d. An equity investment.
    e. None of the above.

CHAPTER 1—SOLUTIONS

Completion Statements

1. consolidation
2. control
3. temporary
4. aggregated, disaggregated
5. general-purpose
6. consolidation worksheet
7. elimination entries
8. reciprocal balance
9. intercompany
10. substitution

True-or-False Statements

1. False	9. True
2. True	10. True
3. False	11. False
4. True	12. False
5. True	13. False
6. False	14. False
7. True	15. False
8. True	

Multiple-Choice Questions

1. d	5. e
2. d	6. b
3. a	7. a
4. c	8. b

CHAPTER 2

INTERNAL EXPANSION: ACCOUNTING FOR WHOLLY OWNED CREATED SUBSIDIARIES SUBSEQUENT TO DATE OF CREATION

CHAPTER HIGHLIGHTS

1. The two methods available for valuing investments in common stock of subsidiaries are the **equity method** and the **cost method.**

2. Regardless of how a parent accounts for its investment in a subsidiary, the **consolidated amounts** are the **same.**

3. The general idea of the **equity method** is that the subsidiary's earnings **belong** to the parent.

4. The **equity method** of valuing an investment in a subsidiary is analogous to the **accrual basis** of accounting in that it reflects the **result** of the economic activities that have occurred at the subsidiary.

5. Under the **equity method,** all dividends declared by the subsidiary (except stock dividends) are treated as a **liquidation** of the investment.

6. Under the **equity method,** the carrying value of the investment is decreased when the subsidiary **declares dividends**—not when it pays dividends.

7. The valuation produced under the **equity method** is not intended to equal the market value of the subsidiary's common stock.

8. The parent stops applying the **equity method** when the subsidiary has exhausted its equity—**unless** the parent is obligated to invest additional funds in the subsidiary to satisfy a potential deficiency to creditors.

9. Under the **cost method,** the earnings of the subsidiary are ignored. The parent reports **investment income** only when the subsidiary **declares dividends,** which the parent reports as Dividend Income.

10. Under the **cost method,** the parent's investment is written down if **serious doubt exists** as to realization of the investment. Any **write-down** made is **permanent.**

11. From the parent's perspective, the **cost method** is unsound.

12. A parent's financial statements are meaningful **internally** only if the **equity method** is used.

13. The **equity method** provides a **built-in self-checking feature** in the consolidation process (consolidated net income equals the parent's net income).

14. When the parent uses the **equity method, all** of the subsidiary's retained earnings are eliminated in consolidation.

15. When the parent uses the **cost method,** the subsidiary's retained earnings (obviously being "undistributed") are added to the parent's retained earnings in preparing consolidated statements.

16. When **parent-company-only statements** are presented in **notes to the consolidated statements** (usually necessary for financial institution subsidiaries of holding companies), the only sensible way to value the parent's Investment in Subsidiary account is the **equity method.**

17. If a subsidiary is **not consolidated** (which is only possible if control does not exist or control is expected to be temporary), then **either** the equity method or the cost method may be used, all **depending on** which is more appropriate in light of why the subsidiary is not consolidated.

18. When a subsidiary is **not consolidated,** and is reported under the **equity method,** the equity method is viewed as a "one-line consolidation."

19. All **intercompany receivables and payables** are eliminated in consolidation.

20. **Intercompany allocations** are usually necessary to properly evaluate the profitability of subsidiaries.

COMPLETION STATEMENTS

1. The two methods of accounting for an investment in a subsidiary are the _____ _____ method and the _____ method.

2. The conceptually correct method of accounting for an investment in a subsidiary is the _____ method.

3. For income tax reporting purposes, the _____ is used in determining when a parent must pay income taxes on the earnings of a subsidiary.

4. Under the **equity method** of accounting, the parent's investment income is appropriately described in the parent's income statement as _____ .

5. Under the **cost method** of accounting, the parent's investment income is appropriately described in the parent's income statement as _____ .

6. Under the **equity method** of accounting, all dividends declared by the subsidiary are treated as a(n) _____ of the parent's investment.

7. Financial statements of the parent that are presented **in notes to the consolidated statements** are called _____ statements.

TRUE-OR-FALSE STATEMENTS

1. T   F   If a subsidiary **is consolidated,** it must be accounted for using the equity method.

2. T   F   Under the equity method, **all** dividends (except stock dividends) declared by the subsidiary are treated as a liquidation of the investment.

3. T   F   Under the **cost method,** the investment account is not reduced for dividends declared by the subsidiary.

4. T   F   Under the **cost method,** the investment account is reduced for dividends when they are received—not when they are paid.

5. T   F   Whether the equity method or the cost method is used to account for an investment in a subsidiary, the consolidated statements are always identical.

6. T   F   The parent's net income equals the consolidated net income only if the parent accounts for its investment in the subsidiary using the **equity method.**

7. T   F   To properly calculate the return on its investment in a subsidiary, the parent must use the carrying value produced under the **equity method.**

8. T   F   When a parent accounts for its investment in a subsidiary using the **equity method,** only the subsidiary's undistributed retained earnings are added to the parent's retained earnings in consolidation.

9. T   F   When a parent accounts for its investment in a subsidiary using the **cost method,** the subsidiary's retained earnings are added to the parent's retained earnings in consolidation.

10. T   F   If the subsidiary is **not consolidated,** the parent can arbitrarily choose between either the equity method or the cost method.

11. T   F   If the subsidiary is **not consolidated,** the equity method can be used only if significant influence exists.

12. T   F   Parent-company-only statements must be included in notes to consolidated statements under *SFAS No. 94.*

MULTIPLE-CHOICE QUESTIONS

Conceptual Questions

1. The **equity method** of accounting for an investment in the common stock of another company **cannot** be used when
   a. The ownership interest exceeds 50%.
   b. The ownership interest is at least 20% but not over 50%.
   c. The ownership interest is above 50% but the parent no longer controls the subsidiary.
   d. The subsidiary's retained earnings become negative.
   e. None of the above.

2. Which of the following statements is false concerning the **equity method** of accounting?
   a. All dividends (except stock dividends) declared by the subsidiary are treated as a liquidation of the investment.
   b. The difference between the equity method and consolidation is the amount of detail reported in the parent's separate statements.
   c. The equity method may be used when a parent company no longer controls a subsidiary providing the parent company is able to exert significant influence.
   d. Dividends are credited to the investment account at their declaration date rather than at the date received.
   e. None of the above.

3. Which of the following statements is **not** one of the merits or features of the **equity method** of accounting?
   a. It is analogous to the accrual basis of accounting.
   b. It provides a built-in self-checking feature in preparing consolidated statements.
   c. It is a logical method for profitable subsidiaries and unprofitable subsidiaries.
   d. It results in an overly conservative valuation of the investment account when a subsidiary has substantial undistributed earnings.
   e. None of the above.

4. Which of the following statements is false concerning the **cost method** of accounting for an investment in a subsidiary?
   a. It may be used when the subsidiary is no longer under the control of the parent.
   b. The carrying value of the investment may be written down below cost.
   c. The carrying value of the investment may be written back up to its original cost subsequent to a write-down below original cost.
   d. Dividends are never treated as a reduction to the carrying value of the investment.
   e. None of the above.

Application Questions

5. On March 31, 19X1, P Company created a wholly owned subsidiary, S Company, with a cash investment of $600,000 in S Company's common stock. For 19X1, S Company had net income of $30,000 each quarter. Also for 19X1, S Company declared and paid cash dividends of $20,000 for each quarter. What is P Company's carrying value of its investment in S Company at December 31, 19X1, under the **equity method?**

    a. $600,000
    b. $630,000
    c. $660,000
    d. $690,000
    e. None of the above.

6. Use the same information as in Question 5. What is the carrying value of the investment in S Company at December 31, 19X1, under the **cost method?**

    a. $600,000
    b. $630,000
    c. $660,000
    d. $690,000
    e. None of the above.

7. Use the same information as in Question 5. What amount appears in P Company's 19X1 separate income statement if P Company accounts for its investment in S Company under the **equity method?**

    a. $-0-
    b. $30,000
    c. $60,000
    d. $90,000
    e. None of the above.

8. Use the same information as in Question 5. What amount appears in P Company's separate 19X1 income statement if P Company accounts for its investment in S Company under the **cost method?**

    a. $-0-
    b. $30,000
    c. $60,000
    d. $80,000
    e. $90,000

9. P Company created S Company on January 1, 19X1, with a $500,000 cash investment. During 19X1, S Company reported $40,000 of net income each quarter. On December 31, 19X1, S Company declared and paid a cash dividend of $120,000. What did the parent earn on its investment during 19X1?

    a. 8% ($40,000/$500,000)
    b. 24% ($120,000/$500,000)
    c. 32% ($160,000/$500,000)
    d. 56% ($280,000/$500,000)
    e. None of the above.

CHAPTER 2—SOLUTIONS

Completion Statements

1. equity, cost
2. equity
3. cash basis
4. equity in net income of subsidiary
5. dividend income
6. liquidation
7. parent-company-only

True-or-False Statements

1. False		6. True
2. True		7. True
3. True		8. False
(only for created		9. True
subsidiaries)		10. False
4. False		11. True
5. True		12. False

Multiple-Choice Questions

1. e
2. b
3. d
4. c
5. b ($600,000 + $90,000 − $60,000 = $630,000)
6. a (original investment of $600,000)
7. d (quarterly earnings of $30,000 × 3 = $90,000)
8. c (quarterly dividends of $20,000 × 3 = $60,000)
9. c

CHAPTER 2—APPENDIX
BRANCH ACCOUNTING

CHAPTER APPENDIX HIGHLIGHTS

1. The **headquarters location** of the legal entity that establishes a branch is referred to as the **home office.**

2. The **outlying location** is commonly referred to as a **branch, division, sales office,** or **store,** all depending on which description is most appropriate.

3. The extent of delegation of **decision-making authority** to outlying management is a **centralization** versus **decentralization** issue.

4. Under a **centralized accounting system,** an outlying location does *not* maintain a separate general ledger in which to record its transactions.

5. Under a **decentralized accounting system,** an outlying location **maintains a separate general ledger** in which to record its transactions.

6. The **Investment in Branch** account is used to keep track and maintain control over (A) the assets transferred to the branch and (B) the increase or decrease in the branch's net assets as a result of the branch's operations.

7. The only equity account used by a branch is the **Home Office Equity** account (a **reciprocal** account to the **Investment in Branch** account).

8. The home office reflects the branch's earnings in its books in an income statement account called **Branch Income** or **Branch Loss.**

9. Branch earnings are viewed as an **operating income** or **loss** because branches do not have interest income, interest expense, or income tax expense.

10. **Fixed assets** of a branch can be recorded on the books of the home office or on the books of the branch. When recorded on the home office books, depreciation expense must be **allocated** to the branch.

11. For **reporting to stockholders,** it is necessary to combine the financial statements of the home office with the financial statements of the branch (using a **combining statement worksheet**).

12. Before the combining statement worksheet is prepared, the **reciprocal** accounts (Investment in Branch and Home Office Equity) **must be in agreement.**

13. The **combining process** is substantively a **substitution process** because: (A) the assets and liabilities of the branch are substituted for the Investment in Branch account in the balance sheet; and (B) the branch's sales, cost of expenses accounts are substituted for the Branch Income account in the income statement.

14. In preparing combined financial statements, a **built-in checking feature** exists because the amounts in the combined column of the worksheet **for net income and retained earnings** will always equal the amounts to be reported in the home office column of the worksheet for these accounts.

COMPLETION STATEMENTS FOR APPENDIX

1. A branch that does **not maintain** a general ledger is said to use a(n) _____ _____ accounting system.

2. A branch that **does maintain** a general ledger is said to use a(n) _____ _____ accounting system.

3. Another term for **intracompany** accounts is _____ accounts.

4. The Investment in Branch account is maintained in a manner that keeps the balance equal to the branch's _____ .

5. The home office records the branch's earnings in an account called _____ _____ .

TRUE-OR-FALSE STATEMENTS FOR APPENDIX

1. T F Under a decentralized accounting system, the fixed assets of a branch **cannot** be maintained or recorded on the books of the home office.

2. T F Under a decentralized accounting system, income taxes on branch earnings are recorded on the books of the branch.

3. T F Home office allocations to a branch have **no** effect on earnings reported to stockholders.

4. T F Earnings reported by a branch are best described as being an **operating income or loss** rather than a **net income or loss.**

5. T F The basic elimination entry is **never** posted to the general ledger.

6. T F Recording branch earnings on the home office's books is analogous to applying the **equity method of accounting** to the earnings of an **investee.**

MULTIPLE-CHOICE QUESTIONS FOR APPENDIX

Conceptual Questions

1. Which of the following accounts is not an **intracompany** account?
    a. Home Office Equity.
    b. Investment in Branch.
    c. Receivable from Branch.
    d. Branch Income.
    e. None of the above.

2. In preparing the combining statement worksheet, which of the following accounts is **not eliminated** (brought to a zero balance in the combined column)?
    a. Branch Income.
    b. Home Office Equity.
    c. Payable to Home Office.
    d. Investment in Branch.
    e. None of the above.

CHAPTER 2—SOLUTIONS FOR APPENDIX

Completion Statements

1. centralized
2. decentralized
3. reciprocal
4. net assets
5. branch income

True-or-False Statements

1. False
2. False
3. True

4. True
5. True
6. True

Multiple-Choice Questions

1. d
2. e

CHAPTER 3
INTRODUCTION TO BUSINESS COMBINATIONS

CHAPTER HIGHLIGHTS

1. Bringing together two separate businesses under common ownership is known as a **business combination.**

2. Whether a business combination is categorized as a **vertical, horizontal,** or **conglomerate** combination has no bearing on how the combination is recorded for financial reporting purposes.

3. The two basic methods of accounting for business combinations are the **pooling of interests method** and the **purchase method.**

4. For a given set of circumstances, only one of the methods will apply.

5. Twelve specific conditions **must** be met for a pooling of interests to be allowed.

6. If all twelve conditions are met, then the pooling of interests method **must** be used.

7. If any of the twelve conditions is not met, then the purchase method **must** be used.

8. The theory underlying **pooling of interests accounting** is that a sale or purchase of a business has **not** occurred.

9. The underlying concept of the **purchase method** is that one company has acquired the business of another company and a sale has occurred.

10. A business combination can be achieved by acquiring the target company's **assets** or the target company's **outstanding common stock.**

11. Many circumstances affect whether the acquiring company should acquire **assets** or **common stock** of the target company.

12. The major **disadvantage** to acquiring common stock is that the acquiring company inherits any unidentified or unknown liabilities of the target company.

13. When the target company's assets are acquired, the acquiring company usually **assumes responsibility** for paying the target company's **recorded liabilities.**

14. When assets are acquired, the newly acquired business is normally referred to as a **division** of the acquiring company.

15. When the target company's common stock is acquired, a **parent-subsidiary** relationship is established.

16. In a **stock-for-stock exchange,** the **exchange ratio** is the number of common shares issued by the acquiring company for each outstanding common share of the target company surrendered.

17. In a **statutory merger,** the target company's equity securities are retired and the corporate existence of the target company is terminated.

18. For income tax reporting purposes, a combination is treated as either a **taxable** combination or a **tax-deferrable** (tax-free) combination.

19. In a **taxable** combination, the buyer **changes the basis of accounting** for what was acquired, whereas the seller reports a gain or loss on the sale for tax purposes.

20. In a **tax-free combination,** no change in basis results and no gain or loss is reportable for tax purposes.

21. Since 1986 there has been virtually no incentive to acquire a company merely because of its **net operating loss carryforward.**

22. The **negotiating position** of the owners of the target business is usually shaped by **income tax considerations.**

23. The **negotiating position** of the acquiring company may be shaped by income tax considerations or financial reporting considerations **depending on management philosophy.**

24. For income tax reporting purposes, the **"taxable" versus "tax-free" terminology** focuses on the impact on the seller (even though there is an impact on the buyer as to whether the buyer can change the basis of accounting for the target company's assets).

25. For financial reporting purposes, the **"purchase" versus "pooling of interests" terminology** focuses on the impact on the acquiring company as to whether it can change the basis of accounting for the target company's assets (even though there is an impact on the target company or its shareholders from a financial reporting perspective).

COMPLETION STATEMENTS

1. The company whose business is being sought is often called the _____ _____ company.

2. Business combinations can be categorized as _____ , _____ _____ , or _____ .

3. An alternative to making a **tender offer** is to seek control in a(n) _____ _____ .

4. The acquisition of a target company's assets or common stock in which the acquirer uses an extremely high percentage of debt to pay for the acquisition is a(n) _____ .

5. The two basic methods of accounting for business combinations are the _____ _____ method and the _____ method.

6. A business may be acquired by acquiring _____ or acquiring _____ .

7. When a target company's assets have been acquired, the acquired operation is normally referred to as a(n) _____ .

8. A company owning more than 50% of the outstanding common stock of another company is referred to as the _____ of that company.

9. A company whose outstanding common stock is more than 50% owned by another company is referred to as a(n) _____ of that company.

10. A corporation that has no revenue-producing operations of its own and only investments in subsidiaries is called a(n) _____ .

11. A business combination in which the target company's corporate existence is terminated is called a(n) _____ .

12. A business combination in which both of the combining companies simultaneously cease their separate corporate existences takes place in a(n) _____ _____ .

13. For business combinations in which the seller does not have to report any profit or pay income taxes on the sale of the business, the Internal Revenue Code refers to such transactions as _____ .

14. A "tax-free" combination is more properly described as a(n) _____ _____ combination.

TRUE-OR-FALSE STATEMENTS

1. T F For a given set of conditions, **either** the purchase method **or** the pooling of interests method may be used to record a business combination.

2. T F To qualify for pooling of interests treatment, a business combination **must** be nontaxable for income tax reporting purposes.

3. T F Goodwill is **never** created when a business combination is recorded using pooling of interests accounting.

4. T F If all 12 conditions for pooling of interests treatment are met, then the combination **must** be accounted for as a pooling of interests.

5.   T   F   Under *APB Opinion No. 17,* "Intangible Assets," goodwill must be amortized over 40 years.

6.   T   F   Under the purchase method of accounting, a target company's assets **must** be revalued to their current values.

7.   T   F   When the target company's common stock is acquired, the acquiring company has the option of assuming the target company's liabilities.

8.   T   F   To obtain pooling of interests accounting treatment, a common stock for common stock exchange must occur.

9.   T   F   To obtain pooling of interests accounting treatment, it is necessary to issue common stock as the consideration given to effect the combination.

10.   T   F   When a target company has contingent liabilities as a result of lawsuits pending, the acquiring company can best insulate itself from becoming responsible for such liabilities by acquiring assets of the target company.

11.   T   F   The best way to force out dissenting shareholders is to use pooling of interests accounting.

12.   T   F   Centralized accounting versus decentralized accounting is an issue only when assets are acquired.

13.   T   F   The Investment in Subsidiary account would **never** be used if the assets of the target company were acquired.

14.   T   F   The underlying concept of a taxable combination is that a **sale** has occurred.

15.   T   F   If a business combination is taxable for tax reporting purposes, it will **always** be a purchase for financial reporting purposes.

16.   T   F   The "change in basis" issue is described as a purchase versus pooling of interests issue for financial reporting and described as a taxable or nontaxable issue for tax reporting.

MULTIPLE-CHOICE QUESTIONS

Conceptual Questions

1. Which of the following items is the critical factor in determining whether goodwill is to be reported?
    a. Assets of the target company must be acquired.
    b. Common stock of the target company must be acquired.
    c. Pooling of interests accounting must be used.
    d. Purchase accounting must be used.
    e. None of the above.

2. Which of the following is the critical factor to **not changing** the basis of accounting of the target company's assets for financial reporting purposes?
    a. Acquiring assets of the target company.
    b. Acquiring common stock of the target company.
    c. Pooling of interests accounting must be used.
    d. Purchase accounting must be used.
    e. None of the above.

3. Which of the following terms would **not** be appropriate or be used in or after the acquisition of the target company's **common stock?**
    a. Exchange ratio.
    b. Parent company.
    c. Shell company.
    d. Subsidiary company.
    e. None of the above.

4. Which of the following terms would **not** be appropriate or would not come into play after the acquisition of a target company's assets?
    a. Subsidiary.
    b. Division.
    c. Nonoperating company.
    d. Shell company.
    e. None of the above.

5. To force out a small percentage of a target company's shareholders who are likely to object to the business combination, the acquiring company would most likely
    a. Acquire common stock.
    b. Effect a statutory merger.
    c. Effect a statutory consolidation.
    d. Form a holding company.
    e. None of the above.

6. Which of the following factors would **favor acquiring common stock** of the target company versus acquiring assets of the target company?
    a. The target company has substantial contingent liabilities.
    b. The target company is a party to a contract that cannot be assigned.
    c. The acquiring company desires access to the target company's cash and highly liquid short-term investments.
    d. The target company has a segment that the acquiring company does not want.
    e. None of the above.

7. The significance to the buyer of a business combination that is **taxable** for tax reporting purposes is
    a. The buyer may have to report goodwill.
    b. The buyer reports a loss equal to the seller's gain.
    c. The buyer is allowed to change the basis of accounting of the target company's assets for tax reporting purposes.
    d. The buyer will be able to utilize the target company's net operating loss carryover.
    e. None of the above.

8. In a business combination that is **taxable** for tax reporting purposes, which of the following parties would be taxed?

	Buyer	Seller
a.	No	Yes
b.	Yes	No
c.	Yes	Yes
d.	No	No

9. Which of the following **always** results in a business combination structured as an exchange of **common stock for common stock?**

   a. Goodwill.
   b. A home office–division relationship.
   c. Pooling of interests accounting treatment.
   d. Taxable transaction for tax reporting purposes.
   e. None of the above.

10. Which of the following **always** results in a business combination achieved by a **cash for common stock exchange?**

   a. Goodwill.
   b. A parent–subsidiary relationship.
   c. A division.
   d. Pooling of interests accounting treatment.
   e. None of the above.

11. Which of the following **always** results in a business combination in which the target company's **assets are acquired** through the **issuance of common stock?**

   a. Pooling of interests accounting treatment.
   b. Goodwill is never reported.
   c. A parent–subsidiary relationship is formed.
   d. A new basis of accounting is established for the target company's assets.
   e. None of the above.

Application Questions

12. P Company gave $500,000 cash for all of the outstanding common stock of S Company. S Company's net assets have a book value of $400,000 and a current value of $480,000. Which entries would be made in each company's books as a result of this transaction?

	P Company	S Company
a.	Debit Investment in Subsidiary for $500,000.	Make no entry.
b.	Debit Investment in Subsidiary for $480,000.	Make no entry.
c.	Debit Investment in Subsidiary for $500,000.	Credit a Gain account for $100,000.
d.	Debit Investment in Subsidiary for $480,000.	Credit a Gain account for $100,000.
e.	None of the above.	

13. P Company gave $800,000 cash for all of the assets of S Company. S Company's assets had a book value of $700,000 and a current value of $740,000. Which entries would be made in each company's books as a result of this transaction?

P Company	S Company
a. Debit Investment in Subsidiary for $800,000.	Credit a Gain account for $100,000.
b. Debit Goodwill for $60,000.	Credit a Gain account for $100,000.
c. Debit Goodwill for $60,000.	Make no entry.
d. Debit Goodwill for $100,000.	Make no entry.
e. None of the above.	

14. P Company issued 60,000 shares of its $1 par value common stock in exchange for all of the $5 par value outstanding common stock of S Company. S Company's assets had a book value of $700,000 and a current value of $780,000. The transaction did **not** qualify as a pooling of interests. P Company's common stock had a market value of $15 per share. What entry would P Company make in recording the transaction?

    a. Debit various assets for $780,000 and debit Goodwill for $120,000.
    b. Debit Investment in Subsidiary for $780,000 and debit Goodwill for $120,000.
    c. Debit Investment in Subsidiary for $700,000.
    d. Debit Investment in Subsidiary for $900,000.
    e. None of the above.

15. P Company issued 50,000 shares of its $1 par value common stock (market value of $14 per share) for all of the assets of S Company. S Company's assets had a book value of $600,000 and a current value of $630,000. The transaction qualified as a pooling of interests. Which entries would be made in each company's books as a result of this combination?

P Company	S Company
a. Debit various assets for $600,000.	Debit Investment in P Company for $700,000.
b. Debit various assets for $630,000 and debit Goodwill for $70,000.	Debit Investment in P Company for $700,000.
c. Debit Investment in Subsidiary for $600,000.	Make no entry.
d. Debit Investment in Subsidiary for $700,000.	Make no entry.
e. None of the above.	

CHAPTER 3—SOLUTIONS

Completion Statements

1. target
2. vertical; horizontal; conglomerate
3. proxy contest
4. leveraged buyout
5. purchase; pooling of interests

6. assets; common stock
7. division
8. parent
9. subsidiary
10. holding company
11. statutory merger
12. statutory consolidation
13. tax-free reorganizations
14. tax-deferred

True-or-False Statements

1. False	9. True
2. False	10. True
3. True	11. False
4. True	12. True
5. False	13. True
6. True	14. True
7. False	15. False
8. False	16. True

Multiple-Choice Questions

1. d	9. e
2. c	10. b
3. c	11. e
4. a	12. a
5. b	13. b
6. b	14. d
7. c	15. a
8. a	

CHAPTER 4

THE PURCHASE METHOD OF ACCOUNTING: WHOLLY OWNED SUBSIDIARIES

CHAPTER HIGHLIGHTS

1. In purchase accounting, the acquiring company's cost is based essentially on the **current value** of the consideration given.

2. If the acquiring company's cost exceeds the current value of the target company's net assets, then **goodwill** exists.

3. Goodwill must be amortized over **no more than** 40 years.

4. If the acquiring company's cost is below the current value of the target company's net assets, then a **bargain purchase element** exists.

5. A bargain purchase element must be **extinguished,** if possible, by allocating it against the current value of certain **noncurrent** assets.

6. Any unextinguished bargain purchase element is reported as a **deferred credit** that must be amortized over a period not to exceed 40 years.

7. The total cost of the acquired business includes **direct costs** (directly traceable) incurred in connection with the acquisition (excluding SEC registration costs).

8. The total cost of the acquired business includes the fair value of any **contingent consideration** that is given subsequent to the acquisition date.

9. Contingent consideration based on **security prices** does not result in an increase in the cost of the acquired business above what was recorded at the acquisition date.

10. Contingent consideration is recorded when it becomes **determinable beyond a reasonable doubt** that it will have to be paid.

11. **Goodwill** is **not** deductible for income tax reporting purposes.

12. **Covenants not to compete** are intangible assets similar to goodwill that **are** deductible for income tax reporting purposes.

13. When assets are acquired, the acquiring company has the option of using **centralized** or **decentralized** accounting.

14. For financial reporting purposes, the **book values** of the acquired business's various assets and liabilities as of the combination date become **irrelevant** to the acquiring company.

15. Under **non-push-down accounting,** the subsidiaries' assets and liabilities are revalued to their current values in the consolidation process.

16. Under **push-down accounting,** the subsidiaries' assets and liabilities are revalued to their current values by making adjustments in the subsidiary's general ledger.

17. When an acquired business has unamortized goodwill on its books at the acquisition date, such "old goodwill" is always assumed to have a zero value and is **never** reported in the consolidated balance sheet.

18. Under **non-push-down accounting,** the amounts reported in the financial statements prepared by the subsidiary are **wholly irrelevant amounts** from the parent's perspective.

19. The amortization of excess cost **elimination entry** is essentially a **reclassification entry** made in consolidation.

20. Regardless of the acquisition date, only the **postacquisition** earnings of the subsidiary are included in consolidated net income.

21. Under the **cost method,** dividends declared by the subsidiary that are in excess of postacquisition earnings are recorded as a **liquidating dividend** (reducing the investment account) rather than being credited to Dividend Income.

22. A continual assessment must be made to determine whether subsequent events and circumstances warrant a **write-down** or **write-off** of any unamortized goodwill.

23. In determining whether goodwill should be written down or written off, the professional literature focuses on **recoverability.** Economically, the focus should be on whether there has been a **loss of value.**

COMPLETION STATEMENTS

1. Goodwill is always determined in a(n) _____ manner.

2. When the acquiring company's total cost is **below** the current value of the target company's net assets, a(n) _____ exists.

3. Goodwill is **effectively** deductible for income tax reporting purposes only if _____ are acquired.

4. Some accountants incorrectly refer to an excess of current value **over** cost as _____ rather than as a bargain purchase element.

5. When a subsidiary acquired in a purchase transaction issues separate financial statements and the parent is a publicly owned company, the presentation of the subsidiary's financial statements on the new basis of accounting is called _____ _____ .

6. When a target company's assets are acquired and decentralized accounting is used, the new operation is referred to as a(n) _____ .

7. The reciprocal account of the Investment in Division account is the _____ _____ account.

8. The revaluation of a subsidiary's assets and liabilities to their current values in the consolidation process is called _____ accounting.

9. When the non-push-down basis of accounting is used, the amounts reported in the financial statements prepared by the subsidiary are _____ amounts.

10. In consolidating a subsidiary's income statement with the income statement of the parent, only the _____ earnings of the subsidiary are reported or included in the consolidated net income.

11. Dividends of a subsidiary that exceed postacquisition earnings are called _____ _____ .

12. In assessing whether goodwill should be written down or written off, professional guidance focuses on _____ .

TRUE-OR-FALSE STATEMENTS

1. T F In purchase accounting, the acquired business's preacquisition earnings are **never** combined with the preacquisition earnings of the acquiring company.

2. T F Costs of registering with the Securities and Exchange Commission any securities given as consideration by the acquiring company are **never** added to the acquiring company's total cost.

3. T F The salary and overhead costs of an internal acquisitions department **may** be allocated to the cost of successful acquisitions.

4. T F In determining the cost of the acquired business when equity securities are issued as consideration, the fair value of the equity securities issued is used—regardless if the fair value of the property acquired is more clearly evident.

5. T F Contingencies based on **other than security prices** cannot result in an increase to the cost of the acquired business above what was recorded at the acquisition date.

6. T   F   Contingencies whose outcomes are **not** currently determinable are record-able when the amount is reasonably estimatable and it is probable that the contingent consideration will be paid.

7. T   F   A **covenant not to compete** is tax deductible.

8. T   F   Goodwill is **not** tax deductible.

9. T   F   Bargain purchase elements must be fully extinguished—no remaining deferred credit balance is reportable.

10. T   F   When a bargain purchase element is present, it clearly suggests that the assets are worth **less** individually than as part of a going business.

11. T   F   The Investment in Subsidiary account is **always** eliminated in consolida-tion regardless of whether the parent paid more or less than the current value of the subsidiary's net assets.

12. T   F   Whether common stock or assets are acquired, goodwill is **always** recorded in a separate general ledger account.

13. T   F   If an acquired business has unamortized goodwill on its books at the acquisition date and common stock is acquired, the subsidiary **must** write off the goodwill in its general ledger.

14. T   F   In applying the equity method of accounting, the subsidiary's earnings from the beginning of the parent's year up to the acquisition date are ignored.

15. T   F   Under generally accepted accounting principles, a subsidiary can be marginally profitable and **not** have to write-down or write-off any unamor-tized goodwill.

MULTIPLE-CHOICE QUESTIONS

Conceptual Questions

1. Which of the following statements is false?
   a. Goodwill is determined in a residual manner.
   b. Goodwill must be amortized over 40 years.
   c. A bargain purchase element that is not fully extinguished is reported as a deferred credit (unextinguished portion only).
   d. In purchase accounting, the acquired business's preacquisition earnings are never combined with the preacquisition earnings of the acquiring com-pany.
   e. None of the above.

2. Which of the following costs **cannot** be added to the total cost of the acquired business?
   a. The fair value of the consideration given.

b. The fair value of any contingent consideration that is given subsequent to the acquisition date.

c. The direct costs (directly traceable) incurred in registering with the Securities and Exchange Commission any securities given as consideration.

d. The present value of debt securities issued.

e. None of the above.

3. P Company acquired 100% of the outstanding common stock of S Company for $800,000 cash. S Company's assets have a book value of $1,500,000 and a current value of $1,750,000. S Company's liabilities have a book value of $1,000,000 and a current value of $1,100,000. What is the amount of goodwill paid for?

    a. $ -0-

    b. $50,000

    c. $150,000

    d. $300,000

    e. None of the above.

4. P Company acquired all of the outstanding common stock of S Company at a total cost of $400,000. S Company's net assets have a book value of $350,000 (including $15,000 of goodwill) and a current value of $430,000 (**excluding** the $15,000 of goodwill). In the consolidated financial statements, which of the following would be reported?

    a. Goodwill of $ -0-

    b. Goodwill of $15,000

    c. A deferred credit of $30,000

    d. A deferred credit of $80,000

    e. Goodwill of $30,000

    f. None of the above.

5. P Company acquired 100% of the outstanding common stock of S Company. In analyzing the conceptual analysis of the investment account, $40,000 is shown in the "Goodwill Element" column. At the combination date, S Company had $5,000 of goodwill on its books. What amount should be reported for goodwill in the consolidated financial statements?

    a. $35,000

    b. $40,000

    c. $45,000

    d. None of the above.

6. During 19X1, S Company (100% owned by P Company) reported net income of $100,000 and declared dividends of $20,000. During 19X1, P Company recorded $5,000 of amortization of cost in excess of book value relating to its investment in S Company. Insofar as the parent is concerned, the true earnings of S Company for 19X1 are

    a. $75,000

    b. $80,000

    c. $95,000

    d. $100,000

    e. None of the above.

7. Assume the parent uses the **equity method** of accounting. Regarding the preparation of the consolidation worksheet, which of the following statements is false?

a. The parent's retained earnings equals the consolidated retained earnings.
b. The parent's net income equals the consolidated net income.
c. The effect of the amortization of excess cost elimination entry is to reduce net income by the amount of the amortization of any cost in excess of book value.
d. The amounts in the subsidiary's column for the income statement section of the worksheet include only amounts subsequent to the acquisition date.
e. None of the above.

Application Questions

8. How much of the following costs and expenses can P Company charge to its Investment in Common Stock of S Company account upon the acquisition of all of the outstanding common stock of S Company in exchange for 100,000 shares of its $1 par value common stock?

Finder's fee	$50,000
Legal fees to prepare the acquisition agreement	30,000
Accounting fees for purchase investigation	25,000
Travel costs	3,000
President's salary (25% of $80,000–the president spent 25% of the year working on the acquisition)	20,000
SEC registration costs of common stock issued	70,000
Pro-rata share of merger and acquisitions departmental expenses	40,000
	$238,000

a. $108,000
b. $128,000
c. $168,000
d. $238,000
e. None of the above.

9. P Company acquired all of the assets of S Company for $500,000 cash. It did not assume any of S Company's liabilities. S Company's assets had a book value of $400,000 and a current value of $450,000. The acquired business is to be accounted for as a decentralized division. What entry would be made to record the combination?

P Company	S Division
a. Debit Home Office Equity for $500,000 and credit Cash for $500,000.	Debit various Assets and Goodwill for $500,000 and credit Home Office Equity for $500,000.
b. Debit Investment in S Division for $500,000 and credit Home Office Equity for $500,000.	Debit various assets and Goodwill for $500,000 and credit Cash for $500,000.
c. Debit Investment in S Division for $500,000 and credit Cash for $500,000.	Debit various Assets and Goodwill for $500,000 and credit Home Office Equity for $500,000.
d. Debit Investment in S Division for $450,000, debit Goodwill for $50,000, and credit Cash for $500,000.	Debit various Assets for $450,000 and credit Home Office Equity for $450,000.
e. None of the above.	

10. Use the same information as in Question 9 but assume all of the common stock was acquired instead of all of the assets. (Change S Division to S Company.)

11. On April 1, 19X1, P Company acquired 100% of the outstanding common stock of S Company for cash of $700,000. For 19X1, S Company had net income of $30,000 each quarter. Also for 19X1, S Company declared and paid cash dividends of $20,000 for each of the first two quarters and $40,000 for each of the last two quarters. Amortization of cost in excess of book value for 19X1 is $12,000. What is P Company's carrying value of its investment in S Company at December 31, 19X1, under the equity method?

    a. $678,000
    b. $681,000
    c. $688,000
    d. $691,000
    d. $700,000

12. Use the same information as in Question 11. What is the carrying value of the investment in S Company at December 31, 19X1, under the cost method?

    a. $678,000
    b. $688,000
    c. $690,000
    d. $700,000
    e. $710,000

13. Use the same information as in Question 11. What amount appears in P Company's income statement if P Company accounts for its investment in S Company under the equity method?

    a. $75,000
    b. $78,000
    c. $85,000
    d. $88,000
    e. $90,000

14. Use the same information as in Question 11. What amount appears in P Company's 19X1 income statement if P Company accounts for its investment in S Company under the cost method?

    a. $-0-
    b. $78,000
    c. $90,000
    d. $100,000
    e. $120,000

15. P Company acquired 100% of the outstanding common stock of S Company on January 1, 19X1, for $500,000 cash. During 19X1, S Company reported $40,000 of net income each quarter. On June 30, 19X1, S Company declared and paid a cash dividend of $200,000. What did the parent earn on its investment during 19X1?

    a. 8% ($40,000/$500,000)
    b. 32% ($160,000/$500,000)
    c. 33% ($160,000/$480,000)
    d. 35% ($160,000/$460,000)

    e. 36% ($160,000/$440,000)

    f. 40% ($200,000/$500,000)

PROBLEMS

Problem 1: Date of Acquisition—Acquisition of Common Stock

Pax Company acquired 100% of the outstanding common stock of Sax Company on April 30, 19X1, by issuing 40,000 shares of its $5 par value common stock (having a market price of $20 per share). Pax incurred legal and accounting fees of $120,000, of which $50,000 pertained to registering the shares issued with the SEC. If Sax's sales for the three years ended April 30, 19X4, exceed $10 million, then Pax must issue an additional 5,000 shares of common stock to Sax's former owners. The balances in the capital accounts of Sax as of the acquisition date are as follows:

Common Stock	$ 60,000
Retained Earnings	640,000
	$700,000

All the assets and liabilities of Sax have a current value equal to their book value, except the following:

	Book Value	Current Value
Patents	$120,000	$280,000
Long-term debt, 9%	400,000	370,000

Sax has $40,000 of goodwill on its books as of the acquisition date that Sax's management feels is fully realizable. Of the $120,000 incurred for legal and accounting fees, $61,000 was paid by April 30, 19X1, and charged to a Deferred Charges account pending consummation of the acquisition. The remaining $59,000 has not been paid or accrued.

Required:
1. Prepare the entry to record the acquisition.
2. Prepare an analysis of the investment account.
3. Prepare the elimination entries for consolidation at April 30, 19X1.

Problem 2: Date of Acquisition—Acquisition of Assets

Pix Company acquired all of the assets of Stix Company on May 1, 19X1, by (A) giving cash of $200,000, (B) issuing 5,000 shares of its $5 par value common stock that had a market value of $50 per share, and (C) assuming responsibility for all of Stix's liabilities having a book value of $260,000 and a current value of $300,000. Stix's assets have a book value of $720,000 and a current value of $690,000. Assume centralized accounting is to be used by Pix.

Required:
Prepare the entries to be recorded by both companies as a result of this business combination.

Problem 3: Subsequent to Date of Acquisition—Midyear Acquisition

Puda Company acquired all of the outstanding common stock of Suda Company on April 1, 19X1, at a total cost of $442,000. Suda's capital accounts at the acquisition date were as follows:

Common Stock .... $ 50,000
Retained Earnings 220,000

The only assets and liabilities of Suda that had current values different from book values were as follows:
    Copyright—undervalued by $60,000 (5-year remaining life)
    Bonds Payable—overvalued by $48,000 (6-year remaining life)
For 19X1, Suda had the following earnings and dividends:

	First Quarter	Remainder of Year	Total
Net income	$20,000	$90,000	$110,000
Dividends declared	10,000	30,000	40,000

Puda has chosen to use (A) the equity method of accounting; (B) straight-line amortization for over- and undervalued items; and (C) a 4-year life for goodwill.

Required:
1. Prepare the journal entries the parent would make for the year ended December 31, 19X1, under the equity method.
2. Prepare an analysis of the investment account as of the acquisition date, and update it for the entries developed in requirement 1.
3. Prepare all consolidation elimination entries at December 31, 19X1.

CHAPTER 4—SOLUTIONS

Completion Statements

1. residual
2. bargain purchase element
3. assets
4. negative goodwill
5. push-down accounting
6. division
7. home office equity
8. non-push-down accounting
9. irrelevant
10. postacquisition
11. liquidating dividends
12. recoverability

True-or-False Statements

1. True		9. False	
2. True		10. False	
3. False		11. True	
4. False		12. False	
5. False		13. False	
6. False		14. True	
7. True		15. True	
8. True			

Multiple-Choice Questions

1. b
2. c
3. c ($800,000 – $650,000 [$1,750,000 – $1,100,000] = $150,000)
4. a
5. b
6. c
7. c
8. a ($50,000 + $30,000 + $25,000 + $3,000 = $108,000)
9. c
10. e (Choice C is correct only for P Company.)
11. a ($700,000 + $90,000 – $100,000 – $12,000 = $678,000)
12. c ($700,000 – $10,000 liquidating dividend = $690,000)
13. b ($90,000 – $12,000 = $78,000)
14. c ($20,000 + $40,000 + $30,000 = $90,000)
15. e ($500,000 + $380,000) ÷ 2 = $440,000 average

Note: The beginning investment of $500,000 can be used only through 6/30/X1. Because of the liquidating dividend of $120,000 on 6/30/X1 ($200,000 – $80,000 of net income), $380,000 is used in the denominator for the second 6 months.

Problems

Problem 1

Requirement 1

```
Investment in Sax Company (40,000 shares × $20
    market price) ..........................................   800,000
        Common Stock (40,000 shares × $5 par) ..........              200,000
        Additional Paid-in Capital ...........................              600,000
    To record issuance of common stock.


Investment in Sax Company ............................    70,000
Additional Paid-in Capital ...............................    50,000
        Deferred Charges ....................................               61,000
        Accrued Liabilities ..................................               59,000
    To record direct acquisition costs of $70,000 and
        $50,000 cost of registering common stock.
```

Note: No entry would be made pertaining to the contingent consideration at this time. Disclosure would be made in the notes to the financial statements.

Requirement 2

Total Cost	=	BOOK VALUE ELEMENT Common Stock	+	Retained Earnings	+	Patents	+	UNDERVALUATION OF NET ASSETS ELEMENT Old Goodwill	+	Long-term Debt	+	GOODWILL ELEMENT
$870,000		$60,000		$640,000		$160,000		$(40,000)		$30,000		$20,000

Problem 1 (continued)

Requirement 3

The basic elimination entry:

Common Stock	60,000	
Retained Earnings	640,000	
Investment in Sax Company		700,000

The excess cost elimination entry:

Patents	160,000	
Goodwill (new)	20,000	
Long-term debt	30,000	
Goodwill (old)		40,000
Investment in Sax Company		170,000

Problem 2

Pix Company

Assets (in total)	690,000	
Goodwill	60,000	
Cash		200,000
Common Stock (5,000 shares × $5 par)		25,000
Additional Paid-in Capital		225,000
Liabilities		300,000
To record the acquisition of Stix Company's assets.		

Stix Company

Cash	200,000	
Liabilities	260,000	
Investment in Pix Company (5,000 shares @ $50/share market value)	250,000	
Loss on Sale of Assets	10,000	
Assets		720,000
To record sale of assets to Pix Company.		

Problem 3

Requirement 1

Investment in Suda Company	90,000	
Equity in Net Income of Subsidiary		90,000
To record share of subsidiary's earnings from April 1, 19X1, to December 31, 19X1.		
Dividends Receivable	30,000	
Investment in Suda Company		30,000
To record dividends from subsidiary for period April 1, 19X1, to December 31, 19X1.		
Equity in Net Income of Subsidiary	27,000	
Investment in Suda Company		27,000
To amortize cost in excess of book value.		

Requirement 2

			BOOK VALUE ELEMENT			
			Retained Earnings			
					Current Year	
	Cost	=	Common Stock +	Prior Periods +	Earnings –	Dividends
Balance, 4/1/X1	$270,000		$50,000	$220,000		
Equity in N.I.	90,000				$ 90,000	
Dividends	(30,000)					$(30,000)
Subtotal	$330,000		$50,000	$220,000	$ 90,000	$(30,000)
				60,000	(90,000)	30,000
Balance, 12/31/X1	$330,000		$50,000	$280,000	$ -0-	$ -0-

| | | | UNDERVALUATION OF NET ASSETS ELEMENT | | |
	Excess Cost	=	Copyright +	Bonds Payable +	GOODWILL ELEMENT
Balance, 4/1/X1	$172,000		$60,000	$48,000	$ 64,000
Amortization	(27,000)		(9,000)[a]	(6,000)[b]	(12,000)[c]
Balance, 12/31/X1	$145,000		$51,000	$42,000	$ 52,000

[a]$60,000 ÷ 5 years × ¾ year equals $9,000
[b]$48,000 ÷ 6 years × ¾ year equals $6,000
[c]$64,000 ÷ 4 years × ¾ year equals $12,000

Requirement 3

The basic elimination entry:

Common Stock	50,000	
Retained Earnings (beginning of year)	220,000	
Equity in Net Income of Subsidiary	90,000	
Dividends Declared		30,000
Investment in Suda Company		330,000

The excess cost elimination entry:

Copyright	51,000	
Bonds Payable	42,000	
Goodwill	52,000	
Investment in Suda Company		145,000

The amortization of excess cost elimination entry:

Cost of Sales	21,000	
Expenses (interest expense)	6,000	
Equity in Net Income of Subsidiary		27,000

CHAPTER 5

THE PURCHASE METHOD OF ACCOUNTING: PARTIALLY OWNED SUBSIDIARIES AND BLOCK ACQUISITIONS

CHAPTER HIGHLIGHTS

1. When the parent owns **less than 100%** of a subsidiary's outstanding common stock, the subsidiary's other stockholders are referred to collectively as the **minority interest.**

2. Under *ARB No. 51,* only **full** consolidation is permitted—**proportional** consolidation is prohibited.

3. Under the **parent company concept,** the parent company is still considered the reporting entity.

4. Under the **parent company concept,** the minority interest in the subsidiary's net income is reported as a **deduction** in arriving at consolidated net income.

5. Under the **parent company concept,** the minority interest in the subsidiary's net assets is reported **outside** of the consolidated stockholders' equity.

6. Under the **economic unit concept,** a **new reporting entity** is deemed to have been created as a result of the consolidation process.

7. Under the **economic unit concept,** the minority interest in the subsidiary's net income is reported as a **division** of the combined net income of the parent and the subsidiary.

8. Under the **economic unit concept,** the minority interest in the subsidiary's net assets is reported as part of consolidated stockholders' equity.

9. Under *ARB No. 51,* **both** the parent company **concept** and the **economic unit concept** are permitted.

10. **Dividends** paid to minority shareholders reduce the amount reported in the consolidated balance sheet as Minority Interest in Net Assets of Subsidiary.

11. **Dividends** paid to minority shareholders of a subsidiary are **never** reported in the consolidated statement of retained earnings.

12. When a subsidiary has **undervalued assets** at the acquisition date, such assets are revalued to 100% of their current value only under the **economic unit concept.**

13. Under the **parent company concept,** a subsidiary's undervalued assets at the acquisition date are only **partially** revalued in consolidation.

14. When control is obtained after two or more **block acquisitions,** the two methods of analyzing the total cost of the investment at the control date are (A) the date of latest purchase method and (B) the step-by-step method.

15. Under the **date of latest purchase method,** the practical (although artificial) assumption is made that **all** of the acquired shares were purchased on the date control was obtained.

16. Under the **step-by-step method,** the cost of each block of stock acquired is separated into its components using data that apply to the date that each block was purchased.

COMPLETION STATEMENTS

1. When the parent owns less than 100% of the subsidiary's outstanding common stock, the subsidiary's remaining shareholders are referred to as the _____ _____ .

2. Consolidating only the parent's ownership interest in each of the items in the subsidiary's financial statements is called _____ consolidation.

3. Consolidating the entire amount of each of the subsidiary's individual assets, liabilities, and income statement accounts with those of the parent is called _____ _____ consolidation.

4. A consolidation theory concerning the treatment of the minority interest that assumes **the reporting entity does not change** as a result of the consolidation process is called the _____ concept.

5. A consolidation theory concerning the treatment of the minority interest that assumes **a new reporting entity is created** as a result of the consolidation process is called the _____ concept.

6. Acquiring control over a company as a result of having purchased common stock **over a period of time** is referred to as having made _____ .

7. When control over a company is achieved as a result of block acquisitions, a technique of analyzing the total cost using data that apply only to the date control is obtained is called _____ .

8. When control over a company is achieved as a result of block acquisitions, a technique of analyzing the total cost using data that apply to the date each block of stock was purchased is called _____ .

TRUE-OR-FALSE STATEMENTS

1. T F Proportional consolidation fits **under** the economic unit concept.

2. T F Proportional consolidation fits **under** the parent company concept.

3. T F Full consolidation fits **under** the economic unit concept.

4. T F Full consolidation fits **under** the parent company concept.

5. T F The parent company concept assumes **no change** in the reporting entity as a result of the consolidation process.

6. T F Under the parent company concept, the minority interest is considered **an equity interest** in the consolidated financial statements.

7. T F When both the parent and the subsidiary are profitable, the consolidated net income is **higher** under the economic unit concept than under the parent company concept.

8. T F *Accounting Research Bulletin No. 51* **disallows** the economic unit concept.

9. T F Dividends paid to minority shareholders are **never** reported in the consolidated statement of retained earnings under the parent company concept.

10. T F *APB Opinion No. 16* does **not** prohibit either partial revaluation or full revaluation of a partially owned subsidiary's assets and liabilities to their current values.

11. T F Full revaluation of a subsidiary's assets and liabilities to their current values is consistent with the parent company concept.

12. T F Under the non-push-down basis of accounting, the amounts reported in the financial statements prepared by the subsidiary are wholly irrelevant amounts.

13. T F *ARB No. 51* allows **both** the step-by-step method and the date of latest purchase method when dealing with block acquisitions.

14. T F The date of latest purchase method **cannot** be used if the 20–50% ownership range is entered into.

15. T F The step-by-step method is the conceptually correct method—**not** the date of latest purchase method.

MULTIPLE-CHOICE QUESTIONS

Conceptual Questions

1. Concerning conceptual consolidation issues, which of the following statements is **false?**
   a. How to present the minority interest is not an issue under proportional consolidation.
   b. Under the parent company concept, the parent company is still considered the reporting entity.
   c. Under the economic unit concept, the parent is not considered the reporting entity.
   d. *APB Opinion No. 16* allows only partial revaluation of a partially owned subsidiary's assets to current value—not full revaluation to 100% of current value.
   e. None of the above.

2. Concerning the manner of reporting dividends paid to minority shareholders, which of the following statements is **false?**
   a. Dividends paid to minority shareholders are added to dividends declared by the parent in preparing the consolidated statement of retained earnings.
   b. Under the parent company concept, dividends paid to minority shareholders reduce the amount reported in the consolidated balance sheet as Minority Interest in Net Assets of Subsidiary.
   c. Under the economic unit concept, dividends paid to minority shareholders reduce the amount reported in the consolidated balance sheet as Minority Interest in Net Assets of Subsidiary.
   d. Unlike dividends paid to the parent, dividends paid to minority shareholders leave the consolidated group.
   e. None of the above.

3. Regarding the presentation of consolidated statements under the parent company concept, which of the following statements is **false?**
   a. The Minority Interest in Net Income amount is shown as a deduction in arriving at consolidated net income.
   b. The Minority Interest in Net Assets of Subsidiary amount is shown between liabilities and stockholders' equity.
   c. The Minority Interest in Net Income amount is a valid business expense in arriving at consolidated net income.
   d. Dividends paid to minority shareholders are eliminated in consolidation.
   e. None of the above.

4. Regarding the presentation of consolidated financial statements under the economic unit concept, which of the following statements is **false?**
   a. The consolidated income statement does **not** include a line item called Minority Interest in Net Income of Subsidiary.
   b. The Minority Interest in Net Assets of Subsidiary amount is shown as part of stockholders' equity.
   c. The Minority Interest in Net Income of Subsidiary amount is an artificial debit that arises on the consolidation worksheet.
   d. Dividends paid to minority shareholders are eliminated in consolidation.
   e. None of the above.

5. Regarding block acquisitions, which of the following statements is **false?**

   a. The date of latest purchase method cannot be used if the 20–50% ownership range has been entered into.

   b. The step-by-step method must be used if the 20–50% ownership range is entered into.

   c. The date of latest purchase method makes an artificial assumption.

   d. The step-by-step method is theoretically more correct than the date of latest purchase method.

   e. None of the above.

Application Questions

6. On April 1, 19X1, P Company acquired 75% of the outstanding common stock of S Company for $600,000 cash. For 19X1, S Company reported $40,000 of net income each quarter and declared dividends of $28,000 each quarter. Also for 19X1, P Company recorded $8,000 of amortization of cost in excess of book value. What should be the carrying value of the parent's investment under the equity method of accounting at December 31, 19X1?

   a. $619,000

   b. $621,000

   c. $626,000

   d. $627,000

   e. $628,000

7. Use the same information as in Question 6. What amount appears in P Company's 19X1 income statement if P Company accounts for its investment in S Company under the equity method?

   a. $63,000

   b. $82,000

   c. $90,000

   d. $112,000

   e. $120,000

8. On May 1, 19X1, Pax Company acquired 75% of the outstanding common stock of Sax Company for $400,000 cash. On this date, Sax had (A) net assets that had a book value of $400,000 and (B) land that had a book value of $200,000 and a current value of $280,000. Goodwill paid for was calculated to be $40,000. At what amount would Sax's land be reported in the consolidated balance sheet at May 1, 19X1, under the parent company concept?

   a. $200,000

   b. $210,000

   c. $240,000

   d. $260,000

   e. $280,000

9. On June 30, 19X1, Pix Company acquired 75% of the outstanding common stock of Slix Company for $480,000 cash. The book value of Slix's net assets is $400,000. Slix's only over- or undervalued asset or liability is a building that has a book value of $450,000 and a current value of $610,000. The building has a remaining life of 10 years. Under the parent company concept, at what amount would the minority interest be reported in the consolidated balance sheet at June 30, 19X1?

a. $100,000
b. $140,000
c. $160,000
d. $400,000
e. None of the above.

10. Use the same information as in Question 9. In addition, assume that Slix reported $80,000 of net income for 19X1 (earned evenly throughout the year) and declared dividends of $16,000 each quarter of 19X1. Under the parent company concept, at what amount would the minority interest be reported in the consolidated balance sheet at December 31, 19X1?

a. $101,500
b. $102,000
c. $104,000
d. $110,000
e. None of the above.

11. Pax Company acquired 80% of the outstanding common stock of Sax Company on January 1, 19X1, for $600,000 cash. On January 3, 19X1 (2 days later), Sax declared and paid a cash dividend of $125,000 (as instructed by Pax). For 19X1, Sax reported $150,000 of net income. For 19X1, Pax had no amortization of cost in excess of book value. What did the parent earn on its investment in 19X1?

a. 16⅔% ($100,000/$600,000)
b. 13⅓% ($80,000/$600,000)
c. 20% ($100,000/$500,000)
d. 24% ($120,000/$500,000)
e. 25% ($150,000/$600,000)

PROBLEM

1. Pix Company acquired 80% of the outstanding common stock of Stix Company on July 1, 19X1, at a total cost of $256,000. Stix's capital accounts at the acquisition date were as follows:

Common stock .... $ 90,000
Retained earnings   110,000

All of Stix's assets and liabilities had current values equal to book values as of the acquisition date, except patents, which had a current value of $80,000 and a book value of $30,000. The patents have a remaining life of 5 years. Goodwill was assigned a 4-year life.

For 19X1, Stix had the following earnings and dividends:

	Jan. 1– June 30, 19X1	July 1– Dec. 31, 19X1	Total
Net income......................	$65,000	$75,000	$140,000
Dividends declared..............	20,000	40,000	60,000

Required:
1. Prepare the journal entries Pix would make for the year ended December 31, 19X1, under the equity method.
2. Prepare an expanded analysis of the investment account as of the acquisition date and update it through December 31, 19X1.

3. Prepare the basic elimination entry, the excess cost elimination entry, and the amortization of excess elimination entry for consolidation at December 31, 19X1.

CHAPTER 5—SOLUTIONS

Completion Statements

1. minority interest
2. proportional
3. full
4. parent company
5. economic unit
6. block acquisitions
7. the date of latest purchase method
8. the step-by-step method

True-or-False Statements

1. False
2. False
3. False
4. False
5. True
6. False
7. True
8. False
9. True
10 True
11. False
12. True
13. True
14 True
15. True

Multiple-Choice Questions

1. d
2. a
3. c
4. c
5. e
6. a ($600,000 + $90,000 share of net income – $63,000 share of dividends – $8,000 of amortization)
7. b ($90,000 share of net income – $8,000 of amortization)
8. d ($200,000 of book value + 75% of undervaluation of $80,000)
9. a (25% of $400,000 book value of net assets)
10. b ($100,000 share of book value of net assets as of June 30, 19X1 + $10,000 share of net income for the last six months of 19X1 – $8,000 share of dividends declared during the last six months of 19X1)
11. d The $500,000 denominator is the beginning investment balance of $600,000 minus the $100,000 dividend (Pax's 80% share) declared on January 3, 19X1.

PROBLEM

1. Investment in Stix Company 60,000
        Equity in Net Income of Subsidiary 60,000
    To record share of earnings of subsidiary
      from July 1, 19X1 to December 31, 19X1
      ($75,000 × 80%).

  Dividends Receivable 32,000
        Investment in Suda Company 32,000
    To record dividends from subsidiary from
      July 1, 19X1, to December 31, 19X1
      ($40,000 × 80%).

  Equity in Net Income of Subsidiary 11,000
        Investment in Stix Company 11,000
    To amortize cost in excess of book value
      ($4,000 for patents and $7,000
      for goodwill).

2.

				BOOK VALUE ELEMENT			
					Retained Earnings		
						Current Year	
Minority Interest (20%)	+	Cost	=	Common Stock	+	Prior Periods	+	Earnings	Dividends
		$160,000		$72,000		$ 88,000			
$40,000				18,000		22,000			
$40,000		$160,000		$90,000		$110,000			
		60,000						$ 60,000	
15,000								15,000	
		(32,000)							$(32,000)
(8,000)									(8,000)
$47,000		$188,000		$90,000		$110,000		$ 75,000	$(40,000)
						(35,000)		(75,000)	40,000
$47,000		$188,000		$90,000		$145,000		$ -0-	$ -0-

| | | UNDERVALUATION OF NET ASSETS ELEMENT | | |
Excess Cost	=	Patents	+	GOODWILL ELEMENT
$96,000		$40,000		$56,000
(11,000)		(4,000)[a]		(7,000)[b]
$85,000		$36,000		$49,000

[a]$40,000 ÷ 5 years × ½ year equals $4,000.
[b]$56,000 ÷ 4 years × ½ year equals $7,000.

3.   The basic elimination entry:

	Dr.	Cr.
Common Stock	90,000	
Retained Earnings—(beginning)	110,000	
Equity in Net Income of Subsidiary	60,000	
Minority Interest in Net Income of Subsidiary	15,000	
Dividends Declared		40,000
Minority Interest in Net Assets of Subsidiary		47,000
Investment in Subsidiary		188,000

The excess cost elimination entry:

	Dr.	Cr.
Patents	36,000	
Goodwill	49,000	
Investment in Subsidiary		85,000

The amortization of excess cost elimination entry:

	Dr.	Cr.
Cost of Sales	11,000	
Equity in Net Income of Subsidiary		11,000

CHAPTER 6

THE POOLING OF INTERESTS METHOD OF ACCOUNTING

CHAPTER HIGHLIGHTS

1. In discussing pooling of interests accounting, it is **not** appropriate to use the terms **acquiring company** or **acquired company** inasmuch as those terms are appropriate only for purchase accounting.

2. In a pooling of interests, each company's stockholders are presumed to have combined or fused their ownership interests in such a manner that each group becomes an owner of the combined, enlarged business.

3. To fuse the two ownership interests, it is necessary for one of the combining companies to issue **common stock.**

4. The only relevance of the **negotiated value** is that it is used to determine how many shares of common stock are to be issued.

5. The relevance of the target company's **book values** is that the basis of accounting does **not** change as a result of the pooling of interests.

6. When financial statements are presented for periods **prior to the combination date,** the earnings and dividends of each company are combined as though the combination had occurred at the **beginning of the earliest period presented**—but only to the extent of the ownership interest combined.

7. The **relative size** of the two combining companies is irrelevant in determining whether pooling of interests accounting treatment is appropriate.

8. **No continuity of interests** need be maintained for a certain period of time **after** the common stock is issued in a combination accounted for as a pooling of interests.

9. **Twelve specific conditions** must be met **before** pooling of interests accounting is permitted.

10. If all twelve conditions are met, then **purchase accounting cannot** be used.

11. Each of the combining companies must be **autonomous** and have been autonomous for **two** years before the combination.

12. Each of the combining companies must be **independent** of the other combining company.

13. In most instances, each combining company is **independent** of the other combining company if **neither** company owns **more than 10%** of the outstanding common stock of the other combining company.

14. A pooling of interests can be effected by a **stock-for-stock** exchange or an **exchange of the assets** of the target company for common stock.

15. The common stock issued in a pooling of interests must have the same **identical rights** to those of its outstanding common stock.

16. In a **common stock-for-common stock exchange,** the company issuing common stock must obtain **at least 90%** of the other combining company's outstanding common stock **subsequent** to the initiation date in exchange for its own common stock.

17. Neither of the combining companies can change or **alter its equity interest** of the voting common stock **in contemplation of a pooling of interests** (within two years before the plan of combination is initiated or between the initiation date and the combination date).

18. The only cash that pooling shareholders may receive is **cash for fractional shares.**

19. The use of **treasury stock** might prevent pooling of interests treatment—this is a case-by-case determination.

20. No agreements to retire or reacquire **any** of the common stock issued to effect the combination are permitted.

21. There can be no **intent or plan to dispose** of a significant part of the assets of the combining companies **within two years** after the combination (some limited exceptions allowed).

22. If **dissenting shareholders** are bought out with cash, then the entire transaction is recorded as a pooling of interests—there is no such thing as recording the transaction as part pooling, part purchase.

23. **Direct costs** and **registration expenses** are both charged to expense in a pooling of interests.

COMPLETION STATEMENTS

1. In a pooling of interests combination, the shareholders, if any, of the target company who receive cash **instead** of common stock of the issuing company are referred to as ⎯⎯⎯⎯⎯⎯⎯⎯⎯ .

2. The two attributes required of the combining companies in a pooling of interests are ⎯⎯⎯⎯⎯⎯⎯⎯⎯ and ⎯⎯⎯⎯⎯⎯⎯⎯⎯ .

3. If the issuing company holds _____ stock, pooling of interests accounting may be **disallowed.**

4. An individual shareholder of the target company in a planned pooling of interests **cannot** at the same time be both a(n) _____ and a(n) _____ _____ .

5. In a pooling of interests, direct costs are charged to _____ .

6. In a pooling of interests, registration costs relating to the common stock issued **must** be charged to _____ .

7. When each of the combining companies has an investment in the other prior to the combination date, this is described as having _____ .

TRUE-OR-FALSE STATEMENTS

1. T   F   It is technically **incorrect** to use the terms **acquiring company** and **acquired company** in a pooling of interests.

2. T   F   In a pooling of interests, the negotiated value of the consideration given is **not** relevant in recording the combination.

3. T   F   Precombination earnings of the target company are **always** combined with the precombination earnings of the company issuing common stock to effect a combination.

4. T   F   In a pooling of interests, each of the combining companies **must** be approximately the same size.

5. T   F   In a pooling of interests involving a common stock for common stock exchange, the shareholders of the target company can immediately sell for cash the common shares received **without** jeopardizing pooling of interests accounting treatment.

6. T   F   The existence of dual intercorporate investments prior to the combination date **violates** the requirement that the companies be independent of each other.

7. T   F   In a pooling of interests, the **larger** of the two combining companies **must** issue the common stock to bring about the pooling.

8. T   F   If each combining company owns no more than 10% of the outstanding common stock of the other combining company, the independence test may still **not** be met.

9. T   F   If assets are exchanged in a business combination, at least 90% of the assets **must** be exchanged.

10. T F Precombination dividends of the target company are **never** added to the precombination dividends of the company issuing common stock in a pooling of interests.

MULTIPLE-CHOICE QUESTIONS

Conceptual Questions

1. A parent company of a 100%-owned subsidiary has a cost that equals the book value of the subsidiary's net assets. This situation could have resulted from any of the following **except**
   a. The parent company formed the subsidiary.
   b. The parent company acquired the subsidiary in a business combination that was recorded as a pooling of interests.
   c. The parent company acquired the subsidiary in a purchase transaction in which a bargain purchase element was present (with the bargain purchase element equaling the amount of the undervaluation of the net assets of the subsidiary).
   d. The parent company acquired the subsidiary in a purchase transaction in which the amount of the bargain purchase element was fully extinguished.
   e. None of the above.

2. One of the conditions or requirements for pooling of interests treatment is
   a. Neither combining company has been autonomous nor a subsidiary of another corporation within two years before the plan of combination is initiated.
   b. Dissenting shareholders cannot receive common stock of the company issuing common stock to bring about the combination.
   c. The issuing company must bring about the combination by issuing treasury stock acquired within two years of the initiation date.
   d. The smaller of the two companies may not be the company that issues common stock to bring about the combination.
   e. None of the above.

3. One of the conditions or requirements for pooling of interests treatment is
   a. Each combining company may alter its own equity interest but is prohibited from altering the equity interest of the other combining company in contemplation of a pooling of interests.
   b. There have been no dual intercorporate investments between the two combining companies for two years preceding the initiation date.
   c. The only cash that may be given to dissenting shareholders is cash given for fractional shares.
   d. The company issuing common stock is prohibited from acquiring any treasury stock for two years subsequent to the consummation date.
   e. None of the above.

4. One of the conditions or requirements for pooling of interests treatment is
   a. Neither of the combining companies on a stand alone basis can have any contingencies pending at the consummation date (such as from a lawsuit outstanding).
   b. Each shareholder of the target company who exchanges common stock for voting common stock of the issuing company must receive that voting common stock in exact proportion to his or her relative common stock interest in the target company before the combination is effected.
   c. The issuing company cannot issue a separate class of common stock (such as Class B) even though such stock has the exact same rights and privileges of the company's already outstanding common stock.
   d. Shares of the target company acquired prior to the initiation date can be used to determine if the 90% requirement has been met.
   e. None of the above.

5. Regarding the presentation of consolidated financial statements for the year ended December 31, 19X1, during which a business combination recorded as a pooling of interests occurred on April 1, 19X1, which of the following statements is correct?
   a. Dividends declared by the subsidiary during the first quarter of 19X1 would be combined with the parent's dividends in the consolidated statement of retained earnings.
   b. Dividends declared by the subsidiary during the last three quarters of 19X1 would be combined with the parent's dividends in the consolidated statement of retained earnings.
   c. Dividends declared by the subsidiary during each of the four quarters would be combined with the parent's dividends in the consolidated statement of retained earnings.
   d. Dividends declared by the subsidiary during any of the four quarters would not be combined with the parent's dividends in the consolidated statement of retained earnings.
   e. None of the above.

6. Regarding the treatment of direct costs and registration expenses in a pooling of interests business combination, which of the following is **false?**
   a. Direct costs cannot be capitalized into the Investment in Subsidiary account.
   b. SEC registration expenses must be expensed in the income statement.
   c. Direct costs must be expensed in the income statement.
   d. SEC registration expenses are to be charged to retained earnings.
   e. None of the above.

Application Questions

7. On July 1, 19X1, Pax Company issued common stock in exchange for all of the outstanding common stock of Sax Company. Earnings and dividend information for 19X1 follow:

	Pax	Sax
Net income (from own separate operations):		
6 months ended June 30, 19X1	$130,000	$ 60,000
6 months ended Dec. 31, 19X1	170,000	80,000
	$300,000	$140,000

Dividends declared and paid:

6 months ended June 30, 19X1	....	$ 25,000	$ 40,000
6 months ended Dec. 31, 19X1	....	75,000	50,000
		$100,000	$ 90,000

Under the pooling of interests method, what is the consolidated net income for 19X1?

a. $240,000   e. $350,000
b. $250,000   f. $360,000
c. $280,000   g. $380,000
d. $330,000   h. $440,000

8. Use the same information as in Question 7. Under the pooling of interests method, what is the amount reported for dividends in the consolidated statement of retained earnings for 19X1?

    a. $100,000
    b. $125,000
    c. $140,000
    d. $150,000
    e. $190,000

9. In recording a business combination accounted for as a pooling of interests, P Company credited Retained Earnings for $50,000, which amount was equal to S Company's retained earnings at the combination date. Just prior to recording the business combination, P Company's retained earnings balance was $300,000. In a consolidated balance sheet prepared as of the combination date, the amount shown for retained earnings is

    a. $50,000
    b. $300,000
    c. $350,000
    d. None of the above.

10. Pax Company combined with Sax Company in a business combination properly accounted for as a pooling of interests. No minority interest resulted. Just prior to recording the combination, the equity accounts of each company were as follows:

	Pax	Sax
Common Stock:		
Par value, $10	$400,000	
Par value, $5		$120,000
Additional paid-in capital	40,000	80,000
Retained earnings	500,000	100,000
	$940,000	$300,000

Pax issued 25,000 shares of its common stock, which had a market value of $18 per share. What is the consolidated retained earnings as of the combination date?

    a. $490,000
    b. $550,000
    c. $590,000
    d. $600,000
    e. None of the above.

11. Use the information in Question 10, but assume the combination did not qualify for pooling of interests treatment. What is the consolidated retained earnings as of the combination date?
   a. $490,000
   b. $500,000
   c. $590,000
   d. $600,000
   e. None of the above.

12. Use the information in Question 10. At what amount would Pax debit its Investment in Subsidiary account in recording the combination as a pooling of interests?
   a. $250,000
   b. $300,000
   c. $450,000
   d. None of the above.

PROBLEM

1. On May 1, 19X2, Pax Company combined with Sax Company in a combination that qualified as a pooling of interests. Pax issued 45,000 shares of its common stock in exchange for 54,000 outstanding shares of Sax. Pax paid $80,000 cash for the remaining 6,000 outstanding shares of Sax. Pax's common stock had a market price of $16 at the combination date, and Sax's common stock had a market price of $13 just prior to the combination. The capital accounts of each company on April 30, 19X2, follow:

	Pax	Sax
Common stock, $10 par value	$ 900,000	
Common stock, $5 par value		$300,000
Additional paid-in capital	160,000	30,000
Retained earnings	1,330,000	270,000

For 19X2, each company—on a stand-alone basis—had the following earnings and dividends:

	Jan. 1– April 30, 19X2	May 1– Dec. 31, 19X2	Total
Pax Company:			
Net income	$250,000	$610,000	$860,000
Dividends declared	144,000	432,000	576,000
Sax Company:			
Net income	$70,000	$120,000	$190,000
Dividends declared	50,000	100,000	150,000

Pax incurred $75,000 of costs directly related to the combination and $35,000 of costs in registering the shares issued with the SEC. These costs are *not* included in the above amounts.

Required:
1. Prepare the entries required at the combination date.
2. Prepare the entries required under the equity method of accounting for 19X2.
3. Prepare an analysis of the Investment account as updated through December 31, 19X2.
4. Prepare the basic elimination entry for consolidation at December 31, 19X2.
5. Prepare a consolidated statement of retained earnings for 19X2.

CHAPTER 6—SOLUTIONS

Completion Statements

1. dissenting shareholders
2. autonomy, independence
3. treasury
4. assenter, dissenter
5. expense
6. expense
7. dual intercorporate investments

True-or-False Statements

1. True	6. False
2. True	7. False
3. True	8. True
4. False	9. False
5. True	10. False

Multiple-Choice Questions

1. d
2. e
3. e
4. b
5. a
6. d
7. h ($300,000 + $140,000 = $440,000)
8. c ($100,000 + $40,000 = $140,000)
9. c ($300,000 + $50,000 = $350,000)
10. c ($500,000 + $100,000 – $10,000 debit to balance = $590,000)
11. b (Pax's retained earnings only)
12. b (Equal to Sax's book value of its net assets)

Problem

1. Entry to record the combination as if it occurred as of the beginning of the year:

Investment in Sax Company (100% of
  Sax's total stockholder's equity
  at December 31, 19X1) 580,000
      Common Stock (45,000 shares × $10 par value)......   450,000
      Cash (to dissenting shareholders)   80,000
      Retained Earnings (100% of Sax's
        Dec. 31, 19X2, retained earnings balance)   250,000

At this point a $200,000 debit is needed to balance the entry:

Additional Paid-in Capital (a $160,000
  debit brings this account to a -0- balance) 160,000
Retained Earnings (residual)............................... 40,000

Note: The effect of the pooling is $210,000 ($250,000–$40,000), and this amount is reported in the consolidated statement of retained earnings for the year 19X2.

Entry to account for costs incurred:

Expenses 110,000
      Accrued Liabilities/Deferred Charges   110,000

2. Investment in Sax Company 190,000
      Equity in Net Income of Subsidiary....................   190,000
    To record equity in earnings of subsidiary
    for 19X2 (100% of $190,000).

Dividends Declared 50,000
      Investment in Sax Company   50,000
    To reflect dividends paid prior to the
    combination date (to Sax shareholders who
    surrendered their stock) as dividends to be
    reported in the consolidated statement of
    retained earnings.

Dividends Receivable...................................... 100,000
      Investment in Sax Company   100,000
    To record dividends declared after the
    combination date

3.

						BOOK VALUE ELEMENT		
						Retained Earnings		
							Current Year	
	Total Cost	=	Common Stock	+	Paid-in Capital	+	Prior Year	+	Earnings	Dividends
Jan 1, 19X2	$ 580,000		$300,000		$30,000		$250,000			
Net income ..	190,000								$ 190,000	
Dividends	(50,000)									$ (50,000)
Dividends	(100,000)									(100,000)
Dec. 31, 19X2..	$ 620,000		$300,000		$30,000		$250,000		$ 190,000	$(150,000)
Reclassify....							40,000		(190,000)	150,000
Dec. 31, 19X2..	$ 620,000		$300,000		$30,000		$290,000		$ -0-	$ -0-

4. The basic elimination entry:

Common Stock	300,000	
Additional Paid-in Capital	30,000	
Retained Earnings (beginning of year)	250,000	
Equity in Net Income of Subsidiary	190,000	
Dividends Declared		150,000
Investment in Sax Company		620,000

5.

Pax Company
Statement of Retained Earnings
For the Year Ended December 31, 19X2

Balance, December 31, 19X1, as previously reported	$1,224,000
Effect of pooling of interests with Sax Company	210,000
Balance, December 31, 19X1, as restated	$1,434,000
Net income for the year	940,000[a]
Subtotal	$2,374,000
Dividends declared	(626,000)[b]
Balance, December 31, 19X2	$1,748,000

[a]Comprised of $860,000 from Pax, $190,000 from Sax, and less $110,000 of expenses incurred.
[b]Comprised of $576,000 for Pax plus $50,000 for Sax that was paid to Sax's shareholders prior to the combination date. (The entire $50,000 is reported even though 10% of Sax's shareholders dissented—Pax obtained a 100% interest in Sax.)

CHAPTER 7
NEW BASIS OF ACCOUNTING

CHAPTER HIGHLIGHTS

Push-down Accounting

1. The push-down basis of accounting issue is whether a subsidiary acquired in a purchase transaction should (A) continue its **old basis** of accounting or (B) establish a **new basis** of accounting based on the parent's acquisition cost.

2. The push-down basis of accounting issue is relevant only if the subsidiary issues financial statements to **outside third parties** (such as lenders) other than its parent company.

3. Conceptually, the push-down accounting controversy is a debate between **relevancy** and **historical cost.**

4. Under the push-down basis of accounting, the subsidiary (A) **adjusts** its assets and liabilities to their current values and records goodwill (B) **eliminates** the balance in its Accumulated Depreciation account(s), and (C) **closes** its Retained Earnings account balance to Additional Paid-in Capital.

5. The rationale underlying push-down accounting is that amounts reported for the acquired operation's assets and liabilities should be the same whether the parent acquired **assets** or **common stock.**

6. In a business combination in which common stock is acquired, the parent controls the **form of the organization**—it has the legal power to liquidate the subsidiary into a division (branch) just as if it had acquired assets instead of common stock.

7. Currently, *Staff Accounting Bulletin No. 54* (issued by the staff of the Securities and Exchange Commission), is the only accounting pronouncement that requires push-down accounting.

8. Under push-down accounting, adjustments to the book values of assets and liabilities that result in **increasing** stockholder's equity are reported in a **Revaluation Capital** account.

9. The **consolidated amounts** are the same regardless of whether or not the subsidiary has applied the push-down basis of accounting.

10. From a **consolidated perspective,** the push-down basis accomplishes in the subsidiary's general ledger what is accomplished on the **consolidation worksheet** when **nonpush-down accounting** is used.

11. In *Staff Accounting Bulletin No. 73,* **parent company debt** relating to the acquisition of the common stock of a company in a **purchase transaction** may have to be recorded on (pushed down to) the subsidiary's books.

Leveraged Buyouts

12. A **leveraged buyout (LBO)** is the acquisition of a target company's assets or common stock in which the acquirer uses an extremely high percentage of debt and thus a very low percentage of equity (usually 10% or lower) to pay for the acquisition.

13. In an LBO, the **debt structure** of the target company is refinanced simultaneously with the acquisition, making an LBO nothing more than **a combination of an acquisition and a debt refinancing.**

14. In most LBOs, management has a major ownership interest as a result of investing its own money. Accordingly, an **alignment of interests** occurs between management's interest and the interest of the remaining stockholders.

15. Most LBOs are not business combinations in the sense of two **operating businesses** being combined. Typically, the acquiring entity is formed by a group of investors for the purpose of acquiring the common stock of the target company.

16. In LBOs, the primary rationale for forming a legal entity solely to acquire the common stock of the target company is that it overcomes the general practice of not allowing personal transactions among stockholders to **pierce the corporate veil** (a form versus substance issue).

17. In LBOs, a more logical reason for forming a legal entity solely to acquire the common stock of the target company is it **facilitates the process** of effecting the transaction.

18. In LBOs, a **change in control** must occur before a new basis of accounting can be used. The change in control must be **genuine, substantive,** and **nontemporary.**

19. If **no change in control occurs** in an LBO (new basis of accounting thus not permitted), a **recapitalization** of equity occurs (usually resulting in negative stockholders' equity).

20. When some of the target company's shareholders in an LBO (that qualifies for new basis of accounting) continue as owners, the issue is whether the target company's assets and liabilities are to be valued **entirely** on the new basis of accounting or only **partially** on the new basis of accounting and partially on the old basis of accounting.

21. In LBOs, shareholders whose continuing ownership percentage **increases** are called **"bulls."**

22. In LBOs, shareholders whose continuing ownership percentage **decreases** are called **"bears."**

23. In LBOs, when the continuing ownership percentage **increases,** carryover of predecessor basis is required unless the continuing ownership percentage does not exceed 5%.

24. In LBOs, when the **continuing ownership percentage decreases,** carryover of predecessor basis is required unless the continuing ownership interest is below 20% (and certain similar 20% tests are met).

COMPLETION STATEMENTS

Push-down Accounting

1. Push-down accounting is presently required by _____ .

2. In applying push-down accounting, the upward revaluation of assets to their current values would require a credit entry to _____
_____ .

3. The alternative to push-down accounting is _____
_____ .

4. Push-down accounting is presently not required for _____ entities.

Leveraged Buyouts

5. In LBOs, the critical issue is whether or not there has been a change in _____
_____ .

6. In an LBO transaction, those shareholders whose continuing ownership interest **increases** are called _____ .

7. In an LBO transaction, those shareholders whose continuing ownership interest **decreases** are called _____ .

TRUE-OR-FALSE STATEMENTS

1. T F Concerning push-down accounting, the SEC has rules pertaining to publicly owned companies, and the FASB has rules pertaining to privately owned companies.

2. T F Push-down accounting is an irrelevant issue from a consolidated perspective.

3. T F Push-down accounting is **less** logical than nonpush-down accounting.

4.   T   F   The consolidation process is **more** involved if push-down accounting has been applied by the subsidiary.

5.   T   F   In applying push-down accounting, the subsidiary's Retained Earnings account is always brought to a zero balance.

6.   T   F   In applying push-down accounting, the subsidiary's Accumulated Depreciation account(s) is always brought to a zero balance.

7.   T   F   In applying push-down accounting, the subsidiary's Additional Paid-in Capital account is always brought to a zero balance.

8.   T   F   In applying push-down accounting, the offsetting entry for adjusting an asset upward to its current value is to the Retained Earnings account.

9.   T   F   After applying push-down accounting, the parent's conceptual analysis of the investment account would **not** show an excess cost element or a goodwill element.

10.   T   F   Push-down accounting could be applied to a leveraged buyout.

11.   T   F   Applying push-down accounting does **not** require any entries on the parent's books.

12.   T   F   Applying push-down accounting would be abandoning the historical cost basis of accounting.

Leveraged Buyouts

13.   T   F   In an LBO, a new basis of accounting can be used only if a change in control has occurred.

14.   T   F   In an LBO, the requirement to create a corporate entity to be used to acquire the common stock of the target company is merely form over substance.

15.   T   F   LBO transactions must be accounted for using the new basis of accounting entirely or the old basis of accounting entirely—never part new basis and part old basis.

16.   T   F   The first step in analyzing an LBO transaction is to determine if a change in control has occurred.

17.   T   F   In an LBO transaction, a change in control may **not** have occurred even though a new group of shareholders owns more than 50% of the common stock.

18.   T   F   In an LBO, if management has more than a 20% ownership interest, the new basis of accounting **cannot** be used.

19. T F In an LBO, if an existing shareholder(s) obtains more than a 50% interest, a new basis of accounting **cannot** be used.

20. T F In an LBO in which a change in control has **not** occurred, cash given to the target company's shareholders that exceeds the book value of the target company's equity results in a charge to equity.

21. T F In an LBO, structuring the transaction to achieve the new basis of accounting to the maximum extent possible is usually of major importance.

22. T F In an LBO in which no continuing ownership occurs, the new basis of accounting is always used in its entirety.

23. T F In an LBO, to the extent that carryover of predecessor basis is required, it is determined using the personal cost basis of the shares owned by these shareholders.

24. T F In an LBO, shareholders whose continuing ownership percentage increases are called "bulls."

25. T F In an LBO, the carryover of predecessor basis is an issue only for bears—not bulls.

26. T F In an LBO, carryover of predecessor basis treatment is **not** required as long as the continuing ownership percentage does not exceed 20%.

27. T F In an LBO, any retained earnings balance at the transaction date is **not** reported in the consolidated balance sheet.

MULTIPLE-CHOICE QUESTIONS

Push-down Accounting

1. In applying push-down accounting in a situation in which the net assets are **undervalued,** which of the following accounts would **not** be adjusted or used?
    a. Revaluation Capital.
    b. Retained Earnings.
    c. Accumulated Depreciation.
    d. Additional Paid-in Capital.
    e. None of the above.

2. In applying push-down accounting in a situation in which the net assets are **overvalued,** which of the following accounts would **not** be adjusted or used?
    a. Revaluation Capital.
    b. Retained Earnings.
    c. Accumulated Depreciation.
    d. Additional Paid-in Capital.
    e. None of the above.

3. The push-down basis of accounting would **not** make sense if the subsidiary
   a. Is 100% owned by the parent.
   b. Is not consolidated.
   c. Was acquired in a leveraged buyout.
   d. Presents its separate financial statements to its lenders.
   e. None of the above.

4. Immediately before applying push-down accounting, the subsidiary has the following account balances:

   Accumulated Depreciation $170,000
   Additional Paid-in Capital $300,000
   Retained Earnings $400,000

   After applying push-down accounting in a situation in which the net assets were neither over- nor undervalued, what would be the proper balance of the Additional Paid-in Capital account?
   a. $ -0-
   b. $470,000
   c. $700,000
   d. $870,000
   e. None of the above.

5. Use the information in Question 4, but answer the question for the Retained Earnings account.
   a. $ -0-
   b. $470,000
   c. $700,000
   d. $870,000
   e. None of the above.

6. Immediately before applying push-down accounting, the subsidiary has the following account balances:

   Additional Paid-in Capital $200,000
   Retained Earnings $500,000

   After applying push-down accounting in a situation in which the net assets were undervalued by $120,000, what would be the proper balance of the Additional Paid-in Capital account?
   a. $ -0-
   b. $120,000
   c. $500,000
   d. $700,000
   e. $820,000

7. Use the information in Question 6, but answer the question for the Retained Earnings account.
   a. $ -0-
   b. $200,000
   c. $320,000
   d. $700,000
   e. $820,000

Leveraged Buyouts

8. In an LBO, which of the following statements is **false** concerning the carrying over of predecessor basis?

    a. It facilitates the recording of the transaction.
    b. It is the equivalent of using part purchase and part pooling of interests.
    c. It has no effect on the amounts reported on a consolidated basis.
    d. It is consistent with the historical cost basis of accounting.
    e. None of the above.

9. In an LBO, which of the following accounts would have a zero balance in the consolidated column immediately after recording the transaction?

    a. Goodwill.
    b. Retained Earnings.
    c. Revaluation Capital.
    d. Additional Paid-in Capital.
    e. None of the above.

10. In an LBO, a new basis of accounting can be used only if

    a. There is no carryover of predecessor basis.
    b. The continuing ownership percentage increases.
    c. The continuing ownership percentage decreases.
    d. There is a change in control.
    e. None of the above.

11. In an LBO, carryover of predecessor basis will **not** be required if the continuing ownership interest is

    a. More than 5%.
    b. More than 20%.
    c. Not more than 5%.
    d. Not more than 20%.
    e. None of the above.

12. In an LBO, carryover of predecessor basis is **not** required for the **bears** if the continuing ownership interest is

    a. More than 5%.
    b. More than 20%.
    c. Not more than 5%.
    d. Not more than 20%.
    e. None of the above.

13. In an LBO, carryover of predecessor basis is **not** required for the **bulls** if the continuing ownership interest is

    a. More than 5%.
    b. More than 20%.
    c. Not more than 5%.
    d. Not more than 20%.
    e. None of the above.

CHAPTER 7—SOLUTIONS

Completion Statements

Push-down Accounting

1. *Staff Accounting Bulletin No. 54* (of the SEC)
2. Revaluation capital
3. non-push-down accounting
4. nonpublicly owned

Leveraged Buyouts

5. control
6. bulls
7. bears

True-or-False Statements

Push-down Accounting

1. False	7. False
2. True	8. False
3. False	9. True
4. False	10. True
5. True	11. True
6. True	12. False

Leveraged Buyouts

13. True	21. True
14. True	22. True
15. False	23. False
16. True	24. True
17. True	25. False
18. False	26. False
19. False	27. True
20. True	

Multiple-Choice Questions

Push-down Accounting

1. e
2. a
3. e
4. c
5. a
6. d
7. a

Leveraged Buyouts

8. a
9. b
10. d
11. c
12. d
13. c

CHAPTER 8

INTERCOMPANY TRANSACTIONS: OVERALL DISCUSSION AND INTERCOMPANY INVENTORY TRANSFERS

CHAPTER HIGHLIGHTS

1. The term **"intercompany transaction"** applies only when a control situation exists.

2. To facilitate the consolidation process, intercompany transactions are normally recorded in **separate general ledger accounts.**

3. Before the consolidation process begins, all intercompany accounts that are to have **reciprocal balances** (both in the income statement and the balance sheet) must be reconciled and adjusted, if necessary, to bring them into agreement.

4. All intercompany transactions are **undone** in consolidation because they are **internal transactions** from a consolidated perspective.

5. All intercompany transactions are **not arms-length transactions;** however, they are still **bonafide transactions** from the perspective of each separate company.

6. All **intercompany transactions** are **related party transactions;** however, not all related party transactions are intercompany transactions.

7. From a consolidated viewpoint, the sale of inventory among entities within a consolidated group is considered merely the **physical movement** from one location to another (similar to the movement of inventory from one division to another division).

8. When inventory is transferred from one company to another within a consolidated group, the amount of profit to be eliminated in consolidation is the **selling entity's gross profit.**

9. When intercompany gross profit on intercompany sales is eliminated in consolidation, **income taxes** that have been provided on such gross profit **must also be eliminated.**

10. Intercompany gross profit on intercompany inventory transfers is **realized** from a consolidated viewpoint only when the inventory has been **resold to an outside unaffiliated customer.**

11. The amount of intercompany gross profit or loss to be eliminated is **not** affected by the existence of a **minority interest.**

12. The amount of intercompany gross profit or loss to be eliminated in consolidation **may be allocated proportionately** between the majority and minority interests (applicable only to **upstream transfers** from partially owned subsidiaries).

13. **Fractional elimination** is **not** permitted under *ARB No. 51*.

14. Intercompany Sales and Intercompany Cost of Sales accounts are eliminated in consolidation **only in years in which intercompany sales occur.** (If unrealized intercompany profit exists at the end of 19X2 as a result of a 19X1 intercompany inventory sale and no 19X2 intercompany inventory transfers occurred, then it would **not** be necessary to eliminate the Intercompany Sales and Intercompany Cost of Sales accounts in consolidation at the end of 19X2, inasmuch as these accounts would have zero balances.)

15. Under existing generally accepted accounting principles, a **partially owned** subsidiary **need not defer** any of its unrealized intercompany gross profit in reporting to its **minority shareholders.**

16. For consolidated reporting purposes, the appropriate valuation of intercompany acquired inventory is the lower of the **selling entity's** cost or the market value.

17. Section 482 of the Internal Revenue Code (which deals with transfer pricing) applies to **all** intercompany transactions—not just inventory transfers.

COMPLETION STATEMENTS

1. An inventory transfer from a parent to a subsidiary is called a(n) _____ _____ transfer.

2. An inventory transfer from a subsidiary to a parent is called a(n) _____ _____ transfer.

3. The measure of profit to be used in calculating the amount of unrealized intercompany profit at a balance sheet date is _____ .

4. Transactions that take place between completely independent parties are called _____ transactions.

5. All intercompany transactions between a parent and a subsidiary are _____ _____ transactions.

6. When a partially owned subsidiary sells inventory at a mark-up to its parent and the parent has not resold all of the inventory by year-end, the intercompany profit on the ending inventory has been _____ from the perspective of the minority shareholders.

7. The section of the Internal Revenue Code that deals with transfer pricing is
_____ .

TRUE-OR-FALSE STATEMENTS

1. T F Even though intercompany transactions are **not** arms-length transactions, such transactions still are bonafide transactions.

2. T F No intercompany eliminations are necessary in the income statement section of the combining statement worksheet when the intercompany sales are **at cost.**

3. T F In eliminating unrealized intercompany profit, the measure of profit is the operating profit.

4. T F In eliminating unrealized intercompany profit, income taxes provided on such profit **must** also be eliminated.

5. T F The amount of intercompany profit or loss to be eliminated is **not** affected by the existence of a minority interest.

6. T F Fractional elimination is **required** under *ARB No. 51*.

7. T F Intercompany profit on **downstream** sales to partially owned subsidiaries is deemed to be realized to the extent of the minority interest.

8. T F When a **partially owned** subsidiary has **upstream** sales, the intercompany profit accruing to the minority shareholders **must** be deferred in the consolidated financial statements.

9. T F When a **partially owned** subsidiary has **upstream** intercompany inventory transfers above cost and a portion of the intercompany profit is unrealized at year-end in the consolidated financial statements, the subsidiary **need not** defer any of the unrealized intercompany profit in reporting to its minority shareholders.

10. T F *ARB No. 51* requires that unrealized intercompany profit be allocated **proportionately** between the controlling interest and the minority interest in preparing consolidated financial statements.

MULTIPLE-CHOICE QUESTIONS

Conceptual Questions

1. Which of the following statements **is** a valid reason for eliminating intercompany transactions in consolidation?
    a. Intercompany transactions are related party transactions.
    b. Intercompany transactions are not bonafide transactions.
    c. It is often impractical and in many cases impossible to determine if intercompany transfer prices approximate prices that could have been obtained with outside independent parties.

    d. The parent company could manipulate the intercompany transfer prices in a manner that is not equitable to the subsidiary.

    e. None of the above.

2. Which of the following statements **is** correct?

    a. Elimination by rearrangement is mandatory under *ARB No. 51.*

    b. Intercompany inventory transfers at cost do not have to be eliminated in consolidation.

    c. If an intercompany inventory transfer is made in 19X1 but the inventory is not resold until 19X2, the intercompany inventory sale must also be eliminated in 19X2.

    d. Downstream intercompany inventory sales do not have to be eliminated if the subsidiary is 100% owned.

    e. None of the above.

3. An intercompany inventory transfer above cost occurred in 19X1. At the end of 19X1, a portion of the transferred inventory remains unsold. Which of the following accounts would **not** require adjustment or elimination in consolidation at the end of 19X1?

    a. Intercompany Cost of Sales.

    b. Intercompany Sales.

    c. Inventory.

    d. Sales.

    e. None of the above.

4. An intercompany inventory transfer above cost occurred in 19X1. In 19X2, this inventory was resold to an outside party. Which of the following accounts **would** require adjustment or elimination in consolidation at the end of 19X2?

    a. Cost of Sales.

    b. Intercompany Cost of Sales.

    c. Intercompany Sales.

    d. Inventory.

    e. None of the above.

5. Concerning the treatment in consolidation of intercompany profit on intercompany inventory sales, which of the following statements **is** correct?

    a. Intercompany profit on downstream sales to a partially owned subsidiary should be considered realized to the extent of the minority interest ownership percentage.

    b. On an upstream sale from a partially owned subsidiary, the intercompany profit that accrues to the minority shareholders need not be deferred in consolidation.

    c. Income taxes on intercompany profit eliminated in consolidation does not have to also be eliminated.

    d. For upstream intercompany transfers from a partially owned subsidiary, the deferral of intercompany profit must be allocated proportionately between the majority interest and the minority interest.

    e. None of the above.

Application Questions

6. In 19X1, P Company sold inventory costing $100,000 to its 75%-owned subsidiary, S Company, for $180,000. At the end of 19X1, S Company reported $54,000 of this inventory in its balance sheet. The amount of unrealized intercompany profit that **cannot** be reported in the consolidated income statement for 19X1 is
   - a. $18,000
   - b. $20,000
   - c. $24,000
   - d. $60,000
   - e. None of the above.

7. Use the information in Question 6, except assume that the sale is upstream.
   - a. $6,000
   - b. $18,000
   - c. $20,000
   - d. $24,000
   - e. None of the above.

8. S Company, a 75%-owned subsidiary of P Company, sold inventory costing $400,000 to its parent for $480,000 in 19X1. P Company resold $408,000 of this inventory in 19X1 for $550,000. For 19X1, S Company reported a net income of $400,000 disregarding any unrealized intercompany profit at the end of 19X1. The amount of unrealized intercompany profit that **cannot** be reported in the consolidated income statement for 19X1 is
   - a. $3,000
   - b. $9,000
   - c. $12,000
   - d. $72,000
   - e. $80,000

9. Refer to the information in Question 8. In the consolidated income statement for 19X1, the minority interest deduction would be reported at
   - a. $88,000
   - b. $91,000
   - c. $97,000
   - d. $100,000
   - e. None of the above.

10. S Company, a 90%-owned subsidiary of P Company, resold in 19X2 for $66,000 inventory that it had acquired from P Company in 19X1 for $50,000. P Company's cost was $40,000. For 19X2, S Company reported a net income of $100,000 disregarding any intercompany profit realized in 19X2. The amount of realized intercompany profit that **can** be reported in the 19X2 consolidated income statement is
    - a. $1,000
    - b. $9,000
    - c. $10,000
    - d. $16,000
    - e. $26,000

11. Refer to the information in Question 10. In preparing consolidated financial statements for 19X2, what is the amount that will be credited to Intercompany Cost of Sales on the worksheet?

    a. $ –0–
    b. $10,000
    c. $16,000
    d. $26,000
    e. None of the above.

12. In 19X2, P Company resold for $85,000 inventory that it had acquired from its 60%-owned subsidiary, S Company, in 19X1 for $70,000. S Company's cost was $50,000. For 19X2, S Company reported a net income of $200,000 disregarding any intercompany profit realized in 19X2. The amount of realized intercompany profit that **can** be reported in the 19X2 consolidated income statement is

    a. $12,000
    b. $15,000
    c. $20,000
    d. $21,000
    e. $35,000

13. Refer to the information in Question 12. In the consolidated income statement for 19X2, the minority interest deduction would be reported at

    a. $72,000
    b. $74,000
    c. $80,000
    d. $86,000
    e. $88,000

14. Refer to the information in Question 12. In preparing consolidated statements for 19X2, what is the amount of the adjustment to the Inventory account on the worksheet?

    a. $ –0–
    b. $12,000
    c. $20,000
    d. $50,000
    e. $70,000

CHAPTER 8—SOLUTIONS

Completion Statements

    1. downstream
    2. upstream
    3. gross profit
    4. arm's-length
    5. related party
    6. realized
    7. Section 482

True-or-False Statements

1. True	6. False
2. False	7. False
3. False	8. True
4. True	9. True
5. True	10. False

Multiple-Choice Questions

1. e
2. e
3. d
4. a
5. e
6. c ($54,000 × 4/9 = $24,000)
7. d ($54,000 × 4/9 = $24,000)
8. c ($72,000 × 16 2/3% = $12,000)
9. c ($400,000 − $12,000 = $388,000; $388,000 × 25% = $97,000)
10. c ($50,000 − $40,000 = $10,000)
11. a (No adjustment is necessary to this account because the intercompany transfer occurred the previous year.)
12. c ($70,000 − $50,000 = $20,000)
13. e ($200,000 + $20,000 = $220,000; $220,000 × 40% = $88,000)
14. a (No adjustment is needed to this account because it has a zero balance—the inventory has been resold.)

CHAPTER 8—APPENDIX

INTRACOMPANY INVENTORY TRANSFERS FOR BRANCHES AND DIVISIONS

CHAPTER APPENDIX HIGHLIGHTS

1. When **inventory is transferred** from the home office to a branch, a sale reportable to the company's stockholders has not occurred. This action is merely the physical movement of inventory within the company (an intracompany transaction).

2. For intracompany inventory transfers, an **intracompany billing** must be prepared to transfer purchases from the books of the home office to the books of the branch. The **Purchases Sent to Branch** account (a **contra purchases** account) is credited by the home office and the **Purchases from Home Office** account is debited by the branch.

3. For intracompany inventory transfers **above cost,** the home office keeps track of the unrealized profit in an account called **Deferred Profit,** which is adjusted at each balance sheet date.

COMPLETION STATEMENTS FOR APPENDIX

1. An account used by a branch under a periodic inventory system to record purchases from the home office is called _____ .

2. An account used by a home office under a periodic inventory system to record inventory transfers to a branch is called _____ .

3. A contra asset account used by a home office in recording inventory shipments to a branch at a mark-up is called _____ .

4. The Purchases Sent to Branch account is substantively a(n) _____ _____ account.

TRUE-OR-FALSE STATEMENTS FOR APPENDIX

1. T F   The Purchases Sent to Branch account and the Purchases from Home Office account are **reciprocal** accounts only if inventory transfers are made at the home office's cost.

2. T F   The Deferred Profit account maintained on the home office's books is substantively a **contra asset** account.

3. T F   In the combining statement worksheet, the combined net income will usually differ from the home office's net income when inventory transfers to the branch are made above cost.

4. T F   In the combining statement worksheet, the recognized profit elimination entry needed when inventory transfers are made above cost is substantively an **adjusting** entry rather than a **reclassification** entry.

MULTIPLE-CHOICE QUESTIONS FOR APPENDIX

Conceptual Questions

1. Under a periodical inventory system, which of the following accounts is **not** used in transferring inventory from a home office to a branch at a mark-up?
    a. Purchases Sent to Branch.
    b. Deferred Profit.
    c. Branch Income.
    d. Home Office Equity.
    e. None of the above.

2. Which of the following accounts is **not closed out** in the year-end closing entries of the home office when a periodic inventory system is used?
    a. Purchases Sent to Branch.
    b. Deferred Profit.
    c. Branch Income.
    d. Cost of Sales.
    e. None of the above.

3. In preparing the combining statement worksheet for a home office and a branch at year-end, which of the following entries would be made in the recognized profit elimination entry?

	Debit	Credit
a.	Branch Income	Deferred Profit
b.	Cost of Sales	Branch Income
c.	Deferred Profit	Cost of Sales
d.	Branch Income	Cost of Sales
e.	None of the above.	

Application Questions

4. A home office ships inventory costing $60,000 to its branch at a transfer price of $75,000. The mark-up as a percentage of the home office cost is

    a. .20%
    b. .25%
    c. 1.25%
    d. 20%
    e. 25%

5. In 19X1, a home office shipped inventory costing $75,000 to its newly established branch at a transfer price of $100,000. In the branch's year-end closing entries at the end of 19X1, the branch charged $60,000 of this inventory to Cost of Sales. The adjusted general ledger balance in the Deferred Profit account at year-end should be

    a. $3,750
    b. $10,000
    c. $15,000
    d. $25,000
    e. None of the above.

6. For the year ended December 31, 19X1, the adjusted financial statements of a home office and its branch show net income of $200,000 and $50,000, respectively. At the end of 19X1, the home office adjusted the Deferred Profit account by debiting it for $16,000, leaving a balance of $9,000. The combined net income for 19X1 is

    a. $184,000
    b. $191,000
    c. $200,000
    d. $250,000
    e. None of the above.

7. For the year ended December 31, 19X1, selected line items from the home office and branch columns of the combining statement worksheet are as follows:

	Home Office	Branch
Cost of sales	$(600,000)	$(300,000)
Branch income	80,000	
Net income	200,000	50,000
Deferred Profit	15,000	

What amount would be reported in the combined column for Cost of Sales?

    a. $850,000
    b. $870,000
    c. $885,000
    d. $900,000
    e. None of the above.

8. Using the information in the preceding question, what is the combined net income as reported in the combined column?
   a. $170,000
   b. $185,000
   c. $200,000
   d. $250,000
   e. None of the above.

CHAPTER 8—SOLUTIONS FOR APPENDIX

Completion Statements

1. Purchases from Home Office
2. Purchases Sent to Branch
3. Deferred Profit
4. Contra purchases account

True-or-False Statements

1. True
2. True
3. False
4. False

Multiple-Choice Questions

1. c
2. b
3. d
4. e
5. b
6. c
7. b ($600,000 + $300,000 − $30,000 [$80,000 − $50,000] = $870,000)
8. c

CHAPTER 9
INTERCOMPANY FIXED ASSET TRANSFERS

CHAPTER HIGHLIGHTS

1. From a consolidated viewpoint, the reported amount for a fixed asset **cannot** change merely because the asset has been moved to a different location within the consolidated group.

2. If an intercompany gain or loss on an intercompany fixed asset transfer is deferred in consolidation, then any income taxes (or tax benefit) provided on the gain or loss **must** also be deferred.

3. In developing elimination entries pertaining to transfers of depreciable fixed assets, it is necessary to use the assets' **new remaining assigned life,** if different from the old remaining life. (The old remaining life is no longer relevant.)

4. The amount of intercompany gain or loss to be eliminated is **not** affected by the existence of a **minority interest.**

5. The amount of intercompany gain or loss to be eliminated in consolidation **may be allocated proportionately** between the majority and minority interests (applicable only to upstream transfers from partially owned subsidiaries).

TRUE-OR-FALSE STATEMENTS

1. T F   Just like fixed asset transfers **above** carrying value, a loss on the transfer of a fixed asset **below** carrying value **must** be deferred in the consolidated financial statements.

2. T F   When depreciable fixed assets are transferred, the acquiring entity must use the **selling entity's** remaining depreciable life.

3. T F   When a **downstream** depreciable asset transfer occurs, the subsidiary must record depreciation expense based on the carrying value of the depreciable asset at the transfer date.

4. T F   When a depreciable asset transfer occurs at **above** the selling entity's carrying value, the historical cost of that asset to be reported in the consolidated balance sheet is the carrying value of the asset at the transfer date.

5. T   F   The principles underlying the treatment of downstream depreciable asset transfers in consolidated financial statements are the **same** as for upstream transfers.

6. T   F   A downstream depreciable asset transfer occurs at **above** cost to a **wholly owned** subsidiary. Once the asset is fully depreciated by the subsidiary, the parent's retained earnings (not consolidated retained earnings) will be the same as if the asset had not been transferred.

7. T   F   A downstream depreciable asset transfer occurs at **above** cost to a **partially owned** subsidiary. Once the asset is fully depreciated by the subsidiary, the parent's retained earnings (not consolidated retained earnings) will be the same as if the asset had not been transferred.

MULTIPLE-CHOICE QUESTIONS

Application Questions

1. On January 2, 19X1, Pax Company sold equipment costing $62,000 to its 90%-owned subsidiary, Sax Company, for $44,000. At the time of the sale, the equipment had a carrying value of $32,000 and a remaining life of 4 years. Each company uses the straight-line depreciation method. What are the cost and accumulated depreciation, respectively, of this equipment in the December 31, 19X1, consolidated balance sheet?

    a. $44,000 and $8,000
    b. $44,000 and $11,000
    c. $62,000 and $8,000
    d. $62,000 and $11,000
    e. None of the above.

2. Use the same information as in Question 1. What is the amount of the adjustment to Depreciation Expense in preparing the consolidation worksheet at December 31, 19X1?

    a. A $3,000 debit.
    b. A $3,000 credit.
    c. A $2,700 debit.
    d. A $2,700 credit.
    e. None of the above.

3. Use the same information as in Question 1. Also assume that Sax reported net income of $500,000 for 19X1. What is the amount of the minority interest deduction in the consolidated income statement for 19X1?

    a. $49,700
    b. $50,000
    c. $50,300
    d. $50,900
    e. None of the above.

4. Use the same information as in Question 1. What is the amount of unrealized inter-company gain or loss that must be deferred at December 31, 19X2 (not 19X1)?

    a. $5,100
    b. $6,000
    c. $10,800
    d. $12,000
    e. None of the above.

5. On January 3, 19X1, S Company, a 75%-owned subsidiary of P Company, sold equipment having a cost of $800,000 and accumulated depreciation of $600,000 to P Company for $360,000. S Company had been using an 8-year life. P Company estimated the equipment would last 4 years. Each company uses the straight-line depreciation method. For 19X1, S Company reported net income of $400,000 exclusive of any intercompany gain on the equipment transfer. What are the cost and accumulated depreciation, respectively, of this equipment in the December 31, 19X1, consolidated balance sheet?

    a. $800,000 and $40,000
    b. $800,000 and $650,000
    c. $800,000 and $690,000
    d. $360,000 and $90,000
    e. $360,000 and $100,000

6. Use the same information as in Question 5. What is the amount of the adjustment to Depreciation Expense in preparing the consolidation worksheet at December 31, 19X1?

    a. A debit of $30,000.
    b. A credit of $30,000.
    c. A debit of $40,000.
    d. A credit of $40,000.
    e. None of the above.

7. Use the same information as in Question 5. What is the amount of the minority interest deduction in the consolidated income statement for 19X1?

    a. $100,000
    b. $110,000
    c. $130,000
    d. $140,000
    e. None of the above.

8. Use the same information as in Question 5. What is the amount of unrealized inter-company gain or loss that must be deferred at December 31, 19X2 (not 19X1)?

    a. $60,000
    b. $80,000
    c. $135,000
    d. $180,000
    e. None of the above.

CHAPTER 9—SOLUTIONS

Completion Statements (None)

True-or-False Statements

1. True
2. False
3. False
4. False
5. True
6. True
7. False

Multiple-Choice Questions

1. e (Accumulated depreciation is $30,000 on 1/2/X1 plus $8,000 of depreciation expense for 19X1.)
2. b ($11,000 of depreciation expense recorded by the subsidiary minus $8,000 of reportable depreciation expense for 19X1)
3. b (10% of $500,000)
4. b (50% of the $12,000 intercompany gain)
5. b (Accumulated depreciation is $600,000 on 1/3/X1 plus $50,000 of depreciation expense for 19X1.)
6. d ($90,000 of depreciation expense recorded by the parent minus $50,000 of reportable depreciation expense for 19X1)
7. b (25% of $440,000) The realized portion of the $160,000 intercompany gain is $40,000.
8. b (50% of the $160,000 intercompany gain)

CHAPTER 10
INTERCOMPANY BOND HOLDINGS

CHAPTER HIGHLIGHTS

1. The purchase by one entity within the consolidated group of any or all of the outstanding bonds of another entity within the consolidated group represents a **constructive retirement** of the bonds.

2. Any **imputed gain or loss** on the constructive retirement of an affiliate's bonds **must** be reported in the consolidated income statement **in the period of purchase.**

3. If the imputed gain or loss on the constructive retirement of an affiliate's bonds is material, it **must** be reported as an **extraordinary item.**

4. The objective of the consolidation procedures is to make the necessary adjustments on the consolidating statement worksheet to reflect, in the consolidated financial statements, amounts that would have existed if the **issuing entity,** rather than the **acquiring entity,** had acquired the bonds.

5. In calculating the gain or loss on the extinguishment of debt, amounts paid by the acquiring entity **for interest** from the last interest payment date to the purchase date **must** be excluded.

6. The amount of the **imputed** gain or loss on the extinguishment of debt that is reported in the period in which the affiliate's bonds are purchased is determined by comparing the **acquisition cost** (excluding amounts paid for interest) to the **applicable percentage of the carrying value** of the bonds payable as of the bond acquisition date.

7. When the **issuing company** has a premium and the **acquiring company** has a discount, a gain always results.

8. When the **issuing company** has a discount and the **acquiring company** has a premium, a loss always results.

9. When each company has a discount or each company has a premium, the net effect is a gain or a loss, depending on which company has the **greater** discount or premium.

10. If the acquiring entity subsequently sells some or all of the intercompany bond holdings (instead of holding them until their maturity date), the sale is treated as the **issuance of bonds** from a consolidated viewpoint.

COMPLETION STATEMENTS

1. The gain or loss on the deemed extinguishment of debt that is reported in the period in which an affiliate's bonds are purchased is a(n) _____ gain or loss.

2. When a parent purchases a portion of its subsidiary's outstanding bonds, the subsidiary should reflect the parent's ownership in the bonds by using _____ _____ accounts.

3. When a gain or loss is to be reported as a result of an intercompany bond acquisition, the gain or loss may have to be reported as a(n) _____ .

4. The purchase by one entity within the consolidated group of any or all of the outstanding bonds represents a(n) _____ retirement of the bonds.

TRUE-OR-FALSE STATEMENTS

1. T   F   A gain or loss as a result of an intercompany bond acquisition is reportable in the consolidated financial statements **only if** the amount is material.

2. T   F   In intercompany bond holdings in which the parent has a **premium** and the subsidiary has a **discount,** a gain will **always** be reported in the consolidated income statement in the year of the bond acquisition.

3. T   F   In intercompany bond holdings in which the issuing company has a **discount** and the acquiring company has a **discount,** a loss will **always** be reported in the consolidated income statement in the year of the bond acquisition.

4. T   F   In intercompany bond holdings in which the issuing company has a **premium** and the acquiring company has a **discount,** a gain will **always** be reported in the consolidated income statement in the year of the bond acquisition.

5. T   F   The Intercompany Interest Income and Intercompany Interest Expense accounts are **always** eliminated in consolidation.

6. T   F   The imputed gain or loss arising from the acquisition of an affiliate's bonds is **always** eliminated in consolidation.

7. T   F   The account Intercompany Bond Premium is **always** eliminated in consolidation in its entirety—regardless of whether the account is on the parent's books or the books of a partially owned subsidiary.

8. T   F   The procedures to determine and account for imputed gains and losses arising from intercompany bond purchases do **not** change if the purchase is made between interest payment dates as opposed to the purchase being made at an interest payment date.

MULTIPLE-CHOICE QUESTIONS

Conceptual Questions

1. Which of the following statements is **false?**
    a. The purchase of a subsidiary's outstanding bonds by the parent company is a constructive retirement of the bonds—not an actual retirement of the bonds.
    b. Any imputed gain or loss on the deemed retirement resulting from an intercompany bond holding must be treated as an extraordinary item regardless of materiality.
    c. When the issuing company has a bond premium and the acquiring company has a discount, a gain on extinguishment of debt will always result.
    d. When each company has a premium in an intercompany bond holding, the effect of the deemed retirement can be a gain or a loss.
    e. None of the above.

2. The gain or loss on the deemed extinguishment of a subsidiary's bonds is to be reported in the consolidated financial statements as a(n)
    a. Extraordinary item, if material.
    b. Extraordinary item, regardless of materiality.
    c. Nonextraordinary item.
    d. Adjustment to intercompany interest income and/or intercompany interest expense.
    e. None of the above.

Application Questions

3. A parent company acquired in the open market 25% of its 100%-owned subsidiary's outstanding 8% bonds for $321,000. The outstanding bonds have a face value of $1,200,000 and a carrying value of $1,160,000 on the acquisition date. The gain or loss to be reported in the consolidated income statement in the bond acquisition is a
    a. Gain of $9,000.
    b. Gain of $11,000.
    c. Loss of $11,000.
    d. Loss of $31,000.
    e. Gain of $31,000.

4. An 80%–subsidiary acquired in the open market 20% of its parent's outstanding 10% bonds for $686,000. The outstanding bonds have a face value of $3,500,000 and a carrying value of $3,555,000. The gain or loss to be reported in the consolidated income statement in the bond acquisition year is a
    a. $3,000 gain.
    b. $3,000 loss.
    c. $25,000 gain.
    d. $25,000 loss.

5. On May 1, 19X1, Pax Company acquired in the open market 30% of the 8% outstanding bonds of Sax Company (its 100%-owned subsidiary) for $280,000. The bonds have a face value of $1,000,000, a carrying value of $1,050,000 on the acquisition date, and a maturity date of December 31, 19X2. Corporate policy specifies straight-line amortization of premiums and discounts resulting from bond issuances and bond investments. Pax reported $500,000 of net income for 19X1—excluding any discount amortization pertaining to its bond investment and excluding any earnings of Sax recordable under the equity method of accounting. Sax reported net income of $100,000 for 19X1, which amount is after reported interest expense of $50,000 on the bonds (net of $30,000 of bond premium amortization for the full calendar year). The gain or loss on the extinguishment of debt for 19X1 in the consolidated income statement is a

   a. Loss of $35,000.
   b. Gain of $35,000.
   c. Loss of $5,000.
   d. Gain of $5,000.
   e. None of the above.

6. Use the same information as in Question 5. The consolidated net income for 19X1 is

   a. $609,000
   b. $615,000
   c. $620,000
   d. $629,000
   e. $635,000

7. Use the same information as in Question 5. Pax should report what amount of intercompany interest income in its separate income statement for 19X1?

   a. $8,000
   b. $16,000
   c. $24,000
   d. $36,000
   e. $44,000

8. Use the same information as in Question 5. Sax should report what amount of intercompany interest expense in its separate income statement for 19X1?

   a. $1,000
   b. $6,000
   c. $10,000
   d. $16,000
   e. $22,000

9. Use the same information as in Question 5. What amount should Pax report in its separate 19X1 income statement for Equity in Net Income of Subsidiary?

   a. $100,000
   b. $109,000
   c. $115,000
   d. $120,000
   e. $121,000

10. Use the same information as in Question 5. What amount should be reported in the consolidated income statement for interest expense?

    a. $30,000
    b. $35,000
    c. $40,000
    d. $50,000
    e. $64,000

11. Use the same information as in Question 5, but assume the subsidiary is only 90%–owned by the parent. The minority interest share of Sax's 19X1 net income as reported in the 19X1 consolidated income statement is

    a. $10,000
    b. $10,600
    c. $10,900
    d. $11,500
    e. $12,100

CHAPTER 10—SOLUTIONS

Completion Statements

    1. imputed
    2. intercompany
    3. extraordinary item
    4. constructive

True-or-False Statements

1. False	5. True
2. False	6. False
3. False	7. True
4. True	8. True

Multiple-Choice Questions

    1. b
    2. a
    3. d (Parent's premium of $21,000 + $10,000 intercompany discount on subsidiary's books)
    4. c (Subsidiary's premium of $14,000 + $11,000 intercompany premium on parent's books)
    5. b (Parent's discount of $20,000 + $15,000 intercompany premium on subsidiary's books)
    6. d ($500,000 + $100,000 + $9,000 for subsidiary's unamortized intercompany premium at 12/31/X1 + $20,000 for parent's unamortized discount at 12/31/X1)
    7. c ($300,000 × 8% × 2/3 yr = $16,000; $16,000 + $8,000 of discount amortization equals $24,000)
    8. c ($300,000 × 8% × 2/3 yr = $16,000; $16,000 − $6,000 of intercompany bond premium amortization equals $10,000)

9. e (for Module 1) ($100,000 + $9,000 for subsidiary's unamortized premium at 12/31/X1 + $12,000 for parent's unamortized discount at 12/31/X1)

   a (for Module 2) ($100,000 reported by the subsidiary for 19X1)

10. c ($700,000 × 8% = $56,000; $56,000 – $21,000 of bond premium amortization equals $35,000)

   ($300,000 × 8% × 1/3 yr = $8,000; $8,000 – $3,000 of bond premium amortization from 1/1/X1 to 4/30/X1 equals $5,000)

   ($35,000 + $5,000 = $40,000)

11. c ($100,000 + $9,000 for unamortized intercompany premium at 12/31/X1 equals $109,000; $109,000 × 10% equals $10,900)

CHAPTER 11

CHANGES IN PARENT'S OWNERSHIP INTEREST AND SUBSIDIARY WITH PREFERRED STOCK

CHAPTER HIGHLIGHTS

1. When some or all of the common stock held by minority stockholders of a subsidiary is acquired by either the parent or the subsidiary, the **purchase method** must be used.

2. If the **parent** acquires any or all of the minority interest, the acquisition is treated merely as a **block acquisition** (the cost of the block must be analyzed and separated into its individual components).

3. If the **subsidiary** acquires any or all of the minority interest, no adjustment is made to the parent's carrying value of its investment in the subsidiary—regardless of whether the purchase price is more or less than the book value per share. (Paying more than book value per share results in an increase to the current value over book value element and/or the goodwill element of the conceptual analysis; paying less than book value per share has the opposite effect.)

4. When a parent **sells a portion of its common stock holdings** in a subsidiary, the theoretically correct method of reducing the investment account is the **average cost method.** (For federal income tax reporting purposes, only the **specific identification method** and the **first-in, first-out method** can be used.)

5. When a parent sells a portion of its common stock holdings in a subsidiary, any gain or loss is **reported currently in the income statement.**

6. When a subsidiary **issues additional common stock** to the public at **below** the book value per share of its common stock, the parent suffers **dilution** of its interest in the subsidiary's net assets. If the shares are issued at **above** the book value, the parent's interest is **increased** (accretion).

7. **Dilution** or **accretion** resulting from a subsidiary issuing additional common stock at below or above book value per share of its common stock results in (A) a **gain or loss** in the parent's income statement (and the consolidated income statement) under the **parent company theory** and (B) an **adjustment to the parent's additional paid-in capital** account (which carries through to the consolidated balance sheet) under the **entity theory.**

8. The position of the AICPA is an **endorsement** of the parent company concept.

9. The position of the SEC is that of **permitting** the use of the parent company concept.

10. A **stock dividend** by a subsidiary has no effect on the parent's books or in consolidation.

11. A subsidiary's **preferred stock** is treated as part of the **minority interest** in the consolidated balance sheet.

12. The **special features of preferred stock** (call features, cumulative as to dividends, and participations) may require that a portion of the subsidiary's retained earnings be shown as part of the **minority interest** in the consolidated balance sheet.

13. When a subsidiary has **cumulative** preferred stock outstanding, the preferred stock dividend requirement must be subtracted from the subsidiary's net income **before** the parent can apply the equity method of accounting.

14. If a parent acquires some or all of a subsidiary's **cumulative** preferred stock, the parent should account for its preferred stock investment using the **equity method of accounting.**

15. If a parent acquires some or all of a subsidiary's preferred stock at above or below the book value of the preferred stock holding, the parent will (A) report a **loss or gain,** respectively, under the **parent company concept** (this loss or gain carries through to the consolidated income statement) or (B) adjust its **Additional Paid-in Capital account** for the difference under the **economic unit concept** (this adjustment carries through to the consolidated balance sheet).

COMPLETION STATEMENTS

1. The acquisition of some or all of the common stock held by minority shareholders of a subsidiary **must** be accounted for using the _____ .

2. When a subsidiary acquires at **above** the book value some or all of the common stock held by minority shareholders, the parent suffers _____ of its interest in the subsidiary's _____ at book value.

3. When a parent disposes of a portion of an interest in a subsidiary, the **conceptually correct** method of determining the amount by which the investment account should be reduced is the _____ method.

4. For income tax reporting purposes, the **only** acceptable methods for reducing the investment account when a parent disposes of a portion of an interest in a subsidiary are the _____ method and the _____ method.

5. When a subsidiary issues additional common stock, two concepts on reporting any increase or decrease in the parent's interest in the subsidiary's net asset at book value are the _____ concept and the _____ concept.

6. When a subsidiary issues additional common stock at above or below book value per share, the use of the **economic unit concept** would result in an entry by the parent to _____ .

7. When a subsidiary issues additional common stock, at above or below book value per share, the use of the **parent company concept** would result in an entry to a(n) _____ account that would be reported currently.

8. When a subsidiary issues additional common stock at **below** book value, the parent's interest in its share of the subsidiary's net assets at book value _____ _____ .

9. When a subsidiary has preferred stock outstanding, the preferred stock **must** be classified as _____ in the consolidated balance sheet (except to the extent it is owned by the parent).

10. When a parent acquires a portion of a subsidiary's outstanding preferred stock at **more** than its share of the preferred stock's book value, a debit would be made to _____ under the economic unit concept, whereas a debit would be made to _____ under the parent company concept.

TRUE-OR-FALSE STATEMENTS

1. T F *APB Opinion No. 16* allows **only** the purchase method to account for the acquisition of minority interests—regardless of whether the parent or the subsidiary acquires the minority interest.

2. T F If the subsidiary acquires all or some of the minority at more or less than book value per share, the parent **must** make an adjustment to the carrying value of its investment account.

3. T F Acquisition of some or all of the minority interest at **more** than book value per share always results in additional goodwill to be reported.

4. T F If a subsidiary acquires **part** of the minority interest at more than book value per share, the remaining minority shareholders as well as the parent suffer dilution.

5. T F When a parent disposes of a portion of its common stock holdings in a subsidiary, the **specific identification** method is acceptable for financial reporting purposes in determining the amount by which the investment account should be reduced.

6. T F The average cost method **cannot** be used for income tax reporting purposes when a parent disposes of a portion of its common stock holdings in a subsidiary.

7. T F The reportable gain or loss on the disposal of a portion of the common stock owned of a subsidiary is determined by comparing the proceeds to the subsidiary's book value of the shares sold.

8. T F When a subsidiary issues additional common stock at **above** the existing book value of its common stock, the parent will **adjust** the carrying value of its investment account accordingly.

9. T F When a subsidiary issues additional common stock at **below** the existing book value of its common stock, the parent's total dollar interest in the subsidiary's net assets at book value **decreases.**

10. T F Under the **economic unit concept,** the sale of a subsidiary's shares (pursuant to a partial disposal) is no different, in substance, from the issuance of additional common shares by the subsidiary.

11. T F Reporting in consolidation a gain or loss resulting from the issuance of additional common stock by a subsidiary would fit under the **parent company concept**—not the **economic unit concept.**

12. T F Under *SAB No. 51,* companies do **not** have to recognize a gain or loss in consolidation when a subsidiary issues additional common stock at above or below book value per share.

MULTIPLE-CHOICE QUESTIONS

Conceptual Questions

1. Regarding the acquisition of some or all of a minority interest, which statement is **false?**
    a. If the parent acquires the minority interest, the purchase method must be used.
    b. If the subsidiary acquires the minority interest, the purchase method must be used.
    c. If the subsidiary pays less than the book value per share, the parent's ownership interest increases—both as to ownership percentage and total dollar interest in the subsidiary's net assets at their book value.
    d. The parent's total carrying value of the investment does not change when the subsidiary acquires the minority interest.
    e. None of the above.

2. Which of the following is disallowed by *APB Opinion No. 16* when a parent acquires some or all of the minority interest?
    a.   The pooling of interests method.
    b.   The cost method.
    c.   The economic unit concept.
    d.   The equity method.
    e.   None of the above.

3. Regarding the disposal of an interest in a subsidiary, which of the following methods is the theoretically correct method for financial reporting?
    a.   The average cost method.
    b.   The first-in, first-out method.
    c.   The last-in, last-out method.
    d.   The specific identification method.
    e.   None of the above.

4. When a parent that has an 80%-owned subsidiary sells 5% of its holdings, which of the following could **not** occur or result?
    a.   The minority interest will increase.
    b.   The carrying value of the investment will decrease.
    c.   A gain or loss on disposal will be reported in consolidation.
    d.   The unamortized amount of goodwill existing at the disposal date will be adjusted downward.
    e.   None of the above.

5. When a subsidiary issues additional common stock at above book value, which of the following could **not** occur or result?
    a.   The minority interest will increase.
    b.   The parent will record a loss that is **not** eliminated in consolidation.
    c.   The parent will make an adjustment to Additional Paid-in Capital if the economic unit concept is used.
    d.   The carrying value of the investment will be adjusted upward.
    e.   None of the above.

6. When a subsidiary issues additional common stock at above book value, which of the following could occur or result?
    a.   The unamortized amount of goodwill existing at the time of issuance must be adjusted accordingly.
    b.   The purchase method of account must be used.
    c.   The carrying value of the investment must be adjusted accordingly.
    d.   If the parent is publicly owned, it must report a gain or loss in its income statement that would not be eliminated in consolidation pursuant to *Staff Accounting Bulletin No. 51*.
    e.   None of the above.

7. Concerning a parent that has an investment in its subsidiary's preferred stock, which of the following statements is **false?**
    a.   The parent should account for its preferred stock holdings using the equity method of accounting.
    b.   Dividends in arrears are treated as accruing to the preferred stock interest only if the preferred stock is cumulative preferred stock.

c.   If the parent's cost of the preferred stock holding differs from its share of the book value of the preferred stock holding, the carrying value of the investment in the preferred stock may be adjusted to such book value.
d.   The subsidiary's preferred stock held by the parent company is treated as part of the minority interest in consolidation.
e.   None of the above.

Application Questions

8. Pax Company owns 60% of the outstanding common stock of Sax Company. Sax acquired 10% of its outstanding common stock from minority shareholders for $70,000 cash when its book value was $400,000. How much dilution did the parent suffer?

   a. $-0-
   b. $10,000
   c. $18,000
   d. $20,000
   e. $42,000

9. Use the same information as in Question 8. How much dilution did the remaining minority shareholders suffer?

   a. $-0-
   b. $ 9,000
   c. $10,000
   d. $20,000
   e. $21,000

10. Pax Company owns 75% of the outstanding common stock of Sax Company. These holdings were acquired in a single block purchase in 19X1. On April 1, 19X3, Pax sold 20% of its holdings in Sax for $60,000. At December 31, 19X2, the carrying value of Pax's investment in Sax was $240,000. During the first quarter of 19X3, Sax reported net income of $40,000 and declared dividends of $20,000. Pax uses the equity method. In Pax's 19X3 income statement, it should report a

   a.   Gain of $ 4,000
   b.   Gain of $ 6,000
   c.   Gain of $ 8,000
   d.   Gain of $ 9,000
   e.   Gain of $12,000

11. Use the same information as in Question 10. In addition, assume that Sax reported net income of $160,000 for the last three quarters of 19X3. Which of the following amounts would be reported in the 19X3 consolidated income statement?

	Equity in Net Income of Subsidiary	Minority Interest in Net Income of Subsidiary
a.	$ -0-	$69,000
b.	$ -0-	$74,000
c.	$ -0-	$80,000
d.	$6,000	$69,000
e.	$6,000	$74,000
f.	$6,000	$80,000

12. On May 1, 19X1, Stix Company, a 75%-owned subsidiary of Pix Company, issued 25,000 shares of its $1 par value common stock to the public for $500,000. Stix had 100,000 shares outstanding having a total book value of $900,000 just prior to this issuance. As a result of this issuance, the amount the parent would report in its 19X1 income statement under the parent company concept is

    a. $-0-
    b.   Gain of $132,000
    c.   Gain of $165,000
    d.   Gain of $206,250
    e.   Gain of $225,000

13. Use the same information as in Question 12, but assume that the economic unit concept is used instead of the parent company concept.

    a. $-0-
    b.   Gain of $132,000
    c.   Gain of $165,000
    d.   Gain of $206,250
    e.   Gain of $225,000

14. On June 1, 19X4, P Company acquired 80% of the outstanding common stock of S Company. On that date, S Company had the following equity balances:

Preferred Stock	$500,000
Common Stock.	100,000
Retained earnings	400,000

The preferred stock has a call premium of $25,000 and cumulative dividends in arrears of $45,000. The amount to be reported for the minority interest in a consolidated balance sheet on that date is

    a. $ 86,000
    b. $100,000
    c. $156,000
    d. $656,000
    e. $670,000

CHAPTER 11—SOLUTIONS

Completion Statements

    1. purchase method
    2. dilution, net assets
    3. average cost
    4. specific identification, first-in first-out
    5. parent company, economic unit
    6. additional paid-in capital
    7. gain or loss income statement
    8. decreases
    9. minority interest
    10. additional paid-in capital, loss on acquisition of minority interest at above book value

True-or-False Statements

1. True	7. False
2. False	8. True
3. False	9. True
4. True	10. False
5. True	11. True
6. True	12. True

Multiple-Choice Questions

1. e
2. a
3. a
4. e
5. b
6. c
7. d
8. d ($30,000 of cost in excess of book value shared 2/3 by parent and 1/3 by remaining shareholders)
9. c
10. d ($60,000 proceeds minus $51,000 carrying value equals $9,000) The $51,000 is 20% of the total carrying value of $255,000 at 4/1/X3 ($240,000 + $30,000 – $15,000).
11. b (25% × $40,000 = $10,000 for the first quarter; 40% × $160,000 = $64,000 for the last three quarters; $74,000 in total)
12. c (Parent's share of book value on 4/30/X1 is $675,000; Parent's share of book value on 5/1/X1 is $840,000; $840,000 – $675,000 = $165,000)
13. a (Under the economic unit concept, the increase in the parent's share of the book value is credited to Additional Paid-in Capital—not the income statement.)
14. d ($500,000 + $20,000 + $25,000 + $45,000 + $66,000 = $656,000) The $66,000 is 20% of the retained earnings allocable to the common shareholders ($400,000 – $25,000 – $45,000 = $330,000).

CHAPTER 12
INDIRECT AND RECIPROCAL HOLDINGS

CHAPTER HIGHLIGHTS

1. An **indirect vertical holding** occurs when a parent owns more than 50% of a subsidiary and that subsidiary, in turn, owns more than 50% of another company.

2. In **indirect vertical holdings,** net income for the top-level parent and consolidated net income are the same and can be determined without consolidation by successive application of the **equity method of accounting,** starting with the **lowest-level** parent within the chain.

3. An **indirect horizontal holding** occurs when one subsidiary holds an investment in another subsidiary of a common parent.

4. In **indirect horizontal holdings,** the equity method of accounting should be used by each **investor subsidiary** even if the ownership percentage is below 20%, because the parent exercises significant influence over the investee subsidiary.

5. **Reciprocal holdings** occur when a subsidiary invests in its parent company's common stock.

6. In **reciprocal holdings,** shares of the parent company held by a subsidiary are **not** to be treated as outstanding stock in the consolidated balance sheet.

7. In **reciprocal holdings,** the cost of the investment in the parent's common stock is treated as a **cost of treasury shares.**

8. In **reciprocal holdings** in which the subsidiary is partially owned, the two schools of thought regarding how the combined earnings should be reported are the **treasury stock method** and the **traditional allocation method.**

9. The **treasury stock method** fits under the **parent company concept.**

10. The **traditional allocation** method fits under the **economic unit concept.**

11. Under the **treasury stock method** used in a reciprocal holding, consolidated net income can be determined by having the parent—but not the subsidiary—apply the **equity method of accounting.**

12. Under the **traditional allocation method** used in a reciprocal holding, consolidated net income is the **sum** of the earnings of the parent and the subsidiary. However, the division of the consolidated net income between the **controlling interests** and the **minority interest** requires the use of **simultaneous equations.**

13. In **reciprocal holdings** in which both the parent and the subsidiary report profits, the consolidated net income reported under the **treasury stock method** will always be **greater than** the earnings calculated as accruing to the controlling interests under the **traditional allocation method.**

14. In **reciprocal holdings** in which the **treasury stock method** is used, the consolidated earnings per share amount is **not** meaningful.

COMPLETION STATEMENTS

1. A relationship in which a subsidiary owns more than 50% of the outstanding common stock of another company is called a(n) _____ holding.

2. A relationship in which a subsidiary owns less than 50% of the outstanding common stock of a sister subsidiary is called a(n) _____ holding.

3. A relationship in which a subsidiary owns some of the outstanding common stock of its parent is called a(n) _____ holding.

4. Two schools of thought dealing with how the combined earnings should be reported in reciprocal holding relationships are the _____ method and the _____ method.

5. The treasury stock method fits under the _____ concept.

6. The traditional allocation method fits under the _____ concept.

7. When indirect holdings exist, consolidated net income can be determined other than by consolidation by using the _____ .

TRUE-OR-FALSE STATEMENTS

1. T   F   In an indirect **vertical** holding, a subsidiary **cannot** be consolidated unless over 50% of the subsidiary's earnings accrue to the top-level parent.

2. T   F   In an indirect **vertical** holding, the consolidation process starts at the lowest parent-subsidiary level and then works upward.

3. T   F   In indirect **horizontal** holdings, the equity method of accounting can be used by an investor subsidiary even if the investor subsidiary owns less than 20% of the sister subsidiary's outstanding common stock.

4. T   F   In indirect **horizontal** holdings, the investor subsidiary's cost of its investment in the sister subsidiary is treated as treasury stock in the consolidated balance sheet.

5. T F A subsidiary theoretically could own **all** of its parent company's outstanding common stock.

6. T F Under *ARB No. 51*, shares of the parent held by a subsidiary **must** be treated as outstanding stock in the consolidated balance sheet.

7. T F The **traditional allocation method** comes **under** the equity method of accounting.

8. T F When the **treasury stock method** is used in a reciprocal holding relationship, the consolidated earnings per share amount is **not** meaningful.

9. T F *ARB No. 51* prohibits **neither** the treasury stock method **nor** the traditional allocation method.

10. T F Under the **traditional allocation method,** simultaneous equations are used to calculate consolidated net income.

MULTIPLE-CHOICE QUESTIONS

Conceptual Questions

1. In indirect vertical holdings
    a. Net income for the top-level parent can be determined only by consolidation.
    b. Net income for the top-level parent can be determined only by successive application of the equity method of accounting.
    c. Net income for the top-level parent is different when determined by consolidation versus successive application of the equity method of accounting.
    d. The minority interest reported in the consolidated financial statements can be determined only by consolidation of all subsidiaries.
    e. None of the above.

2. In indirect horizontal holdings
    a. Net income for the top-level parent can be determined only by consolidation.
    b. Net income for the top-level parent can be determined only after each investor and investee has applied the equity method of accounting.
    c. A subsidiary is also a parent.
    d. A minority interest will always be reported in the consolidated financial statements.
    e. None of the above.

3. In reciprocal holdings
    a. A subsidiary **cannot** also be a parent.
    b. Both the treasury stock method and the traditional allocation method are in accordance with generally accepted accounting principles.
    c. The consolidated earnings per share amount under the traditional allocation method is **not** meaningful.
    d. Pursuant to the treasury stock method (that fits under the parent company concept), the cost of a subsidiary's investment in the parent's common stock must be treated as a cost of treasury shares.
    e. None of the above.

4. In reciprocal holdings
   a. A minority interest will never be reported in the consolidated financial statements.
   b. The traditional allocation method fits under the treasury stock method.
   c. The cost of a subsidiary's investment in the parent's common stock is treated as a cost of treasury shares in the consolidated financial statements regardless of whether the treasury stock method or the traditional allocation method is used.
   d. A subsidiary can never own more than 50% of its parent's outstanding common stock.
   e. None of the above.

Application Questions

5. Pax Company owns 80% of the common stock of Sax Company. Sax owns 75% of the common stock of Tax Company. For 19X5, each company had $500,000 of earnings from its own separate operations, exclusive of earnings on its investment in affiliates and amortization of cost in excess of book value. For 19X5, Pax and Sax had amortization of cost in excess of book value of $50,000 and $60,000 respectively. The consolidated net income for 19X5 is
   a. $1,102,000
   b. $1,112,000
   c. $1,114,000
   d. $1,124,000
   e. $1,160,000

6. Use the same information as in Question 5. In the consolidated income statement for 19X5, the minority interest in net income of subsidiaries would be reported at
   a. $225,000
   b. $266,000
   c. $276,000
   d. $288,000
   e. $300,000

7. Pix Company owns 80% of the common stock of Stix Company and 60% of the common stock of Tix Company. Stix owns 10% of the common stock of Tix. For 19X7, each company had $500,000 of earnings from its own separate operations, exclusive of earnings on investments in affiliates and amortization of cost in excess of book value. For 19X7, Pix had amortization of cost in excess of book value of $30,000 relating to Stix and $20,000 relating to Tix. The consolidated net income for 19X7 is
   a. $1,190,000
   b. $1,196,000
   c. $1,198,000
   d. $1,204,000
   e. $1,250,000

8. Use the same information as in Question 7. In the consolidated income statement for 19X7, the minority interest in net income of subsidiaries would be reported at
   a. $246,000
   b. $252,000
   c. $254,000

    d. $250,000

    e. $260,000

9. Pax Company owns 60% of the common stock of Sax Company. Sax owns 10% of the common stock of Pax. For 19X1, each had net income of $500,000 from its own separate operations, exclusive of earnings on its investment in the other. Under a proper presentation under the traditional allocation method, consolidated net income that accrues to the controlling shareholders is

    a. $734,042

    b. $765,957

    c. $800,000

    d. $830,000

    e. $1,000,000

10. Use the same information as in Question 9. Under the traditional allocation method, consolidated net income that accrues to the minority shareholders is

    a. $200,000

    b. $220,000

    c. $234,043

    d. $250,000

    e. None of the above.

CHAPTER 12—SOLUTIONS

Completion Statements

    1. indirect vertical
    2. indirect horizontal
    3. reciprocal
    4. treasury stock, traditional allocation
    5. parent company
    6. economic unit
    7. equity method

True-or-False Statements

    1. False   6. False
    2. True   7. False
    3. True   8. True
    4. False   9. True
    5. True   10. False

Multiple-Choice Questions

    1. e
    2. e
    3. b
    4. c
    5. a ($500,000 × 75% = $375,000; $375,000 − $60,000 = $315,000; $315,000 + $500,000 = $815,000; $815,000 × 80% = $652,000; $652,000 + $500,000 − $50,000 = $1,102,000)
    6. d ($125,000 for Tax plus $163,000 for Sax equals $288,000)

7. a ($500,000 × 10% = $50,000; $50,000 + $500,000 = $550,000;
      $550,000 × 80% = $440,000; $440,000 – $30,000 = $410,000;
      $500,000 × 60% = $300,000; $300,000 – $20,000 = $280,000;
      $410,000 per above plus $280,000 per above plus $500,000
      equals $1,190,000)

8. e ($110,000 for Stix plus $150,000 for Tix equals $260,000)

9. b   P = $500,000 + .60($500,000 + .10 × P)
          P = $500,000 + $300,000 + .06P
      .94P = $800,000
          P = $851,064
      $851,064 × 90% = $765,957

10. c (Total income of $1,000,000 – $765,957 per above equals
       $234,043)

CHAPTER 13

INCOME TAXES, EARNINGS PER SHARE, AND CONSOLIDATED STATEMENT OF CASH FLOWS

CHAPTER HIGHLIGHTS

Income Taxes

1. A parent company may file a consolidated income tax return with **only** its **domestic** subsidiaries.

2. The **major advantages** to filing a **consolidated income tax return** are being able to (A) offset losses against profits, (B) defer the recognition of profit resulting from intercompany transactions, and (C) eliminate paying taxes on intercompany dividends.

3. The **major disadvantages** to filing a **consolidated income tax return** are (A) the deferral of losses on intercompany transactions and (B) the greater risk of the alternative minimum tax.

4. The dividends received deduction is applicable *only* to dividends received from **domestic subsidiaries** that file **separate** income tax returns.

5. **Foreign tax credits** apply *only* to foreign subsidiaries.

6. The two kinds of **foreign tax credits** are (A) foreign income taxes and (B) dividend withholding taxes.

7. **Dividend withholding taxes** are a tax to the **recipient** and are **always** recorded on the parent's books—never on the books of the foreign subsidiary.

8. **Dividend withholding taxes** are withheld by the foreign government **when a dividend is remitted.**

9. Parent companies **must** provide income taxes on earnings of their subsidiaries unless (A) the subsidiary's earnings can be remitted in a **tax-free liquidation** or (B) the earnings have been or will be **invested indefinitely.**

10. Two examples of evidence required to satisfy the "invested indefinitely" condition are (A) **experience** and (B) **future programs of operations.**

11. For **purchase** business combinations (as opposed to pooling of interests business combinations), deferred taxes **must** be recorded at the combination date for differences between the assigned values of assets and liabilities of the acquired business and the tax basis of those assets and liabilities.

12. Deferred income taxes are **not** to be provided on goodwill.

13. Recording deferred income taxes at the combination date will **not** be necessary, in most cases, in which the purchase business combination is **taxable.** (Typically, the assigned values of assets for financial reporting purposes also become the tax basis of those assets for tax reporting purposes.)

Earnings Per Share

14. When a subsidiary has **common stock equivalents** or **other potentially dilutive securities** outstanding, the parent company will use a different amount than the earnings it has recorded under the equity method of accounting to compute consolidated primary and fully diluted earnings per share.

15. Instead of using the parent's ownership percentage times the subsidiary's net income (the equity method of accounting), a ratio (developed by analyzing the denominators used in the subsidiary's earnings per share calculations) is applied to the subsidiary's numerators used in its earnings per share calculations to obtain the amount of the subsidiary's earnings that the parent can include in its consolidated earnings per share calculations.

Consolidated Statement of Cash Flows

16. The **two approaches** that can be used to prepare the consolidated statement of cash flows are (A) combining the separate company statements of cash flow and (B) analyzing the changes in the consolidated balance sheets.

17. When **no intercompany** inventory, fixed asset, or bond transactions have occurred, combining the separate company statements of cash flow is a more practical approach.

18. **Dividends paid**—not dividends declared—to minority shareholders constitute a use of cash and are shown as such in the consolidated statement of cash flows.

19. The **minority interest deduction** in the consolidated income statement does **not** require the use of cash, and it is added back to consolidated net income in arriving at consolidated cash provided from operations.

20. When the parent or the subsidiary acquires some or all of the **minority interest,** the amount paid is reported as a use of cash in the consolidated statement of cash flows.

COMPLETION STATEMENTS

Income Taxes

1. A parent company can file a consolidated tax return with **only** its _____ _____ subsidiaries.

2. An advantage of filing a consolidated income tax return is that _____ are **not** taxable to the parent.

3. The provision of the tax law that allows a major portion of a domestic subsidiary's dividends to be **not** taxable to the parent company is referred to as the _____ _____ .

4. A parent company does **not** have to provide income taxes on undistributed earnings of its subsidiaries if either the _____ condition or the _____ _____ condition is met.

5. Two examples of **evidence** to satisfy the invested indefinitely condition are _____ _____ and _____ .

6. The dividend withholding tax is a tax to the _____ .

7. The dividend withholding tax is recorded as an expense on the _____ books.

8. Dividend withholding taxes are **not** applicable to _____ subsidiaries.

TRUE-OR-FALSE STATEMENTS

Income Taxes

1. T   F   A parent can **never** file a consolidated federal income tax return with a **foreign** subsidiary.

2. T   F   An advantage of a consolidated federal income tax return is that intercompany **losses** on intercompany transactions are deductible **currently** rather than being deferred.

3. T   F   The dividend received deduction is **not** applicable when the parent files a consolidated federal income tax return.

4. T   F   The tax-free liquidation condition applies **only** to foreign subsidiaries.

5. T   F   The **invested indefinitely** condition applies to **all** of a subsidiary's earnings—**not** just the undistributed earnings.

6. T   F   The Internal Revenue Code taxes earnings of foreign subsidiaries of domestic companies on the **cash basis.**

7. T   F   The dividend withholding tax is **never** recorded as an expense on the foreign subsidiary's books.

8. T   F   The dividend received deduction is **not** applicable to **foreign** subsidiaries.

9. T   F   Recognizing deferred taxes at the combination date is generally an issue with **taxable** purchase business combinations—not **nontaxable** purchase combinations.

Earnings Per Share

10. T   F   When a subsidiary is partially owned and has potentially dilutive securities outstanding, the parent must take such potential dilution into consideration in applying the equity method of accounting.

11. T   F   A parent company that did not have to calculate a fully diluted earnings-per-share amount on a stand alone basis **may** have to present a fully diluted earnings-per-share amount on a consolidated basis if a subsidiary has "other potentially dilutive securities" outstanding.

12. T   F   When a subsidiary has common stock equivalents or other potentially dilutive securities outstanding, the parent will **not** use the earnings it has recorded under the equity method of accounting in calculating consolidated earnings per share.

Consolidated Statement of Cash Flows

13. T   F   Dividends declared by a subsidiary but **not paid** are **not** shown in the consolidated statement of cash flows.

14. T   F   When a subsidiary acquires a portion of the minority interest for cash, the cash payment will be shown in the consolidated statement of cash flows as a separate line item.

MULTIPLE-CHOICE QUESTIONS

Income Taxes

1. A parent company may file a consolidated tax return with
    a. Only domestic subsidiaries.
    b. Only foreign subsidiaries.
    c. Both domestic and foreign subsidiaries.
    d. Neither domestic nor foreign subsidiaries.
    e. None of the above.

2. Intercompany dividends from a subsidiary are **not** taxable to the parent company only if
    a. The parent-subsidiary relationship came about in a taxable transaction.
    b. The parent-subsidiary relationship came about in a nontaxable transaction.
    c. The parent formed the subsidiary (no business combination involved).
    d. The subsidiary is wholly owned.
    e. None of the above.

3. Which of the following is **not** an advantage of filing a consolidated income tax return?

    a. Intercompany dividends are not taxable to the parent at all.

    b. Operating losses of companies within the consolidated group that do not generate profits can offset profits of other members of the consolidated group.

    c. Losses on intercompany transactions are deferred.

    d. The group may be able to use a member's excess foreign tax credit.

    e. None of the above.

4. A parent and its **domestic** subsidiary file separate federal income tax returns. In general, for financial reporting purposes, the parent must provide income taxes on

    a. Dividends received from the subsidiary (the cash receipt).

    b. Dividends declared by the subsidiary (the accrual of the dividend).

    c. The earnings of the subsidiary.

    d. Neither the dividends nor the earnings of the subsidiary.

    e. None of the above.

5. A parent and its **foreign** subsidiary file separate income tax returns. In general, for financial reporting purposes, the parent must provide income taxes on

    a. Dividends received from the subsidiary (the cash receipt).

    b. Dividends declared by the subsidiary (the accrual of the dividend).

    c. The earnings of the subsidiary.

    d. Neither the dividends nor the earnings of the subsidiary.

    e. None of the above.

6. A parent and its **foreign** subsidiary file separate income tax returns. In general, for tax reporting purposes, the parent must pay income taxes on

    a. Dividends received from the subsidiary (the cash receipt).

    b. Dividends declared by the subsidiary (the accrual of the dividend).

    c. The earnings of the subsidiary.

    d. Neither the dividends nor the earnings of the subsidiary.

    e. None of the above.

7. For financial reporting purposes, parent companies **must** provide income taxes on their entire share of their subsidiaries earnings

    a. If less than 100% of the subsidiary's earnings are being invested indefinitely.

    b. If the subsidiary is a domestic subsidiary—no allowable exceptions.

    c. If the subsidiary is a foreign subsidiary—no allowable exceptions.

    d. If the subsidiary consistently does not declare or pay cash dividends.

    e. None of the above.

8. Deferred income taxes must be recognized at the business combination date if

    a. The combination is a pooling of interests.

    b. The combination is a purchase.

    c. The combination is nontaxable.

    d. The parent and subsidiary will **not** be filing consolidated income tax returns.

    e. None of the above.

9. Stix Company is a 100%-owned domestic subsidiary of Pix Company. For 19X1, Stix had $500,000 of pretax income and $300,000 of net income. A tax rate of 40% is assumed. At the end of 19X1, Pix had Stix declare and pay a dividend of $100,000. Pix intends to have Stix declare and pay an additional dividend of $25,000 in the first quarter of 19X2 when more cash is available. The remaining $175,000 of 19X1 earnings is expected to be invested indefinitely. For 19X1, Pix should provide income taxes relating to Stix of

    a. $-0-
    b. $2,000
    c. $8,000
    d. $10,000
    e. $24,000

10. Use the same information as in Question 9. How much federal income taxes will Pix pay for 19X1 (based on the parent's separate federal income tax return) as a result of owning Stix?

    a. $-0-
    b. $2,000
    c. $8,000
    d. $10,000
    e. $24,000

11. Pax Company owns 100% of the common stock of Sax Company, a foreign subsidiary located in a country that has a 30% income tax rate and a 10% dividend withholding tax. Assume the income tax rate in the United States is 40%. Sax reported net income of $700,000 for 19X1 and remitted $350,000 of these earnings as dividends to the parent in 19X1. Pax intends to have Sax remit another $140,000 of these earnings to the parent in the first quarter of 19X2 when more cash becomes available. The remaining $210,000 of 19X1 earnings is expected to be invested indefinitely. What is the total amount of income taxes relating to the foreign subsidiary that should be provided on the parent's books for 19X1?

    a. $-0-
    b. $6,000
    c. $15,000
    d. $21,000
    e. $30,000

12. Use the same information as in Question 11. How much federal income tax will Pax pay for 19X1 (based on Pax's federal income tax return) as a result of owning Sax?

    a. $-0-
    b. $6,000
    c. $15,000
    d. $21,000
    e. $30,000

Earnings Per Share

13. In calculating consolidated earnings per share when a subsidiary has potentially dilutive securities, the parent

    a.   Will use the dividends received from the subsidiary rather than the earnings recorded under the equity method of accounting.

b. May have to present a consolidated fully diluted earnings per share amount if the subsidiary has "other potentially dilutive securities" outstanding even though the parent does not have any such securities outstanding.

c. Will make adjustments to its denominator used in computing parent company earnings per share.

d. Will use the earnings recorded under the equity method of accounting.

e. None of the above.

14. P Company owns 100% of the outstanding common stock of S Company. For 19X1, S Company reported net income of $300,000. In addition to its 20,000 shares of common stock owned by the parent, S Company has outstanding warrants to purchase 10,000 shares of its common stock. These warrants were outstanding during all of 19X1, and 5,000 shares of common stock were assumed to be repurchased under the treasury stock method for earnings per share purposes. P Company reported net income of $500,000 for 19X1 from its own separate operations, exclusive of any earnings of S Company. For primary earnings per share on a consolidated basis, the numerator in this calculation is

a. $500,000
b. $700,000
c. $740,000
d. $800,000
e. None of the above.

15. Use the same information as in Question 14. What is the consolidated net income?

a. $500,000
b. $700,000
c. $740,000
d. $800,000
e. None of the above.

Consolidated Statement of Cash Flows

16. In the consolidated statement of cash flows presented using the **indirect** method, which of the following amounts is shown as a separate line item?

a. Dividends paid to the parent by the subsidiary.
b. Dividends paid to minority shareholders of the subsidiary.
c. Equity in reported net income of subsidiary.
d. Minority interest in net assets of subsidiary.
e. None of the above.

17. Sax Company is an 80%-owned subsidiary of Pax Company. For 19X1, Sax reported net income of $300,000, declared dividends of $200,000, and paid dividends of $150,000 ($50,000 remains unpaid at year-end). In the consolidated statement of cash flows for 19X1, what amount would be reported for dividends assuming the parent declared *and paid* $500,000 of dividends?

a. $500,000
b. $530,000
c. $540,000
d. $560,000
e. None of the above.

18. Use the same information as in Question 17. In the consolidated statement of cash flows for 19X1, what amount would be reported for each of the following accounts?

	Equity in Net Income of Subsidiary	Minority Interest in Net Income of Subsidiary
a.	$240,000	$60,000
b.	$240,000	-0-
c.	-0-	-0-
d.	-0-	$60,000
e.	None of the above.	

CHAPTER 13—SOLUTIONS

Completion Statements

1. domestic
2. intercompany dividends
3. dividends received deduction
4. tax-free liquidation, invested indefinitely
5. experience, future programs of operations
6. recipient
7. parent's
8. domestic

True-or-False Statements

1. True		8. True	
2. False		9. False	
3. True		10. False	
4. False		11. True	
5. False		12. True	
6. True		13. True	
7. True		14. True	

Multiple-Choice Questions

1. a
2. e
3. c
4. c
5. c
6. a
7. e
8. b
9. a   (100% dividend received deduction applies because of 100% ownership)
10. a   (100% dividend received deduction applies because of 100% ownership)

11. d ($490,000 of 19X1 earnings are to be remitted to the parent; $490,000 ÷ 70% equals $700,000; $700,000 × 40% U.S. tax rate equals $280,000; $280,000 − $210,000 of foreign income tax credits and minus $49,000 of dividend withholding tax credits equals $21,000)

12. c ($350,000 of cash dividends received ÷ 70% equals $500,000; $500,000 × 40% U.S. tax rate equals $200,000; $200,000 − $150,000 of foreign income tax credits and minus $35,000 of dividend withholding tax credits equals $15,000)

13. b

14. c ($500,000 of parent's earnings plus $240,000 of the subsidiary's earnings) The $240,000 is 80% (20,000/25,000) of the subsidiary's reported net income of $300,000.

15. d ($500,000 + $300,000)

16. b

17. b ($500,000 + $30,000) The $30,000 is the dividends paid to the minority shareholders (20% × $150,000).

18. d ($300,000 × 20% = $60,000)

CHAPTER 14
REPORTING DISAGGREGATED INFORMATION

CHAPTER HIGHLIGHTS

Segment Reporting

1. Segment information (different industries and/or foreign operations) was mandated because of the **limitations** of consolidated financial statements.

2. Segment reporting is applicable **only** to **public enterprises.**

3. Segment reporting is **not** applicable to **interim financial statements.**

4. In presenting segment information (either industry or geographic), **intrasegment** sales **need not** be disclosed.

5. In presenting segment information (either industry or geographic) **intersegment** sales **must** be disclosed separately.

6. The following information must be presented for each **reportable industry segment** (A) revenues from sales to unaffiliated customers and sales to other industry segments, (B) operating profit or loss, and (C) identifiable assets. (In addition, disclosures are also required of capital expenditures, depreciation, depletion, and amortization.)

7. The FASB did **not** establish a basis to set prices for sales or transfers between segments.

8. **Transfer pricing** is more likely to take place **within** an industry segment than **between** industry segments.

9. In dealing with segment information, the term "intercompany" is not relevant—the relevant terms are **intersegment** and **intrasegment.**

10. When determining an industry segment's **operating profit or loss,** the operating expenses subtracted from revenue may include (A) directly traceable costs and (B) an allocated portion of **common costs** that benefit two or more industry segments.

11. Some of the items that **cannot** be added or deducted, as the case may be, in computing an industry segment's operating profit or loss are (A) revenue earned at the corporate level (not being derived from an industry segment's operations), (B) gen-

eral corporate expenses, (C) interest expense, (D) domestic and foreign income taxes, (E) extraordinary items, and (F) minority interest.

12. A component of an enterprise is an **industry segment** if it has sales to unaffiliated customers.

13. Not all industry segments are **reportable** industry segments—**three** tests must be performed to determine if an industry segment is a **reportable** industry segment. (Only one of the three tests need be satisfied.)

14. In describing an enterprise's industry segments, the **product** or **service** of each industry segment **must** be identified.

15. In determining **reportable** industry segments, enough individual segments must be shown so that at least 75% of the combined revenues (from **sales to unaffiliated customers** of all industry segments) is shown by reportable segments.

16. **Foreign operations** are operations located outside of the United States that generate sales to unaffiliated customers or between geographic areas within the enterprise.

17. In presenting information about **foreign operations,** disclosure is required of (A) revenues (both to unaffiliated customers and intergeographic shown separately), (B) identifiable assets, and (C) operating profit or loss (or net income, or some other measure of profitability).

18. When **sales to unaffiliated foreign customers** by a domestic company (export sales) are 10% or more of total revenue from sales to unaffiliated customers, the total export sales must be separately reported, in total and by geographic area.

19. When an enterprise has revenues **from any single customer** in excess of 10% of total revenues, it must disclose the following information (A) the fact of such revenues, (B) the amount of revenues from each customer (but not the identity of each such customer), and (C) the industry segment making the sales to each such customer.

Disposals of Segments

20. The results of operations of a **discontinued segment** and any gain or loss on the disposal must be reported separately from continuing operations.

21. **Discontinued operations** are always presented on a **net of tax expense** (or tax benefit) **basis.**

22. The "Income (loss) from Operations" line of the "Discontinued Operations" section of the income statement includes operations **only** from the beginning of the year up to the **measurement date.**

23. The "Loss on Disposal" line of the "Discontinued Operations" section of the income statement includes operations from the **measurement date** to the **disposal date** (as well as the actual or estimated loss on disposal of the segment).

24. In reporting the **disposal of a segment,** it may be necessary to expense in the current year **operating losses expected to be incurred in the following year** (up to the estimated disposal date).

COMPLETION STATEMENTS

Segment Reporting

1. Intercompany sales that occur within a vertically integrated operation are called _____ .

2. Intercompany sales that occur between industry segments are called _____ _____ .

3. The revenue of an industry segment **includes** _____ sales but **excludes** _____ sales.

4. To determine if an industry segment is a **reportable** industry segment, it is necessary to perform a test based on _____ , a test based on _____ , and a test based on _____ .

5. In presenting industry segment information, the three items that must be **reconciled** to amounts in the consolidated financial statements are _____ , _____ , and _____ .

6. In addition to industry segment information and geographic segment information, *SFAS No. 14* also calls for disclosures pertaining to _____ and _____ .

7. The revenues test and the identifiable assets test used to determine if a geographic area is separately reportable are based on _____ .

8. Enough individual industry segments must be presented so that at least 75% of sales to _____ of all industry segments is shown by reportable segments.

Disposals of Segments

9. The date on which management commits itself to a formal plan to dispose of a segment of the business is called the _____ date.

10. The date of closing the sale if the disposal is by sale or the date that operations cease if the disposal is by abandonment is called the _____ date.

TRUE-OR-FALSE STATEMENTS

Segment Reporting

1. T　F　Segment reporting is required of **only** publicly owned companies.

2.   T   F   Segment reporting is required for **interim** financial statements of publicly owned companies.

3.   T   F   **Intersegment** sales do **not** need to be disclosed in presenting industry segment information.

4.   T   F   **Intrasegment** sales do **not** need to be disclosed in presenting industry segment information.

5.   T   F   The definition of **revenue** under *SFAS No. 14* **excludes** revenues from intersegment sales or transfers.

6.   T   F   Management has the latitude to **not** provide industry segment information for an industry segment that satisfies one of the three tests for determining reportable industry segments.

7.   T   F   One of the tests used to determine if a foreign operation is a **reportable** foreign operation is based on operating profit or loss.

8.   T   F   In presenting information about foreign operations, information about profitability of individual foreign operations by geographic area is **not** required.

9.   T   F   In disclosing information about major customers, it is **not** necessary to disclose the identity of each such customer.

10.   T   F   In presenting geographic area information, *SFAS No. 14* prohibits the deduction of foreign income taxes in presenting information regarding profitability.

11.   T   F   In presenting industry segment information, *SFAS No. 14* requires that an enterprise's internal data by organizational, divisional, or parent-subsidiary lines be used.

12.   T   F   In computing an industry segment's operating profit or loss, operating expenses that are allocated on an arbitrary basis **must** be excluded from the determination of an industry segment's operating profit or loss even though such operating expenses may be **common costs** that benefit two or more segments.

13.   T   F   Operating expenses that are **directly traceable** to an industry segment **must** be deducted in determining an industry segment's operating profit or loss.

Disposals of Segments

14.   T   F   Severance pay and employee relocation expenses are included in determining the gain or loss on disposal of a segment.

15.   T   F   The income or loss from operations during the phase-out period covers the period from the measurement date to the disposal date.

16. T F   The category within the discontinued operations section of the income statement called "Income (Loss) from Operations of Discontinued Division" includes operating losses during the phase-out period.

MULTIPLE-CHOICE QUESTIONS

Segment Reporting

1. Which of the following items is **not** part of the additional disclosure requirements of *SFAS No. 14?*
    a. Major customers.
    b. Major industries.
    c. Export sales.
    d. Foreign operations.
    e. None of the above.

2. Which of the following items are **not** used in one of the three 10% tests for determining reportable industry segments?
    a. Identifiable assets.
    b. Operating profit or loss.
    c. Total intersegment revenues.
    d. Total revenues (intersegment sales and sales to unaffiliated customers combined).
    e. None of the above.

3. Which of the following items are **not** required to be disclosed for reportable industry segments?
    a. Total revenues (intersegment sales and sales to unaffiliated customers combined).
    b. Intersegment revenues.
    c. Revenues from sales to unaffiliated customers.
    d. Operating profit or loss.
    e. None of the above.

4. Which of the following items are **not** required to be disclosed for reportable industry segments?
    a. Depreciation expense.
    b. Net income.
    c. Capital expenditures.
    d. Equity in net income of unconsolidated subsidiary whose operations are vertically integrated with the operations of a reportable industry segment.
    e. None of the above.

5. *SFAS No. 14* specifies that certain items are **not** to be added or deducted, as the case may be, in computing an industry segment's operating profit or loss. Which of the following items is *not* one of those items?
    a. Extraordinary items.
    b. Minority interest.
    c. General corporate expenses.
    d. Loss on discontinued operations.
    e. None of the above.

6. *SFAS No. 14* specifies that certain items are **not** to be added or deducted, as the case may be, in computing an industry segment's operating profit or loss. Which of the following items is **not** one of those items?
    a.   Domestic income taxes.
    b.   Foreign income taxes.
    c.   Interest expense.
    d.   Depreciation expense.
    e.   None of the above.

7. Which of the following categories would be an allowable description of an enterprise's industry segments?
    a.   Manufacturing.
    b.   Wholesaling.
    c.   Retailing.
    d.   Consumer products.
    e.   None of the above.

8. Which of the following items is **not** included in the definition of revenues?
    a.   Sales to unaffiliated customers.
    b.   Intercompany sales within a vertically integrated segment.
    c.   Intercompany sales to other segments.
    d.   Intersegment transfers.
    e.   None of the above.

9. Which of the following information is **not** required to be presented for a reportable foreign geographic area?
    a.   Total revenue (intergeographic sales and sales to unaffiliated customers combined).
    b.   Total sales to unaffiliated customers.
    c.   Operating profit or loss or net income (or some other measure of profitability between the two).
    d.   Identifiable assets.
    e.   None of the above.

10. The revenues test for determining if a foreign operation is a reportable foreign operation is based on
    a.   Total revenues of the foreign operation (intergeographic sales and sales to unaffiliated customers combined).
    b.   Consolidated revenues in the consolidated income statement.
    c.   Intergeographic sales.
    d.   Total revenues of the foreign operation (intergeographic and intrageographic sales and sales to unaffiliated customers combined).
    e.   None of the above.

11. Which of the following information is **not** required to be disclosed about major customers under *SFAS No. 14?*
    a.   The industry segment making sales to each customer.
    b.   The amount of revenues from each major customer.
    c.   The fact that the enterprise has revenues from one or more single customers in excess of 10% of total revenues.

    d. The identity of each major customer.
    e. None of the above.

12. An enterprise that operates in several industries has (A) sales to unaffiliated cus-
    tomers of $10,000,000, (B) intrasegment sales of $1,000,000, and (C) intersegment
    sales of $2,000,000. In making the 10% of revenues test, the 10% is applied to
    a. $2,000,000
    b. $10,000,000
    c. $11,000,000
    d. $12,000,000
    e. $13,000,000

13. Use the same information as in Question 12. In applying the 75% test, the 75% is
    applied to
    a. $2,000,000
    b. $10,000,000
    c. $11,000,000
    d. $12,000,000
    e. $13,000,000

14. An enterprise that operates in several geographic areas has (A) sales to unaffiliated
    customers of $20,000,000, (B) intrageographic intercompany sales of $3,000,000,
    and (C) intergeographic intercompany sales of $4,000,000. In making the 10% of
    revenues test for determining reportable geographic areas, the 10% is applied to
    a. $4,000,000
    b. $20,000,000
    c. $23,000,000
    d. $24,000,000
    e. $27,000,000

15. Pana Company operates in several lines of business, all of which are solely manu-
    facturing operations. For 19X1, Pana had the following items:

    Sales to unaffiliated customers $5,000,000
    Intrasegment sales 1,000,000
    Interest income on intercompany loans 100,000

    Pana has a reportable industry segment if that segment's revenues exceed
    a. $5,000,000
    b. $5,100,000
    c. $6,000,000
    d. $6,100,000
    e. Segment reporting is not required because Pana has only manufacturing
        operations.

16. Use the same information as in Question 15, but assume that Pana has $1,000,000
    of Intersegment sales rather than $1,000,000 of intrasegment sales. Pana has a
    reportable industry segment if that segment's revenues exceed
    a. $5,000,000
    b. $5,100,000
    c. $6,000,000
    d. $6,100,000
    e. None of the above.

17. Pox Company has only two industry segments. These segments had the following sales, costs, and expenses for 19X1:

	Segment A	Segment B
Sales (to unaffiliated customers)	$ 6,000,000	$ 4,000,000
Intersegment sales	500,000	
Cost of sales	(3,000,000)	(2,500,000)
Selling and administrative expenses	(2,000,000)	(1,000,000)
Subtotal	$ 1,500,000	$ 500,000

For 19X1, Pox's central research and development division incurred $600,000 of expenses, which benefit both of the two industry segments and are not included in the above amounts. Also for 19X1, Pox's corporate headquarters expenses were $300,000, exclusive of interest expense incurred of $200,000. Costs are appropriately allocated to the segments based on the ratio of a segment's income before allocable costs to total income before allocable costs. What is the operating profit to be disclosed for Segment A for 19X1?

   a. $675,000
   b. $800,000
   c. $825,000
   d. $1,050,000
   e. $1,500,000

18. Pix Company has two industry segments, both of which are reportable industry segments. For 19X2, the segment information is provided:

	Segment A	Segment B
Sales to unaffiliated customers	$800,000	$700,000
Intersegment sales	100,000	
Intrasegment sales		400,000
Operating profit (includes unrealized profit below)	300,000	200,000
Intersegment gross profit that is unrealized at the end of 19X2	40,000	
Intrasegment gross profit that is unrealized at the end of 19X2		30,000

What is the reportable operating profit for each segment for 19X2 as reported by segment?

	Segment A	Segment B
a.	$300,000	$200,000
b.	$260,000	$170,000
c.	$300,000	$170,000
d.	$260,000	$200,000
e.	None of the above.	

19. Use the same information as in Question 18, but also assume that at the end of 19X1 (not 19X2) Segment A had $25,000 of unrealized **inter**segment profit and Segment B had $10,000 of unrealized **intra**segment profit. What is the consolidated operating profit for 19X1?

   a. $430,000
   b. $460,000
   c. $465,000

d. $485,000
e. $515,000

Disposals of Segments

20. The income statement category "Income (Loss) from Operations of Discontinued Division" includes operations for the period
    a. From the beginning of the year to the disposal date.
    b. From the measurement date to the end of the year.
    c. From the beginning of the year to the end of the year.
    d. From the beginning of the year to the measurement date.
    e. None of the above.

21. Parker Company decided on May 1, 19X1, to dispose of its pencil manufacturing division. Data for this division follows:

    Operating loss from January 1, 19X1,
        through April 30, 19X1 .... $(300,000)
    Operating loss from May 1, 19X1,
        through December 31, 19X1 .... (250,000)
    Anticipated operating loss from
        January 1, 19X2, to March 31, 19X2 (the
        expected date the division will be sold) .... (100,000)
    Estimated loss on the sale of the
        division's assets on March 31, 19X2 .... (700,000)

    All of Parker's other divisions are highly profitable. Parker has a 40% income tax rate applicable to the company as a whole. What amount would Parker report for 19X1 in the income statement line item "Loss from Operations of Discontinued Pencil Division"?
    a. $(180,000)
    b. $(300,000)
    c. $(330,000)
    d. $(390,000)
    e. $(550,000)

22. Use the same information as in Question 20. What amount would Parker report for 19X1 in the income statement line item "Loss on Disposal of Pencil Division"?
    a. $-0-
    b. $(420,000)
    c. $(480,000)
    d. $(630,000)
    e. $(700,000)

CHAPTER 14—SOLUTIONS

Completion Statements

Segment Reporting

1. intrasegment sales
2. intersegment sales

3. intersegment, intrasegment
4. revenues, operating profit or loss, identifiable assets
5. revenues, operating profit or loss, identifiable assets
6. export sales, major customers
7. consolidated amounts
8. unaffiliated customers

Disposals of Segments

9. measurement
10. disposal

True-or-False Statements

Segment Reporting

1. True
2. False
3. False
4. True
5. False
6. True
7. False
8. False
9. True
10. False
11. False
12. False
13. True

Disposals of Segments

14. True
15. True
16. False

Multiple-Choice Questions

Segment Reporting

1. e
2. c
3. a
4. b
5. e
6. d
7. e
8. b
9. a
10. b
11. d
12. d
13. b
14. b

15. a
16. c
17. d   ($1,500,000 – $450,000 of allocable central research and development expenses). The $450,000 amount is 75% of the $600,000 incurred; the 75% is derived from $1,500,000/$2,000,000.
18. c   ($300,000 for Segment A—no adjustments are made in the column that presents data for Segment A)
($170,000 for Segment B—this is the $200,000 operating profit minus $30,000 of unrealized intrasegment profit at 12/31/X2)
19. c   ($300,000 for Segment A plus $180,000 for Segment B minus $15,000 in the adjustments column equals $465,000). The $15,000 is $40,000 of unrealized intersegment profit at 12/31/X2 net of $25,000 of unrealized intersegment profit at 12/31/X1 that was realized in 19X2.

Disposals of Segments

20. d
21. a   ($300,000 operating loss net of $120,000 income tax benefit equals $180,000)
22. d   ($250,000 + $100,000 + $700,000 = $1,050,000; $1,050,000 net of income tax benefit of $420,000 equals $630,000)

CHAPTER 15
TRANSLATION OF FOREIGN CURRENCY TRANSACTIONS

CHAPTER HIGHLIGHTS

Currency Exchange Rates

1. The number of units of a foreign currency needed to acquire one U.S. dollar is the **indirect** quotation of the exchange rate.

2. The number of units of the U.S. dollar needed to acquire one unit of the foreign currency is the **direct** quotation of the exchange rate.

3. Exchange rates at which currencies could be converted immediately (for settlement in two days) are called **spot** rates.

4. Exchange rates at which currencies could be converted at a future stipulated date are called **future** or **forward** rates.

5. Exchange rates determined by market conditions are commonly called **floating** or **free** exchange rates.

6. A **strengthening** of the dollar or a **weakening** of the foreign currency causes the direct exchange rate to decrease.

7. Under the floating exchange rate system, the price of a foreign currency (the exchange rate) is determined by the **laws of supply and demand.**

8. **Supply** is the quantity of a currency that companies and individuals are trying to sell.

9. **Demand** is the quantity of a currency that companies and individuals are trying to buy.

10. In the long run, neither a **foreign trade deficit** nor a **foreign investment deficit** affect exchange rates because they result in offsetting demand.

11. Under the theory of **purchasing power parity** (discussed in the appendix), the differential rate of inflation between two countries can be expected over the long run to result in an **equal but opposite** change in the exchange rate between the two currencies.

Importing and Exporting Transactions

12. **Foreign currency transactions** are transactions that require settlement (payment or receipt) in a foreign currency.

13. The process of actually exchanging one currency for another currency is called **conversion.**

14. The process of expressing amounts stated in one currency in terms of another currency by using appropriate currency exchange rates is called **translation.**

15. A foreign transaction in which settlement is stipulated in a specific currency is said to be **denominated** in that particular currency.

16. A company that has a liability in a foreign currency is said to be in an **exposed liability position.**

17. A company that has a receivable in a foreign currency is said to be in an **exposed asset position.**

18. In a foreign transaction, the **order date** is the date a purchase order or sales order is issued.

19. In a foreign transaction, the **transaction date** is the date on which the transaction is initially recordable under generally accepted accounting principles.

20. In a foreign transaction, the **settlement date** is the date that payment or receipt is required.

21. Under *SFAS No. 52*, all FC receivables and payables are adjusted to the **spot rate at each intervening balance sheet reporting date.**

22. *Under SFAS No. 52*, adjustments to FC receivables and FC payables between the transaction date and the settlement date are reported **currently in the income statement as FC transaction gains or losses.** No adjustment is ever made to the amount initially recorded as sales in an exporting transaction or as inventory in an importing transaction. This is the **"two-transaction** (two separate decisions) **perspective."**

23. FC transaction gains and losses on importing and exporting transactions are (A) **one-sided** and (B) usually **reported net** in the income statement.

24. FC transaction gains and losses recognized in the income statement **at intervening balance sheet dates** are (A) **unrealized** in nature and (B) **not taxable** (for gains) or **tax deductible** (for losses) until realized.

25. In settling foreign currency transactions, companies usually use **bank wire transfers.**

26. In bank wire transfers, no currency **physically changes hands** or **physically moves in or out of a country.**

27. Domestic **importers** (A) have exposed FC payables, (B) are **concerned** about direct rate **increases,** and (C) **desire** direct rate **decreases.**

28. Domestic **exporters** (A) have exposed FC receivables, (B) are **concerned** about direct rate **decreases,** and (C) **desire** direct rate **increases.**

Managing Foreign Currency Exposures

29. The three types of foreign currency exposures that companies can manage are (A) **existing asset and liability exposures,** (B) **anticipatory future transactions,** and (C) **strategic** or **competitive exposures.** Item C is the potential for **loss of** anticipatory future transactions as opposed to the potential for **loss on** a transaction in either item A or B.

30. Companies manage their foreign currency exposures by a technique called **hedging.**

31. In hedging, the idea is to **create an offsetting position** (counterbalancing) to the exposed position so as to have a gain on the hedging transaction in the event of a loss on the **hedged item** (the specific foreign currency exposure).

32. The **financial instrument** used to achieve the hedge is commonly called the **hedging instrument.**

33. The most commonly used hedging instruments are (A) **forward exchange contracts** (which result in two-sided hedges) and (B) **foreign currency options** (which result in one-sided hedges).

34. **Eliminating foreign currency exposure** has a **cost,** which is reflected in (A) the forward rate for a forward exchange contract or (B) the cost (premium) of acquiring a foreign currency option.

35. "**Hedge accounting**" is defined as a special treatment that achieves both **(A) counterbalancing** and (B) either **concurrent recognition** or **concurrent deferral** of mark-to-market adjustments.

Forward Exchange Contracts

36. A **forward exchange contract** is an agreement to buy or sell a foreign currency **at a specified future date** (usually within 12 months) **at a specified exchange rate,** commonly called the **forward rate.** Forward exchange contracts are **customizable** as to **amount** and **duration** (within limits).

37. In a forward exchange contract, each party to the contract **must execute** (fulfill its contractual obligation) **at the expiration date.**

38. A forward exchange contract to **buy foreign currency** requires the buyer to **take delivery** of the foreign currency from the FC dealer. A forward exchange contract to **sell foreign currency** requires the seller to **make delivery** of the foreign currency to the FC dealer.

39. Forward exchange contracts are **executory contracts** for which **no general ledger entries** need be recorded on the books at the time they are entered into.

40. Adjustments made to forward exchange contracts (and foreign currency options, which are covered in detail later) at intervening balance sheet reporting dates are **unrealized gains and losses.**

41. **Obligations** under forward exchange contracts are reported at the **net amount** in the balance sheet—only if the **legal right of setoff** exists (usually the case).

42. Under *SFAS No. 52*, gains and losses from hedging FC receivables and FC payables are recognized currently in the income statement.

43. The difference that usually exists between the forward rate and the spot rate is attributable to (A) the **difference in interest rates** obtainable on the two currencies in the international money market for the duration of the contract and (B) the **fee or commission charged by the FC dealer** for assuming the risk that the exchange rate could change adversely.

44. In a forward exchange contract in which the **forward rate is higher than the spot rate,** the buying or selling of a foreign currency is said to be done at a premium.

45. In a forward exchange contract in which the **forward rate is lower than the spot rate,** the buying or selling of a foreign currency is said to be done at a discount.

46. In forward exchange contracts, **premiums and discounts** are often viewed as the **cost of obtaining the hedge,** which is analogous to an insurance premium that should be amortized based on the passage of time—thus they are viewed as a **time value element.**

47. In forward exchange contracts, the two methods that can be used **to determine the value of the net position** with the FC dealer are (A) **split accounting** (accounting for premiums and discounts as a time value element separate from the intrinsic value element) and (B) **nonsplit accounting** (not accounting for premiums and discounts separately from the intrinsic value element).

48. Under *SFAS No. 52*, **premiums and discounts** on forward exchange contracts that are **hedges** (as opposed to speculations) are (A) accounted for **separately** (split-accounting) and (B) **amortized over the life of the contract to income** (with the exception discussed in the following highlight point).

49. Under *SFAS No. 52*, FC transaction gains and losses on **hedges of identifiable foreign currency commitments** up to the transaction date **may** be deferred and treated as an adjustment to the cost of the item acquired or the sales price of the item sold. (Premium and discount amortization during this period may also be given this treatment.)

50. For a forward exchange contract (and foreign currency options as well) **to qualify as a hedge of an identifiable foreign currency commitment,** the FC transaction must (A) be designated as a hedge of that commitment, (B) be effective, and (C) be firm.

51. Under *SFAS No. 52*, FC transaction gains and losses on forward exchange contracts that are entered into for **speculating** are recognized currently in the income statement—the net position at each intervening balance sheet reporting date is always determined by **using the forward rate available for the remaining period of the contract.** Accordingly, such transactions do not give rise to accounting recognition of premiums and discounts. (Thus nonsplit accounting is automatically used.)

Foreign Currency Options

52. In a foreign currency option contract, one party has the right to buy or sell a specific quantity of currency **at a specified rate** (called the exercise or strike price) **during a specified future period.**

53. In a foreign currency option, the **option holder** can choose **not to exercise the option** and therefore walk away from the contract. Thus only the person granting the option (the FC dealer) has a **commitment to execute.**

54. In a foreign currency option contract, only the possibility of a **gain** exists for the **option holder.** In contrast, only the possibility of a **loss** exists for the **option writer** (usually the FC dealer). (Infrequently, companies will **reverse roles with the FC dealer and write options** just as FC dealers do, thus giving the FC dealer the option to exercise the option.)

55. When the relationship between the **exercise price** and the **spot price** is **favorable to the holder**—in reverse position for puts than for calls—the option is said to be **"in the money,"** in which case the option holder would exercise the option.

56. When the relationship between the **exercise price** and the **spot price** is **unfavorable to the holder**—in reverse position for puts than for calls—the option is said to be **"out of the money,"** in which case the option holder would **not** exercise the option.

57. **Split accounting** in the context of options refers to accounting for the **time value** element separately from the **intrinsic value** element. If at the inception of an option contract, the option is **not** in the money, the entire premium is the time value element.

58. Under *SFAS No. 52*, **hedge accounting** is appropriate when **foreign currency options** are used to (A) hedge existing exposed assets and liabilities and (B) hedge identifiable foreign currency commitments (even though *SFAS No. 52* does not specifically mention foreign currency options as a hedging instrument).

59. *EITF 90-17*, which applies only to **foreign currency options having little or no intrinsic value when designated as a hedge,** allows hedge accounting for certain anticipatory transactions **other than just identifiable foreign currency commitments** (making it less restrictive than *SFAS No. 52*).

60. *EITF 90-17 (consistent with SFAS No. 52)* **prohibits** hedge accounting for **strategic or competitive hedges.**

COMPLETION STATEMENTS

Currency Exchange Rates

1. Actually changing one currency into another currency is called _____ _____ .

2. The process of expressing amounts stated in one currency in terms of another currency is called _____ .

3. Translation is performed by using _____ .

4. The number of units of the foreign currency needed to acquire one unit of the domestic currency is the _____ quotation of the exchange rate.

5. The number of units of the domestic currency needed to acquire one unit of the foreign currency is the _____ quotation of the exchange rate.

6. Exchange rates at which currencies could be converted immediately (for settlement in two days) are termed _____ rates.

7. Exchange rates for which conversion can be made at some stipulated date in the future are called _____ or _____ rates.

8. Exchange rates determined by market conditions are commonly called _____ or _____ rates.

9. A change in a floating exchange rate is appropriately referred to as a(n) _____ or _____ of one currency in relation to another.

Importing and Exporting Transactions

10. In an importing or exporting transaction involving credit terms, the date on which payment is made is called the _____ date.

11. In accounting for foreign currency transactions, the FASB adopted the _____ _____ perspective and rejected the _____ perspective.

12. In accounting for foreign currency transactions, FC receivables and FC payables are adjusted to reflect the current exchange rate at each _____ date.

13. In accounting for foreign currency transactions, adjustments arising out of adjusting FC receivables and FC payables are reported in the income statement as _____ .

14. In settling foreign currency transactions, companies usually use _____ .

15. A company that has a receivable in a foreign currency is said to be in a(n) _____ _____ position.

Managing Foreign Currency Exposures

16. Companies manage their foreign currency exposures by a technique called _____ _____ .

17. The three categories of foreign currency exposures that can be managed are (A) _____ , (B) _____ , and (C) _____ .

18. Hedging a noncancellable sales order is a hedge of a(n) _____ _____ anticipatory transaction.

19. Hedging a foreign subsidiary's budgeted net income is a hedge of a(n) _____ _____ anticipatory transaction.

20. A specific foreign currency exposure being hedged is commonly called the _____ .

21. The financial instrument used to achieve the hedge is commonly called the _____ .

22. The two most commonly used hedging instruments to hedge foreign currency exposures are (1) _____ and (2) _____ .

23. Forward exchange contracts result in a(n) _____ hedge because both the downside risk and the upside potential on the hedged item are _____ .

24. Foreign currency options result in a(n) _____ hedge because only the downside risk on the hedged item is _____ .

25. _____ is a special accounting treatment that achieves both (A) counterbalancing and (B) either concurrent recognition or concurrent deferral of mark-to-market adjustments.

Forward Exchange Contracts

26. A forward exchange contract is an agreement to buy or sell a foreign currency (technically exchange different currencies) at a specified _____ _____ and at a specified _____ .

27. In a forward exchange contract, each party must _____ its _____ at the expiration date.

28. In a forward exchange contract to buy a foreign currency, the buyer must _____ delivery at the expiration date.

29. Forward exchange contracts are _____ in nature.

30. Adjustments to forward exchange contracts at intervening balance sheet reporting dates are _____ FC transaction gains and losses.

31. The fair value obligations of each party in a forward exchange contract are usually reported at _____ in the balance sheet because of the _____ .

32. The difference between the spot rate and the forward is called a(n) _____ _____ or a(n) _____ and is viewed as being a(n) _____ element.

33. Entering into a forward exchange contract to buy a foreign currency at more than the spot rate will result in a(n) _____ that will eventually _____ stockholders' equity.

34. Accounting for premiums and discounts separately from the intrinsic value is called _____ .

35. For a forward exchange contract to qualify as a hedge of an identifiable foreign currency commitment, the foreign currency must be _____ as a hedge, be _____ , and the foreign currency commitment must be _____ .

36. Entering into a forward exchange contract for purposes other than hedging is _____ .

Foreign Currency Options

37. In a foreign currency option, one party has the contractual right to buy or sell a specific quantity of currency at a(n) _____ during a(n) _____ .

38. An option to buy is a(n) _____ . An option to sell is a(n) _____ .

39. The party with the contractual right is the _____ .

40. The party with the obligation to honor the option contract is the _____ .

41. The price paid to acquire an option is called the _____ .

42. An option worth exercising is said to be _____ .

43. Split accounting in the context of options refers to accounting for the _____ _____ separately from the _____ .

44. *EITF 90-17* is less restrictive than *SFAS No. 52* because it also allows hedge accounting treatment for both _____ and _____ .

TRUE-OR-FALSE STATEMENTS

Currency Exchange Rates

1.   T   F   **Conversion** and **translation** are interchangeable terms.

2.   T   F   To express a foreign currency amount in U.S. dollars, the foreign currency amount is **multiplied** by the **direct** exchange rate.

3.   T   F   Forward exchange rates are always higher than spot rates.

4.   T   F   A **strengthening of a foreign currency** has the same impact on the exchange rate as the **weakening of the U.S. dollar.**

5.   T   F   A **strengthening** of the U.S. dollar causes the **direct** exchange rate to increase.

6.   T   F   To obtain the indirect exchange rate from the direct exchange rate, one divides by the U.S. dollar amount in the direct exchange rate.

7.   T   F   Exchange rates are determined by **supply** and **demand.**

8.   T   F   **Supply** is the quantity of a currency that exists.

9.   T   F   The foreign trade deficit of the United States is a major cause of the weakening of the U.S. dollar (in the long run).

10.   T   F   If a country has a foreign **trade** deficit, it will also have a foreign **investment** deficit. (Assume no service deficit or surplus.)

11.   T   F   **Appendix Question:** If Great Britain has **more** inflation than the United States, the **direct** exchange rate between the two currencies would be expected to increase under purchasing **power parity theory.**

Importing and Exporting Transactions

12.   T   F   **Denominated** means the currency in which **settlement** must be made.

13.   T   F   Importing and exporting transactions are **measured** in one currency and **denominated** in a different currency.

14.   T   F   An importing transaction is initially recorded on the books at the **order** (or **commitment**) date.

15.   T   F   In importing and exporting transactions, the **transaction date** and the **settlement date** can never coincide.

16.   T   F   In importing and exporting transactions, **bank wire transfers** must be used.

17.   T   F   Under the **two-transaction perspective,** there cannot be any **intervening balance sheet dates** for which foreign currency receivables or payables would have to be adjusted.

18. T F Under the **two-transaction perspective,** changes in the exchange rate between the **transaction date** and the **settlement date** would **never** result in an adjustment to the amount initially recorded as a sale in an **exporting transaction.**

19. T F Under the **one-transaction perspective,** FC transaction gains or losses are not reported currently in the income statement.

20. T F If a **domestic importer** has an FC transaction **gain,** the **foreign exporter** will have an FC transaction **loss.**

21. T F **FC transaction gains and losses** recognized at intervening balance sheet reporting dates are always **unrealized.**

22. T F From the perspective of both domestic importers and domestic exporters who have exposed positions, it is better to have the **direct** exchange rate **increase** than decrease.

Managing Foreign Currency Exposures

23. T F Companies can hedge **firmly committed anticipatory transactions** but they cannot hedge **other probable anticipatory transactions.**

24. T F Companies **can** hedge **strategic** or **competitive** exposures.

25. T F Hedging an FC Payable is protecting against the **loss of** an **anticipatory future transaction.**

26. T F Hedging an FC Receivable is protecting against the **loss on** an **anticipatory future transaction.**

27. T F Hedging a domestic company's budgeted export sales is **not** a **strategic hedge.**

28. T F Forward exchange contracts and foreign currency options are defined as **hedging instruments.**

29. T F **Hedge accounting** is required if **forward exchange contracts** are used.

30. T F **Hedge accounting** is optional if **foreign currency options** are used.

31. T F **Hedge accounting** is **not** defined as accounting for the time value element separately from the intrinsic value element.

Forward Exchange Contracts

32. T F In a forward exchange contract, there is potential for either a gain or a loss.

33. T F Forward exchange contracts can be **tailored to the exposure** as to **both** (A) the quantity of currency and (B) the duration of the exposure.

34. T   F   In forward exchange contracts, one party to the contract—but not both—must always **deliver a currency** to the other party.

35. T   F   In a forward exchange contract to **sell** a foreign currency, the seller must **make delivery** of the foreign currency to the FC dealer.

36. T   F   In practice, the **obligations of each party** in a forward exchange contract are recorded on the books at the **inception of the contract.**

37. T   F   Just like the issuance of a purchase order, forward exchange contracts are **executory in nature.**

38. T   F   In a forward exchange contract entered into for hedging purposes, recording adjustments for the change in the spot rate is accounting for the **intrinsic value element.**

39. T   F   The accounting for an **importing transaction** and the accounting for a **related hedging transaction** using a forward exchange contract are **completely independent of each other.**

40. T   F   When a domestic exporter desires to hedge an FC Receivable using a forward exchange contract, the exporter will contract to **sell** a specified number of foreign currency units.

41. T   F   Reporting in the balance sheet the fair value of the net position of the obligations of each party to a forward exchange contract is mandatory under U.S. GAAP.

42. T   F   In a forward exchange contract, the process of amortizing the premium or discount to income over the life of the forward contract is called **split-accounting.**

43. T   F   In a forward exchange contract in which a foreign currency is being sold at **less than** the spot rate, a **discount** exists.

44. T   F   In a forward exchange contract that hedges an FC Receivable, the **amortization of a premium** would result in a **debit** being made to the income statement.

45. T   F   In a forward exchange contract that hedges an FC Payable, the **amortization of a discount** would result in a **credit** being made to the income statement.

46. T   F   In a forward exchange contract involving **buying** a foreign currency, the buyer is said to be **"long"** in that currency—not "short" in that currency.

47. T   F   Under *SFAS No. 52*, any FC transaction gain or loss on a forward exchange contract used to hedge **an exposed asset or liability position** must be recognized currently in the income statement.

48. T   F   Under *SFAS No. 52*, any FC transaction gain or loss on a forward exchange contract used to hedge an **identifiable foreign currency commitment** must be deferred until the transaction date.

49. T   F   In a forward exchange contract, the determination of whether a hedge has been **effective** is always an after-the-fact determination.

50. T   F   In **speculating** using a forward exchange contract, a doubling of an exposed position occurs instead of a counterbalancing of the exposed position.

51. T   F   Under *SFAS No. 52*, FC transaction gains and losses resulting from **speculating** using a forward exchange contract **cannot be deferred.**

Foreign Currency Options

52. T   F   In a foreign currency option written by an FC dealer, the FC dealer always has a contractual obligation to **deliver** a foreign currency to the option holder if the option holder exercises the option.

53. T   F   In a foreign currency option, the option writer has potential loss exposure—not the option holder.

54. T   F   An option to **buy** is referred to as a **"call."**

55. T   F   Options have **premiums** but not discounts.

56. T   F   An option that is **"out of the money"** has no **intrinsic value.**

57. T   F   An option that is **"out of the money"** has no **time value.**

58. T   F   Split accounting is not a possibility for foreign currency options.

59. T   F   To **"write" an option,** an entity must be an FC dealer. Thus, a domestic importer or exporter could not write an option—such entities can only be option holders.

60. T   F   *EITF 90-17*, which applies to foreign currency options having little or no intrinsic value when designated as a hedge, allows hedge accounting treatment for **all probable anticipatory transactions**—not just identifiable foreign currency commitments as under *SFAS No. 52.*

MULTIPLE-CHOICE QUESTIONS

Currency Exchange Rates

1. To express 1,000 French francs in U.S. dollars, it is necessary to
    a. Divide the **indirect** exchange rate by 1,000 francs.
    b. Multiply the **indirect** exchange rate by 1,000 francs.
    c. Divide the 1,000 francs by the **direct** exchange rate.
    d. Multiply the 1,000 francs by the **direct** exchange rate.
    e. None of the above.

2. Exchange rates determined by **market conditions** are called
    a. Spot rates.
    b. Floating rates.

c.   Official rates.
d.   Forward rates.
e.   None of the above.

3. In the **long run,** the changes in exchange rates can best be attributed to
   a.   Foreign trade deficits or surpluses.
   b.   Foreign investment deficits or surpluses.
   c.   Differential trade deficits or surpluses.
   d.   Differential rates of inflation.
   e.   None of the above.

Importing and Exporting Transactions

4. In an importing or exporting transaction involving a foreign currency and credit terms (for which **no hedging** is done), which of the following dates would **never** be of concern or have accounting significance?
   a.   The issuance date of the purchase or sales order.
   b.   The transaction date.
   c.   The settlement date.
   d.   The intervening balance sheet date(s).
   e.   None of the above.

5. For an **importing transaction** denominated in a foreign currency, any change in the exchange rate between the purchase order issuance date and the transaction date is reported as
   a.   An adjustment to the foreign currency receivable.
   b.   A gain or loss to be added or subtracted from the initially recorded cost of inventory.
   c.   A gain or loss in the current income statement.
   d.   A deferred gain or loss in the balance sheet pending settlement.
   e.   None of the above.

6. For an **exporting transaction** denominated in a foreign currency, any change in the exchange rate between the transaction date and any intervening balance sheet date is reported as
   a.   An adjustment to the foreign currency payable.
   b.   A gain or loss to be added or subtracted from the initially recorded amount of the sale.
   c.   A gain or loss in the current income statement.
   d.   A deferred gain or loss in the balance sheet pending settlement.
   e.   None of the above.

7. Under *SFAS No. 52,* which of the following statements is **true** regarding a change in the exchange rate during the period of time involving an **unhedged importing transaction** requiring settlement in a foreign currency?
   a.   Any gain or loss preceding the transaction date must be deferred until the transaction date.
   b.   Any gain or loss preceding the settlement date must be deferred until the settlement date.
   c.   Any gain or loss between the transaction date and the settlement date must be deferred until the settlement date.

d. Any gain or loss between the transaction date and the settlement date must be recognized currently in the income statement.
e. None of the above.

Managing Foreign Currency Exposures

8. Which of the following is **not** a foreign currency exposure that a company could manage by hedging?
    a. A net monetary position.
    b. A net asset (investment) position.
    c. An outstanding purchase order issued to a foreign vendor.
    d. A foreign subsidiary's budgeted net income.
    e. None of the above.

9. Which of the following is **not** a foreign currency exposure that a company could manage by hedging?
    a. A foreign currency payable that is unpaid at the agreed upon settlement date and is expected to be paid in 15 days.
    b. An outstanding sales order from a foreign customer.
    c. A foreign subsidiary's budgeted dividend remittances.
    d. A potential loss of sales to foreign customers because of a possible adverse change in the exchange rate.
    e. None of the above.

10. A domestic exporter has a **foreign currency receivable** that is due in 60 days. The exporter desires zero foreign currency exposure and uses only forward exchange contracts. The exporter expects the foreign currency to **strengthen** during the next 60 days. Accordingly, the exporter should
    a. Enter into a hedging transaction to **buy** a specified number of foreign currency units.
    b. Enter into a hedging transaction to **sell** a specified number of foreign currency units.
    c. Not enter into a hedging transaction.
    d. None of the above.

11. A domestic importer has a **foreign currency payable** that is due in 90 days. The importer selectively hedges depending on its expectation of future exchange rate changes and uses only forward exchange contracts. The importer expects the foreign currency to **strengthen** during the next 90 days. Accordingly, the importer should
    a. Enter into a hedging transaction to **buy** a specified number of foreign currency units.
    b. Enter into a hedging transaction to **sell** a specified number of foreign currency units.
    c. Not enter into a hedging transaction.
    d. None of the above.

Forward Exchange Contracts

12. Which of the following statements is **true** regarding forward exchange contracts?
    a. Only one party must make or take delivery of a currency.

    b.   The contract can be customized as to the quantity of the foreign currency but not as to the duration of the contract.

    c.   Receivables and payables (from a GAAP perspective) are created at the time the contract is entered into.

    d.   Premiums can exist but not discounts.

    e.   None of the above.

13. A company that enters into a forward exchange contract to **buy** a foreign currency at **less than** the spot rate (direct quotation) will have a

    a.   Premium that will be amortized as a debit balance.

    b.   Premium that will be amortized as a credit balance.

    c.   Discount that will be amortized as a debit balance.

    d.   Discount that will be amortized as a credit balance.

    e.   None of the above.

14. A company that enters into a forward exchange contract to **sell** a foreign currency at **more than** the spot rate (direct quotation) will have a

    a.   Premium that will be amortized as a debit balance.

    b.   Premium that will be amortized as a credit balance.

    c.   Discount that will be amortized as a debit balance.

    d.   Discount that will be amortized as a credit balance.

    e.   None of the above.

15. On December 1, 19X1, Camico, Inc., entered into a 60-day forward exchange contract involving 100,000 British pounds to hedge **an exposed liability position.** The following exchange rates (direct quotation) are assumed:

	Spot Rate	Forward Rate (for January 30, 19X2)
December 1, 19X1	$1.80	$1.85
December 31, 19X1	1.82	1.84
January 30, 19X2	1.79	n/a

What is the FC transaction gain or loss to be reported in the 19X1 income statement on the hedging transaction?

    a. $-0-

    b. $1,000 gain

    c. $1,000 loss

    d. $2,000 gain

    e. $2,000 loss

16. Use the same information as in Question 15, but assume that the hedging transaction pertains to **a noncancellable contract involving the purchase of special equipment** to be received (delivered) on January 30, 19X2.

17. Use the same information as in Question 15, but assume that the forward exchange contract pertains to **speculation** in foreign currency.

Foreign Currency Options

18. Which of the following statements concerning foreign currency options is **true?**

    a.   They are usually less expensive than forward exchange contracts.

    b.   Only the writer of the option can exercise the option.

c. The writer of the option can only have a loss—never a gain.

d. A put option is "in the money" if the exercise price is below the spot rate (direct quotation).

e. None of the above.

19. Which of the following statements concerning foreign currency options is **false?**

a. A time value element will always exist but not always an intrinsic value element.

b. A call option is "in the money" if the exercise price is below the spot rate (direct quotation).

c. Only one party has the right to walk away from the contract.

d. The premium is paid only if the option holder does not exercise the option.

e. None of the above.

20. On January 1, 19X3, Callo, Inc., purchased an "out of the money" 365-day foreign currency option involving 1,000,000 LCUs at a premium of $2,000. The purpose of the option was to hedge Callo's budgeted 19X3 export sales. The exercise price is $.40 (direct quotation). On June 30, 19X3, the spot rate was $.43. What is the net position with the FC dealer to be reported in Callo's June 30, 19X3, balance sheet?

a. $-0-

b. $1,000 payable

c. $29,000 receivable

d. $30,000 receivable

e. $31,000 receivable

21. Use the same information as in Question 20, but further assume that the actual 19X3 export sales as of June 30, 19X3, were 300,000 LCUs. What is the allowable deferred FC transaction gain at June 30, 19X3?

a. $-0-

b. $9,000

c. $21,000

d. $30,000

e. None of the above.

Appendix Question

22. On January 1, 19X1, the exchange rate (direct quotation) is $1.00. Management forecasts that the U.S. will have 10% inflation during 19X1 and that the foreign country will have 5% inflation during 19X1. Under purchasing power parity theory, what is the expected exchange rate at December 31, 19X1?

a. $0.952

b. $0.955

c. $1.047

d. $1.050

e. $1.100

CHAPTER 15—SOLUTIONS

Completion Statements

Currency Exchange Rates

1. conversion
2. translation
3. foreign currency exchange rates
4. indirect
5. direct
6. spot
7. future, forward
8. floating, free
9. strengthening, weakening

Importing and Exporting Transactions

10. settlement
11. two-transaction, one-transaction
12. intervening balance sheet
13. foreign currency transaction gains and losses
14. bank wire transfers
15. exposed asset

Managing Foreign Currency Exposures

16. hedging
17. existing assets and liabilities, anticipatory future transactions, strategic (or competitive) exposures
18. firmly committed
19. other probable
20. hedged item
21. hedging instrument
22. forward exchange contracts, foreign currency options
23. two-sided, counterbalanced
24. one-sided, counterbalanced
25. Hedge accounting

Forward Exchange Contracts

26. exchange rate, future date
27. fulfill, obligation
28. take
29. executory
30. unrealized
31. the net position, legal right of setoff
32. premium, discount, time value
33. premium, decrease
34. split accounting
35. designated, effective, firm
36. speculating

Foreign Currency Options

37. specified exchange rate, specified period
38. call, put
39. option holder
40. option writer
41. premium
42. "in the money"
43. time value element, intrinsic value element
44. identifiable foreign currency commitments, certain other probable anticipatory transactions

True-or-False Statements

Currency Exchange Rates

1. False
2. True
3. False
4. True
5. False
6. True
7. True
8. False
9. False
10. True
11. False

Importing and Exporting Transactions

12. True
13. False (not by both parties—only one party)
14. False
15. False (true only when credit terms are granted and used)
16. False
17. False
18. True
19. True
20. False
21. True
22. False

Managing Foreign Currency Exposures

23. False (can hedge anything they want to)
24. True (but they cannot get hedge accounting treatment)
25. False (loss on)
26. False (this is an existing asset)
27. True (hedge of an other probable anticipatory transaction)
28. False
29. False
30. False
31. True

Forward Exchange Contracts

32. True
33. True
34. False
35. True
36. False
37. True
38. True
39. True
40. True
41. False (only optional)
42. False
43. True
44. False
45. True
46. True
47. True
48. False (*may* be deferred)
49. True
50. False
51. True

Foreign Currency Options

52. False (true only for calls—not puts)
53. True
54. True
55. True
56. True
57. False
58. False
59. False (infrequently, corporations write options)
60. False (allowed only for certain probable anticipatory transactions)

Multiple-Choice Questions

Currency Exchange Rates

1. d
2. b
3. d

Importing and Exporting Transactions

4. a
5. e
6. c
7. d

Managing Foreign Currency Exposures

8. e
9. e
10. b
11. a

Forward Exchange Contracts

12. e
13. d
14. b
15. d
16. a
17. c

Foreign Currency Options

18. c
19. d
20. e
21. c

Appendix Question

22. c

CHAPTER 16

TRANSLATION OF FOREIGN CURRENCY FINANCIAL STATEMENTS: CONCEPTS

CHAPTER HIGHLIGHTS

1. All foreign subsidiaries **must be consolidated** unless **control is lacking** or control is expected to be **temporary**, in which case consolidation is **not** allowed.

2. A domestic company becomes subject to a foreign country's income taxes when its foreign activities are deemed to represent the **physical presence** of the U.S. company in the foreign country.

3. Intercountry inventory transfers involving branches, divisions, and subsidiaries must be made at **fair transfer prices** that are supportable for income tax reporting purposes.

4. For U.S. income tax reporting purposes, the earnings of a **foreign branch** are taxed currently in the U.S., whereas the earnings of a **foreign subsidiary** are not taxed until the earnings are paid out in the form of dividends.

5. Three major reasons for U.S. companies to **manufacture overseas** instead of domestically are (A) low labor costs, (B) low or no foreign income taxes, and (C) not having to deal with continual changes in the exchange rate.

6. The major **risks of investing abroad** are (A) expropriation, (B) devaluation, (C) currency transfer restrictions, and (D) wars and civil disorders.

7. Accounting principles and practices overseas are substantially different from U.S. accounting principles and practices.

8. **Before** a foreign unit's financial statements can be expressed in U.S. dollars, it is necessary to **restate** such financial statements to reflect U.S. GAAP.

9. The **monetary-nonmonetary** classification scheme pertains **only** to assets and liabilities—not to any other accounts.

10. **Monetary** items include cash and accounts that are contractually obligated to be settled in cash.

11. The only sensible way to translate **monetary** items is to use the exchange rate in effect at the balance sheet date (a current exchange rate).

12. The two schools of thought regarding how to translate **nonmonetary** accounts are: (A) the foreign currency unit of measure approach, and (B) the U.S. dollar unit of measure approach.

13. Under the **foreign currency unit of measure approach,** no distinction is made between monetary and nonmonetary accounts—both types are translated at the exchange rate in effect at the balance sheet date. Consequently, the same **relationships of items** that exist in the foreign currency financial statements are maintained in the translated U.S. dollar financial statements. (For example, if Cash is 10% of total assets in French francs, then Cash will be 10% of total assets in U.S. dollars.)

14. The only translation method that fits under the **foreign currency unit of measure approach** is the **current-rate method.** The focus of this method is on the parent's **net investment.**

15. Under the **foreign currency unit of measure approach** (current rate method), the effect of a change in the exchange rate is charged or credited **directly to stockholders' equity** (bypassing the income statement) [called a "translation adjustment," as explained in Chapter 17].

16. Under the **U.S. dollar unit of measure approach,** nonmonetary accounts are translated using **historical exchange rates** so as to obtain the dollar equivalent of the transaction at the time the transaction occurred. Consequently, the relationships of items that exist in the foreign currency financial statements are **not** maintained in the translated U.S. dollar financial statements. (For example, if Cash is 10% of total assets in French francs, then Cash will usually **never** be 10% of total assets in U.S. dollars.)

17. The three translation methods that fit under the **U.S. dollar unit of measure approach** are (A) the temporal method, (B) the monetary-nonmonetary method, and (C) the current-noncurrent method. The focus of the first two methods is on the **net monetary position.**

18. Under the **U.S. dollar unit of measure approach** (the temporal method), the effect of a change in the exchange rate is reported currently in the income statement [called a "foreign currency transaction gain or loss," as explained in Chapter 17].

19. *SFAS No. 52* mandates the **functional currency concept** be used to determine whether a given foreign unit's financial statements are to be translated using the foreign currency unit of measure approach or the U.S. dollar unit of measure approach.

COMPLETION STATEMENTS

1. In determining whether a U.S. company is subject to a foreign country's income taxes, it is necessary to determine whether the U.S. company has a(n) _____ _____ in the foreign country.

2. A domestic company that transfers inventory to its foreign marketing branch or subsidiary must take into consideration rules dealing with _____ so that gross profit is not artificially shifted between countries to evade income taxes.

3. Before a foreign subsidiary's financial statements can be translated into U.S. dollars, they must be _____ to reflect U.S. GAAP.

4. Assets and liabilities may be conveniently grouped into _____ and _____ classifications.

5. Monetary items include cash and accounts that are _____ to be settled in cash.

6. The unit of measure approach under which all transactions are translated in a manner that produces the dollar equivalent of the transaction at the time the transaction occurred is called the _____ .

7. The focus for translation methods (other than the current-noncurrent method) that fit under the U.S. dollar unit of measure approach is the _____ .

8. An excess of monetary assets over monetary liabilities is referred to as a(n) _____ .

9. An excess of monetary liabilities over monetary assets is referred to as a(n) _____ .

10. The unit of measure approach under which the relationships of items in the financial statements is maintained is called the _____ .

11. The focus of the current rate method of translation is on the _____ of the parent.

12. For a specific foreign operation, it is first necessary to determine that operation's _____ in order to know how to express the foreign unit's financial statements in U.S. dollars.

13. Under the foreign currency unit of measure approach, translation adjustments are charged or credited directly to _____ .

14. Under the U.S. dollar unit of measure approach, foreign currency transaction gains and losses are charged or credited directly to _____ .

TRUE-OR-FALSE STATEMENTS

1. T F A U.S. company that has a **sales office** in a foreign country—but not a warehouse or factory—will generally **not** be subject to the foreign country's income taxes.

2. T F A domestic company that sells inventory to its foreign manufacturing unit must take into consideration the **fair transfer pricing rules** regardless of whether the foreign operation is a branch, division, or subsidiary.

3. T F For U.S. income tax reporting purposes, a major distinction between a **foreign branch** and a **foreign subsidiary** of a domestic company is that the earnings of the branch are currently taxable in the U.S., whereas the earnings of the subsidiary are **not** taxable until remitted as dividends.

4. T F When **foreign currency financial statements** are prepared using accounting principles and practices that are materially different from U.S. GAAP, such statements must be **restated** to U.S. GAAP after they are translated into dollars.

5. T F The **monetary-nonmonetary** classification system applies **only** to assets and liabilities—not to any other accounts.

6. T F An investment in the common stock of IBM Corporation is an example of a **monetary** item.

7. T F The only translation method that fits under the foreign currency unit of measure approach is the **current-noncurrent** method.

8. T F The **current rate** method of translation does **not** fit under the **U.S. dollar unit of measure approach.**

9. T F The focus of the **current rate** method is on the **net monetary position** of the foreign operation.

10. T F Under *SFAS No. 52*, the **U.S. dollar unit of measure approach** is **not** permitted.

11. T F The "disappearing plant" problem does **not** exist when the **foreign currency unit of measure approach** is used.

12. T F Under the **current-rate** method of translation, **nonmonetary** accounts are expressed in dollars at their current values.

13. T F The focus of the **current-rate** method of translation is always on the **net investment** of the parent—never the net monetary position.

14. T F When the **current-rate** method of translation is used, the effect of changes in the exchange rate is charged directly to **stockholders' equity**—not to the income statement.

15. T F If a company reports the effects of changes in the exchange rate currently in its income statement, then it **must** be using the **U.S. dollar unit of measure approach**.

MULTIPLE-CHOICE QUESTIONS

Conceptual Questions

1. Which of the following located in or taking place in a foreign country would **not** result in the foreign activity becoming subject to the foreign country's income taxes?
   a. A warehouse.
   b. A sales office.
   c. Employees conducting activities on behalf of the U.S. home office.
   d. A manufacturing plant.
   e. None of the above.

2. Which of the following accounts is **not** a monetary item?
   a. Accounts receivable.
   b. Bonds payable.
   c. Investment in bonds of IBM Corporation.
   d. Income taxes currently payable.
   e. None of the above.

3. A foreign operation that has **monetary liabilities** exceeding **monetary assets** must use the
   a. Foreign currency unit of measure approach.
   b. U.S. dollar unit of measure approach.
   c. Monetary-nonmonetary method of translation.
   d. Current-rate method of translation.
   e. None of the above.

4. When the **direct** exchange rate **increases** during the year and a **favorable** effect for this change in the exchange rate is reported currently in the income statement, the foreign unit had to be in a
   a. Net monetary asset position.
   b. Net monetary liability position.
   c. Net monetary position.
   d. Net asset position.
   e. Net liability position.

5. When the **direct** exchange rate **decreases** during the year and an **unfavorable** effect for this change in the exchange rate is charged directly to stockholders' equity, the foreign unit had to be in a
   a. Net monetary asset position.
   b. Net monetary liability position.
   c. Net monetary position.
   d. Net asset position.
   e. Net liability position.

6. A translation method that does not achieve a **U.S. dollar unit of measure approach** is the
   a. Current-noncurrent method.
   b. Current rate method.
   c. Monetary-nonmonetary method.

    d.   Temporal method.

    e.   None of the above.

7. A unique aspect of the **foreign currency unit of measure approach** (current rate method) is that it maintains the relationship of items in translation in

    a.   The balance sheet only.

    b.   The income statement only.

    c.   The balance sheet and the income statement.

    d.   Neither the balance sheet nor the income statement.

    e.   None of the above.

8. A unique aspect of the **U.S. dollar unit of measure approach** (temporal method) is that it maintains the relationship of items in translation in

    a.   The balance sheet only.

    b.   The income statement only.

    c.   The balance sheet and the income statement.

    d.   Neither the balance sheet nor the income statement

    e.   None of the above.

Application Questions

9. On January 1, 19X1, a foreign unit of a domestic company acquired a parcel of land at a cost of 100,000 LCUs (local currency units). During 19X1, the inflation rate in the foreign country was 25%. The direct exchange rate was $.50 on January 1, 19X1, and $.44 on December 31, 19X1. At what amount would the land be expressed in dollars in the December 31, 19X1, translated balance sheet using the **foreign currency unit of measure approach?**

    a. $40,000

    b. $44,000

    c. $50,000

    d. $55,000

    e. $62,500

10. Use the same information as in Question 9. At what amount would the land be expressed in dollars in the December 31, 19X1, translated balance sheet using the **U.S. dollar unit of measure approach?**

    a. $40,000

    b. $44,000

    c. $50,000

    d. $55,000

    e. $62,500

11. Candu Company has a foreign subsidiary for which the average balances of its individual assets and liabilities during 19X1 were as follows:

	Units of Foreign Currency
Cash	60,000
Accounts Receivable	440,000
Inventory	400,000
Fixed Assets, net	1,100,000
	2,000,000
Accounts Payable and Accruals	350,000
Current portion of long-term debt	250,000
Long-term Debt	1,200,000
	1,800,000

Under the **foreign currency unit of measure approach,** what was the relevant average financial position during 19X1?

   a.   Net asset position of 200,000 LCUs.
   b.   Net monetary asset position of 200,000 LCUs.
   c.   Net monetary liability position of 100,000 LCUs.
   d.   Net monetary liability position of 1,300,000 LCUs.
   e.   None of the above.

12. Use the same information as in Question 11. Under the **U.S. dollar unit of measure approach,** what was the relevant average financial position during 19X1?

   a.   Net asset position of 200,000 LCUs.
   b.   Net monetary asset position of 200,000 LCUs.
   c.   Net monetary liability position of 100,000 LCUs.
   d.   Net monetary liability position of 1,300,000 LCUs.
   e.   None of the above.

13. Condor Company has a foreign subsidiary in a country in which the **direct** exchange rate **increased** from $.80 at January 1, 19X1, to $.90 at December 31, 19X1. During 19X1, the foreign subsidiary had (A) an average net asset position of 500,000 LCUs and (B) an average net monetary liability position of 300,000 LCUs. Under the **U.S. dollar unit of measure approach,** what is the effect of the change in the exchange rate for 19X1?

   a. $30,000 favorable.
   b. $30,000 unfavorable.
   c. $50,000 favorable.
   d. $50,000 unfavorable.
   e.   None of the above.

14. Use the same information as in Question 13. Under the **foreign currency unit of measure approach,** what is the effect of the change in the exchange rate for 19X1?

   a. $30,000 favorable.
   b. $30,000 unfavorable.
   c. $50,000 favorable.
   d. $50,000 unfavorable.
   e.   None of the above.

CHAPTER 16—SOLUTIONS

Completion Statements

1. physical presence
2. fair-transfer pricing
3. restated
4. monetary, nonmonetary
5. contractually obligated
6. U.S. dollar unit of measure approach
7. net monetary position
8. net monetary asset position
9. net monetary liability position
10. foreign currency unit of measure approach
11. net investment
12. functional currency
13. stockholders' equity
14. the income statement

True-or-False Statements

1.	False	9.	False
2.	True	10.	False
3.	True	11.	False
4.	False	12.	False
5.	True	13.	True
6.	False	14.	True
7.	False	15.	True
8.	True		

Multiple-Choice Questions

1.	e	8.	d
2.	e	9.	b
3.	e	10.	c
4.	a	11.	a
5.	d	12.	d
6.	b	13.	b
7.	c	14.	c

CHAPTER 17

TRANSLATION OF FOREIGN CURRENCY FINANCIAL STATEMENTS: PRACTICE

CHAPTER HIGHLIGHTS

1. Each foreign operation is **presumed** to have a **functional currency**—the currency it primarily uses to generate and expend cash (the currency in which it **primarily conducts its operations**).

2. Foreign operations that are **relatively self-contained and independent** of the parent's operations have the foreign currency as the functional currency.

3. Foreign operations that are **not** relatively self-contained and independent of the parent's operations have the U.S. dollar as the functional currency.

4. The determination of the functional currency must be based on the **economic facts**—it cannot be an arbitrary selection.

5. For **operations in highly inflationary economies** (ones that have a cumulative inflation rate of approximately 100% or more over a three-year period), the U.S. dollar is considered to be the functional currency.

6. When the **foreign currency is the functional currency,** the "translation" process is used (the current rate method, which achieves a foreign currency unit of measure).

7. When the **U.S. dollar is the functional currency,** the remeasurement process is used (the temporal method, which achieves a U.S. dollar unit of measure).

8. "Translation" is the process of going **from the functional currency to the reporting currency** of the parent.

9. "Remeasurement" is the process of **going from a nonfunctional to the functional currency** (which usually is also the reporting currency of the parent).

10. The effect of a change in the exchange rate in "translation" situations is called a **translation adjustment,** which is charged or credited directly to stockholders' equity (bypassing the income statement until the investment in the foreign operation is sold or liquidated).

11. The effect of a change in the exchange rate in "remeasurement" situations is called a **foreign currency transaction gain or loss,** which is reported currently in the income statement.

12. A **minority** of foreign operations may require **both** the remeasurement process and the translation process—the vast majority of foreign operations will require only one or the other.

13. The basic procedures **before** performing **either** the translation process or the remeasurement process are (A) restating foreign currency financial statements to reflect U.S. GAAP, (B) adjusting foreign currency receivables and payables to reflect the current exchange rate at the balance sheet date, and (C) reconciling inter- or intracompany receivable and payable accounts.

14. For **both** the translation process and the remeasurement process, the **current exchange rate** is defined as (A) the exchange rate existing at the balance sheet date (when dealing with the balance sheet) and (B) the exchange rate in effect when an item is recognized in the income statement (when dealing with the income statement).

15. In dealing with the income statement, **average exchange rates** may be used instead of the individual current exchange rates **providing the results** approximate the amounts obtainable if the current exchange rates were used.

16. When the **foreign currency is the functional currency,** the current year translation adjustment can be calculated by **analyzing the net assets** of the foreign operation for the year.

17. When the **U.S. dollar is the functional currency,** the foreign currency transaction gain or loss from remeasurement can be calculated by **analyzing the monetary assets and monetary liabilities** for the year.

18. The **cumulative translation adjustment** account (used in only the "translation" process) is (A) a translation worksheet account and (B) a general ledger account **only** in the parent's general ledger.

19. In the remeasurement process, **a combination of current and historical exchange rates** are used in both the balance sheet and the income statement—only current exchange rates are used in the translation process.

20. **Realization review procedures in U.S. dollars** are required after the remeasurement process **but not** after the translation process.

21. When the **foreign currency is the functional currency,** adjustments made to the parent company's long-term intercompany receivable or payable to reflect the current exchange rate (occurs only when the receivable or payable is denominated in a foreign currency) are charged or credited **to the cumulative translation adjustment account**—not to the income statement.

22. When **intercompany inventory transfers** are made from a parent to a foreign subsidiary, the calculation of any unrealized intercompany gross profit is made using the exchange rates existing **at the time of the transfer**—not the exchange rate existing at the balance sheet date.

23. In **recording dividends receivable** from a foreign subsidiary, the parent uses the exchange rate **existing at the declaration date.** Any changes in the exchange rate between the declaration date and the remittance date are foreign currency transaction gains or losses that are to be **reported currently in the income statement.**

COMPLETION STATEMENTS

1. The currency which a foreign operation primarily uses to generate and expend cash is called its _____ .

2. When a foreign unit's functional currency is its local currency, the process of expressing the foreign currency financial statements in dollars is called _____
_____ .

3. When a foreign unit's functional currency is the U.S. dollar, the process of expressing the foreign currency financial statements in dollars is called _____
_____ .

4. Translation is the process of going from a functional currency to the _____
_____ currency.

5. Remeasurement is the process of going from a nonfunctional currency to the _____ currency.

6. When the current rate method is used, the effect of a change in the exchange rate is called a _____ .

7. When the temporal method is used, the effect of a change in the exchange rate is called a _____ .

8. The current exchange rate as used in translating the income statement is the exchange rate in effect when an item is _____ in the income statement.

9. In the **translation** process, the translation adjustment is charged or credited to an account called _____ .

10. After expressing foreign currency financial statements in U.S. dollars using the remeasurement process, it is necessary to review the nonmonetary assets as to whether they are _____ in U.S. dollars.

11. A foreign subsidiary of a domestic company has an intercompany payable to the parent. The foreign subsidiary will have to adjust the payable to reflect the current exchange rate only if the intercompany payable is _____ in U.S. dollars.

TRUE-OR-FALSE STATEMENTS

1. T   F   The functional currency of a foreign operation is always the currency in which it legally must keep its books.

2. T   F   The functional currency of a foreign operation that is relatively self-contained and independent of the parent's operations would most likely be the local currency of the foreign operation—not the U.S. dollar.

3. T   F   A factor pointing to the U.S. dollar as the functional currency is a low volume of intercompany transactions.

4. T   F   The fact that a foreign subsidiary pays quarterly dividends to the parent points to the U.S. dollar as the functional currency.

5. T   F   The determination of the functional currency must be based on economic facts—it cannot be an arbitrary selection.

6. T   F   A **highly inflationary economy** is defined as one that has inflation of approximately 100% or more per year.

7. T   F   For operations in **highly inflationary economies** (as defined in *FASB Statement No. 52*), the U.S. dollar is deemed to be the functional currency.

8. T   F   **Translation** is the process of going from the reporting currency to the functional currency.

9. T   F   **Remeasurement** is the process of going from a nonfunctional currency to the functional currency.

10. T   F   The effect of a change in the exchange rate from the **remeasurement** process is charged directly to stockholders' equity.

11. T   F   Because intercompany receivables and payables are eliminated in consolidation, it is **not** necessary to adjust these accounts to reflect the current exchange rate at the balance sheet date prior to translation.

12. T   F   The definition of the current exchange rate in *SFAS No. 52* is different for the balance sheet than for the income statement.

13. T   F   In the translation process, the same exchange rates used to translate sales would be used to translate cost of goods sold.

14. T   F   In translating the income statement, it is possible to use 260 (52 weeks times 5 days per week) different exchange rates for an entire year.

15. T   F   The Cumulative Translation Adjustment account is a general ledger account in both the parent's and the subsidiary's general ledgers.

16. T   F   In translating the dividends declared amount in the statement of retained earnings, the exchange rate in effect at the payment date is used.

17. T   F   Translation adjustments reported as a separate component of stockholders' equity are charged or credited directly to retained earnings when the investment is sold or liquidated.

18. T   F   In the **remeasurement process,** the same exchange rates used to remeasure sales would be used to remeasure cost of goods sold.

19. T   F   Nonmonetary assets must be reviewed for realization in dollars after the remeasurement process, but not after the translation process.

20. T   F   In determining the amount of intercompany gross profit to be eliminated resulting from intercompany transactions with foreign units, the exchange rate existing at the time of the transfer must be used.

MULTIPLE-CHOICE QUESTIONS

Conceptual Questions

1. Which of the following factors **points to the foreign currency** as being the functional currency of a foreign unit?
   a. The foreign operation keeps its books in the local currency of the foreign country in which it is located.
   b. The foreign subsidiary does not pay dividends to the parent.
   c. The foreign unit's sales market is entirely in the foreign country in which it is located.
   d. There is a high volume of intercompany inventory transfers.
   e. None of the above.

2. Which of the following factors **points to the U.S. dollar** as being the functional currency of a foreign unit?
   a. The foreign subsidiary pays dividends equal to its net income each year.
   b. The foreign operation is relatively self-contained and independent of the parent's operations.
   c. The foreign unit is heavily financed by local borrowings from banks in the foreign country.
   d. The inflation rate in the foreign country is less than 10% per year.
   e. None of the above.

3. Regarding foreign operations **located in highly inflationary economies,** which of the following statements is correct?
   a. Historical cost amounts are to be restated for inflation prior to translation.
   b. If the cumulative inflation rate over a 3-year period is 100% or more, the foreign currency must be used as the functional currency—no exceptions are allowed.
   c. If the cumulative inflation rate over a 3-year period is 100% or more, the U.S. dollar must be used as the functional currency—no exceptions are allowed.
   d. A cumulative inflation rate over a 3-year period of 95% could be sufficient grounds for using the U.S. dollar as the functional currency if the economic factors do not clearly point to there being a functional currency.
   e. None of the above.

4. The translation process may be described as the process of
   a. Expressing functional currency amounts in the reporting currency.
   b. Applying exchange rates to a foreign operation's financial statements when they are not stated in the functional currency.
   c. Expressing nonfunctional currency amounts in the reporting currency.
   d. Going from a nonfunctional currency to the functional currency.
   e. None of the above.

5. What is the effect of a change in the exchange rate called under the **foreign currency unit of measure approach** (current rate method)?
   a. Translation gain or loss.
   b. Translation adjustment.
   c. Foreign currency transaction gain or loss.
   d. Functional currency adjustment.
   e. Functional currency gain or loss.

6. What is the effect of a change in the exchange rate called under the **U.S. dollar unit of measure approach** (temporal method)?
   a. Translation gain or loss.
   b. Translation adjustment.
   c. Foreign currency transaction gain or loss.
   d. Functional currency adjustment.
   e. Functional currency gain or loss.

7. The Cumulative Translation Adjustment account that is used as a result of the translation process is
   a. A general ledger account in the books of the foreign subsidiary.
   b. A general ledger account in both the parent's books and the foreign subsidiary's books.
   c. A general ledger account only in the parent's books and an account that exists on the translation worksheet.
   d. An account that exists only on the translation worksheet and not in any general ledger.
   e. None of the above.

8. The remeasurement process may be described as a process of
   a. Going from a functional currency to a nonfunctional currency.
   b. Going from a nonfunctional currency to a functional currency.
   c. Going from a functional currency to the reporting currency.
   d. Going from a nonfunctional currency to the reporting currency.
   e. None of the above.

9. On December 27, 19X1, a foreign subsidiary declared a dividend of 100,000 LCUs (local currency units). The dividend is payable in LCUs and was paid on January 4, 19X2. The direct exchange rate was $.49 on the declaration date, $.52 on December 31, 19X1, and $.48 on the payment date. The **functional currency is the foreign currency** (the LCU). At December 31, 19X1, the parent would
   a. Adjust the Investment in Subsidiary account and adjust the Dividends Receivable account.
   b. Adjust the Investment in Subsidiary account and credit the Foreign Currency Transaction Gain account.

    c.   Adjust the Dividends Receivable account and credit the Foreign Currency Transaction Gain account.

    d.   Adjust the Dividends Receivable account and credit the Cumulative Translation Adjustment account.

    e.   Make no entry.

10. Answer the same question as in Question 9, except that the **functional currency is the U.S. dollar.**

Application Questions

11. Which exchange rates should be used in expressing the following accounts in dollars when the **foreign currency is the functional currency?**

	Inventory	Deferred Income Taxes Payable
a.	Current	Current
b.	Historical	Historical
c.	Current	Historical
d.	Historical	Current
e.	None of the above.	

12. Answer the same question as in Question 11, except that the **functional currency is the U.S. dollar.**

13. Which exchange rates should be used in expressing the following accounts in dollars when the **foreign currency is the functional currency?**

	Sales	Patent Amortization Expense
a.	Current	Current
b.	Historical	Historical
c.	Current	Historical
d.	Historical	Current
e.	None of the above.	

14. Answer the same question as in Question 13, except that the **functional currency is the U.S. dollar.**

15. For 19X3, a foreign subsidiary reported 600,000 LCUs (local currency units) of depreciation expense. Of this amount, 400,000 of LCUs pertained to fixed assets acquired at the beginning of 19X1 when the relationship between the two currencies was $1 equals 4 LCUs. The remaining 200,000 of LCUs pertained to fixed assets acquired at the beginning of 19X3 when the relationship between the two currencies was $1 equals 5 LCUs. For 19X3, the average exchange rate was $1 equals 6 LCUs. At December 31, 19X3, the exchange rate was $1 equals 8 LCUs. What is the depreciation expense in dollars if the **functional currency is the LCU?**

    a. $75,000

    b. $100,000

    c. $140,000

    d. $2,600,000

    e. $3,600,000

    f. $4,800,000

16. Answer the same question as in Question 15, except that the **functional currency is the U.S. dollar.**

17. A domestic parent company sold inventory costing $80,000 to its foreign subsidiary for $100,000. At year-end, the subsidiary reported in its balance sheet 60,000 LCUs of this inventory. At the time of the sale, $1 equalled 5 LCUs. At year-end, $1 equals 4 LCUs. How much intercompany profit must be deferred in the consolidated income statement at year-end assuming the **functional currency is the LCU?**

   a. $2,400
   b. $3,000
   c. $12,000
   d. $15,000
   e. None of the above.

18. Answer the same question as in Question 17, except that the **functional currency is the U.S. dollar.**

CHAPTER 17—SOLUTIONS

Completion Statements

1. functional currency
2. translation
3. remeasurement
4. reporting
5. functional
6. translation adjustment
7. foreign currency transaction gain or loss
8. recognized
9. cumulative translation adjustment
10. realizable
11. denominated

True-or-False Statements

1. False
2. True
3. False
4. False
5. True
6. False
7. True
8. False
9. True
10. False

11. False
12. True
13. True
14. True
15. False
16. False
17. False
18. False
19. True
20. True

Multiple-Choice Questions

1. c
2. e
3. d
4. a
5. b

6. c
7. c
8. b
9. c
10. c
11. a
12. d
13. a
14. c
15. b (600,000 LCU ÷ 6 equals $100,000)
16. c (400,000 LCU ÷ 4 equals $100,000; 200,000 LCU ÷ 5 equals $40,000; $100,000 + $40,000 equals $140,000)
17. a
18. a

CHAPTER 18

FOREIGN CURRENCY TRANSLATIONS: EVALUATING THE VALIDITY OF THE FUNCTIONAL CURRENCY CONCEPT

CHAPTER HIGHLIGHTS

1. Under **purchasing power parity theory,** the differential rate of inflation between two countries can be expected to result over the long run in an **equal but opposite** change in the exchange rate between the two currencies.

2. **Foreign inflation** drives the direct exchange rate **down.**

3. **Domestic inflation** drives the direct exchange rate **up.**

4. Under the **PPP current-value approach,** long-lived assets are adjusted upward for foreign inflation and then translated at the **current rate** existing at the balance sheet date.

5. The **disappearing plant problem** does not occur under the PPP current-value approach.

6. Economically, **increases** in the direct exchange rate resulting from **domestic inflation** lead to **unrealized nominal inflation holding gains.**

7. A **nominal gain** means "in name only." Economically, no gain has occurred because no increase in **purchasing power** has occurred.

8. A **real gain** is a true economic gain as a result of an entity having more **purchasing power** than at an earlier time.

9. Economically, **decreases** in the direct exchange rate resulting from **foreign inflation** result in **unrealized inflationary holding gains** to the extent the foreign unit has **nonindexed** debt financing of fixed assets. Economically, such gains are real.

10. The **current rate method** properly reports the effect of both **domestic inflation** and **noninflationary factors** on the exchange rate—but not the effects of **foreign inflation.**

11. The **temporal method** properly reports the effects of **foreign inflation** on the exchange rate—but not the effects of **domestic inflation** and **noninflationary factors.**

12. The **temporal method** is ideally suited for **highly inflationary economies** in which foreign inflation is the dominant cause of exchange rate changes.

13. The **current rate method** is ideally suited for **nonhighly inflationary economies** in which noninflationary factors are the dominant cause of exchange rate changes.

14. The **temporal method** achieves **inflationary accounting reporting results** for foreign inflation—this is not acknowledged in *SFAS No. 52.*

15. *SFAS No. 52's* two translation methods produce major reporting inconsistencies **when foreign inflation occurs.** Under the **temporal method,** unrealized inflationary holding gains are reported currently in the income statement. Under the **current rate method,** unrealized inflationary holding gains are not reported at all (a zero net effect is reported).

16. The **disappearing plant problem** can occur under both the temporal method and the current rate method.

17. *SFAS 52* links the manner in which foreign operations are conducted (determining the **functional currency**) to how fixed assets should be valued in translation. This linkage is erroneous (authors' opinion).

18. The functional currency concept is **not** necessary to allow the use of **multiple units of measure.**

19. Multiple units of measure could have been implemented by the FASB merely by allowing firms to **judgmentally select** either the current rate method or the temporal method.

20. *SFAS No. 52's* translation methods do **not** always (A) reflect the **true economic effect** of exchange rate changes (missing the mark) or (B) achieve reporting results that are **generally compatible** with the economic effect of exchange rate changes (missing the mark by such a wide amount that it reports the opposite effect as to direction—not degree).

21. To the extent the direct exchange rate has decreased because of foreign inflation, the **temporal method** results in adjusting foreign fixed assets for **the effects of foreign inflation.** When such financial statements are consolidated with the parent's domestic financial statements, this results in a **mixing of valuation bases.**

22. To the extent the direct exchange rate has increased because of domestic inflation, the **current rate method** results in adjusting foreign fixed assets for **the effects of domestic inflation.** When such financial statements are consolidated with the parent's domestic financial statements, this results in a **mixing of valuation bases.**

23. Great care must be taken in using financial statements translated using the translation methods required by *SFAS No. 52*. In situations in which the translated amounts **cannot be relied upon,** it may be necessary to develop more meaningful numbers using the PPP current-value approach.

24. The most common situation in which the translated results under *SFAS No. 52* **cannot be relied upon** is using the current rate method when the foreign country consistently has **higher inflation than the U.S.** This creates the disappearing plant problem.

COMPLETION STATEMENTS

1. Long-term exchange rate changes are best explained by _____ _____ theory.

2. The focus of the PPP current-value approach is on the _____ _____ .

3. A problem that occurs under both the temporal method and the current rate method is the _____ problem.

4. The direct exchange rate **decreases** as a result of _____ .

5. The direct exchange rate **increases** as a result of _____ .

6. A gain in name only is a(n) _____ gain.

7. A gain that is **not** in name only is a(n) _____ gain.

8. Under the **current rate method,** an increase in the direct exchange rate caused by **domestic inflation** results in reporting an unrealized _____ _____ .

9. Under the **temporal method,** a decrease in the direct exchange rate caused by **foreign inflation** results in reporting an unrealized _____ _____ when fixed assets are financed by nonindexed local currency debt.

10. The **temporal method** is no more able to produce realistic results when high _____ inflation is the dominant exchange rate change factor than the **current rate method** is able to produce reliable results when high _____ inflation is the dominant exchange rate change factor.

11. *SFAS No. 52* is based on whether a foreign unit is _____ or _____ .

12. *SFAS No. 8* used a(n) _____ unit of measure, which was the

13. *SFAS No. 52* uses _____ units of measure, which are the _____ and the _____ .

14. Under the temporal method, **the disappearing plant problem** occurs if _____ inflation exceeds _____ inflation.

15. Under the current rate method, **the disappearing plant problem** occurs if _____ inflation exceeds _____ inflation.

TRUE-OR-FALSE STATEMENTS

1. T F If foreign inflation **exceeds** domestic inflation, the direct exchange rate should **increase** under PPP theory.

2. T F Under the **PPP current-value approach,** the focus is on the net asset (net investment) position.

3. T F Under the PPP current-value approach, the relationships that exist in the inflation adjusted foreign balance sheet are maintained in translation.

4. T F The disappearing plant problem does **not** occur under the PPP current value approach.

5. T F An **increase** in the direct exchange rate as a result of domestic inflation results in a realized nominal inflationary holding gain.

6. T F A **decrease** in the direct exchange rate as a result of foreign inflation results in an unrealized inflationary holding gain to the extent foreign fixed assets are financed with nonindexed debt.

7. T F A **nominal** gain means an unrealized gain.

8. T F A **real** gain means a realized gain.

9. T F Inflationary holding gains can be either nominal or real.

10. T F The **current rate method** properly reports the economic effect of **foreign** inflation.

11. T F The **current rate method** properly reports the economic effect of **domestic** inflation.

12. T F The **current rate** method properly reports the economic effect of **noninflationary factors.**

13. T F The **temporal method** properly reports the economic effect of **foreign** inflation.

14. T F The **temporal method** properly reports the economic effect of **domestic** inflation.

15. T F The **temporal method** properly reports the economic effect of **noninflationary factors.**

16. T F Mixing of valuation bases (foreign fixed assets and domestic fixed assets) can occur under the **temporal method.**

17. T F Mixing of valuation bases (foreign fixed assets and domestic fixed assets) can occur under the **current rate** method.

18. T F The disappearing plant problem **can occur** under the **current rate method** but **not** under the **temporal method.**

19. T F The disappearing plant problem **can occur** under the **temporal method** but **not** under the **current rate method.**

20. T F The functional currency concept **is** needed to use multiple units of measure.

21. T F Under *SFAS No. 52*, an **autonomous** foreign unit in a nonhighly inflationary environment would use the current rate method.

22. T F The problem with *SFAS No. 8* was that it did **not** account differently for different economic facts.

23. T F The problem with *SFAS No. 8* was that it was **not** based on dealing with causes of exchange rate changes.

24. T F The PPP current-value approach results in mixing different valuation bases (for domestic fixed assets and foreign fixed assets).

MULTIPLE-CHOICE QUESTIONS

Conceptual Questions

1. Unrealized nominal inflationary holding gains resulting from the exchange rate change effect of **domestic inflation** are reported
    a. Only under the current rate method.
    b. Only under the temporal method.
    c. Only under the PPP current value approach.
    d. Under the current rate method and the PPP current value approach.
    e. Under the temporal method and the PPP current value approach.

2. Unrealized inflationary holding gains resulting from the exchange rate change effect of **foreign inflation** are reported
    a. Only under the current rate method.
    b. Only under the temporal method.
    c. Only under the PPP current value approach.
    d. Under the current rate method and the PPP current value approach.
    e. Under the temporal method and the PPP current value approach.

3. The disappearing plant problem can occur

    a.   Only under the current rate method.

    b.   Only under the temporal method.

    c.   Under both the current rate method and the temporal method.

    d.   Under the current rate method and the PPP current value approach.

    e.   Under the temporal method and the PPP current value approach.

4. The mixing of valuation bases (foreign fixed assets and domestic fixed assets) occurs

    a.   Only under the current rate method.

    b.   Only under the temporal method.

    c.   Only under the PPP current value approach.

    d.   Under the current rate method, the temporal method, and the PPP current value approach.

    e.   None of the above.

Application Questions

5. On January 1, 19X1, the direct exchange rate was $.55. At December 31, 19X1, the direct exchange rate was $.49. During 19X1, the U.S. had 4% inflation, and the foreign country had 10% inflation. How much of the change in the exchange rate was the result of **foreign inflation?**

    a. $.02

    b. $(.02)

    c. $.05

    d. $(.05)

    e. $.03

    f. $(.03)

6. Use the information in Question 5. How much of the change in the exchange rate was the result of **domestic inflation?**

    a. $.02

    b. $(.02)

    c. $.05

    d. $(.05)

    e. $.03

    f. $(.03)

7. Use the information in Question 5. How much of the change in the exchange rate was the result of **noninflationary factors?**

    a. $.02

    b. $(.02)

    c. $.05

    d. $(.05)

    e. $.03

    f. $(.03)

8. During 19X1, a foreign subsidiary had fixed assets of 100,000 LCUs that were financed with nonindexed local currency debt. Assume that the direct exchange rate **decreased** by $.08 during 19X1, all of which was the result of **foreign infla-tion.** How much would the consolidated stockholders' equity increase or decrease under the following translation methods?

	Current Rate Method	Temporal Method
a.	$ -0-	$ -0-
b.	$ -0-	$ 8,000
c.	$ 8,000	$ -0-
d.	$ 8,000	$ 8,000
e.	$ -0-	$(8,000)
f.	$(8,000)	$ -0-
g.	$(8,000)	$(8,000)

9. During 19X1, a foreign subsidiary had fixed assets of 100,000 LCUs that were financed with nonindexed local currency debt. Assume that the direct exchange rate **increased** by $.09 during 19X1, all of which was the result of **domestic infla-tion.** How much would the consolidated stockholders' equity increase or decrease under the following translation methods?

	Current Rate Method	Temporal Method
a.	$ -0-	$ -0-
b.	$ -0-	$ 9,000
c.	$ 9,000	$ -0-
d.	$ 9,000	$ 9,000
e.	$ -0-	$(9,000)
f.	$(9,000)	$ -0-
g.	$(9,000)	$(9,000)

CHAPTER 18—SOLUTIONS

Completion Statements

1. purchasing power parity
2. net asset (net investment) position
3. disappearing plant
4. foreign inflation
5. domestic inflation
6. nominal
7. real
8. nominal inflationary holding gain
9. inflationary holding gain
10. domestic, foreign
11. autonomous, nonautonomous
12. single, U.S. dollar
13. multiple, U.S. dollar, local currency
14. domestic, foreign
15. foreign, domestic

True-or-False Statements

1.	False	13.	True
2.	True	14.	False
3.	True	15.	False
4.	True	16.	True
5.	False (it is unrealized)	17.	True
6.	True	18.	False
7.	Falsc	19.	False
8.	False	20.	False
9.	True	21.	True
10.	False	22.	False
11.	True	23.	True
12.	True	24.	True

Multiple-Choice Questions

1.	d	6.	a
2.	e	7.	f
3.	c	8.	b
4.	d	9.	e
5.	d		

CHAPTER 19
INTERIM REPORTING

CHAPTER HIGHLIGHTS

1. Quarterly financial reporting is **not** required by any official accounting pronouncement.

2. Quarterly financial reporting is required by the New York Stock Exchange, the American Stock Exchange, and the Securities and Exchange Commission (for publicly owned companies).

3. The **fundamental conceptual issue** concerning interim financial statements is whether or not they should be prepared using the same accounting principles and practices used to prepare annual financial statements.

4. Under the **discrete view,** no distinction is made between interim reporting and annual reporting—the same accounting principles and practices used for annual reporting are used for interim reporting.

5. Under the **integral view,** interim periods are viewed as an integral part of an annual period in such a way that special accrual and deferral techniques are used at interim dates even though such practices cannot be used at annual reporting dates.

6. *APB Opinion No. 28* prescribes a combination discrete-integral approach.

7. **Revenues** are to be recognized as earned during an interim period on the same basis as followed for the full year.

8. **Costs associated with revenues** (product costs) are to be accounted for at interim dates using the same pricing methods and procedures as used at annual reporting dates with the following exceptions (**all of which are optional**):
   a. **Estimated gross profit rates** may be used to determine cost of goods sold during interim periods.
   b. **Liquidation at an interim date of LIFO base-period inventories** may be disregarded if the company expects to replace the quantities by the end of the annual period.
   c. **Temporary declines in market prices** at interim dates **need not** be recognized at interim dates. (Subsequent recoveries of losses recognized may be recognized, but only to the extent of previously recognized losses.)
   d. **Planned volume variances** expected to be absorbed by year-end **may be** deferred at interim dates.

9. **All other costs and expenses** (nonproduct costs) are to be charged to interim periods as incurred unless they can be identified with the activities or benefits of other interim periods, in which case they **may** be (an optional treatment) allocated among interim periods.

10. Companies having **seasonal businesses** must disclose the seasonal nature of their activities.

11. **Changes in the estimated tax rate** for the year are treated as a change in estimate, the effect of which is to be reported in the interim period in which the change in estimate occurs—**no retroactive restatement** of prior interim periods is made, nor may the cumulative effect be allocated on a prospective basis over the current and remaining interim periods.

12. **Extraordinary, unusual, and infrequently occurring items** and disposals of segments are reported in the period in which they occur.

13. **Contingencies** are reported using the same practices as used for annual reporting.

14. **Changes in accounting principles** made in other than the first interim period are to result in the restatement of the prior interim periods just as if the change had been made at the beginning of the year.

15. **Changes in accounting estimates** are accounted for on a prospective basis in the interim period in which the change is made.

16. Previously issued interim reports are restated for **corrections of an error** (if material, of course).

17. *APB Opinion No. 28* calls for specified income statement items to be presented in interim reports plus other disclosures.

18. **Interim financial reports** need **not** be audited nor reviewed by outside certified public accountants.

19. **Quarterly financial information included in the annual report** of a publicly owned company must be reviewed by the outside auditors.

20. For publicly owned companies, the SEC permits quarterly financial information included in the annual report to be presented **outside the notes to the annual financial statements.**

COMPLETION STATEMENTS

1. A school of thought that an interim period is a self-contained segment of history that must stand on its own is called the _____ .

2. A school of thought that an interim period is an essential part of an annual period is called the _____ .

3. For quarterly financial data presented in the annual report of publicly owned companies, outside auditors of such companies are required to perform _____ _____ on such data.

4. Under *APB Opinion No. 28,* revenues are to be accounted for using the _____ _____ view.

5. Under *APB Opinion No. 28,* income taxes are to be accounted for using the _____ _____ view.

6. Under *APB Opinion No. 28,* extraordinary items are to be accounted for using the _____ view.

7. In interim reporting, changes in accounting estimates are to be accounted for _____ _____ .

8. In interim reporting, changes in accounting principles that are made in other than the first interim reporting quarter are to be accounted for _____ .

TRUE-OR-FALSE STATEMENTS

1. T   F   Quarterly financial reporting is required by *APB Opinion No. 28.*

2. T   F   Under the **discrete view,** the same accounting principles and practices used to prepare annual reports are used for interim reporting.

3. T   F   Under the **integral view,** special deferral and accrual practices are used for interim reporting purposes that may not be used for annual reporting purposes.

4. T   F   Under *APB Opinion No. 28,* a company having **seasonal revenues must** report such revenues in the interim period in which they are earned—they cannot be allocated over the full year.

5. T   F   Under *APB Opinion No. 28,* **costs associated with revenues** (product costs) are to be charged to interim periods as incurred, or be allocated among interim periods based on an estimate of time expired, benefit received, or activity associated with the period.

6. T   F   For interim reporting purposes, **declines in market prices for inventories** at interim dates are to be recognized at the interim date even though such declines are expected to be recovered by the end of the annual period.

7. T   F   For interim reporting purposes, **overhead volume variances** that are planned and expected to be absorbed by the end of the annual period must be deferred at interim reporting dates.

8. T   F   For interim reporting purposes, it is perfectly acceptable to determine cost of goods sold using estimated gross profit rates.

9. T F If at an interim reporting date a company liquidates a portion of its LIFO based-period inventories that it expects to replace by the end of the annual period, cost of goods sold for the interim period will include the expected cost of replacing the liquidated LIFO base.

10. T F Costs of periodic advertising campaigns and charitable contributions are examples of expenditures that may **not** be allocated among interim periods but must be expensed in the interim period in which incurred.

11. T F Major annual repairs and social security taxes are examples of expenditures that **must** be allocated among interim periods instead of being expensed in the interim period in which incurred.

12. T F If the estimated tax rate for the year changes as the year proceeds, the effect of the change is included in the appropriate interim period as a change in accounting estimate—no retroactive restatement of prior interim periods is allowed.

13. T F In computing the estimated tax rate for the year, an excess of depreciation for tax reporting purposes over depreciation for financial reporting purposes would **not** enter into the calculation.

14. T F Extraordinary, unusual, and infrequently occurring items **must** be reported in the interim period in which they occur—they cannot be allocated among interim periods.

15. T F In a company's second quarter, an error is found in the previously issued first quarter report. The correction **must** be charged or credited to income in the second quarter regardless of materiality—no retroactive restatement of the first quarter is permitted.

16. T F Changes in accounting estimates **must** be accounted for in the interim period in which the change is made on a prospective basis—no retroactive restatement to the beginning of the first interim reporting period is permitted.

17. T F Changes in accounting principles that are made in other than the first quarter will result in a restatement of **all** of the prior interim reporting periods of the current year.

18. T F Outside auditors are required to review interim financial data before it is released to the public.

19. T F Quarterly financial data **may** be presented outside of the notes to the annual financial statements.

20. T F If quarterly financial data is presented outside of the notes to the annual financial statements, the outside auditors are **not** required to perform review procedures on the data.

MULTIPLE-CHOICE QUESTIONS

Conceptual Questions

1. Which of the following is **not** an argument in support of the discrete view?
   a. The function of accounting is to record transactions and events as they occur.
   b. An interim period must stand on its own.
   c. The period of time for which results of operations are determined should not influence how such transactions and events are reported.
   d. Accruals and deferrals that are not allowable at year-end are also not allowable at interim dates.
   e. None of the above.

2. Under the integral view (in its pure form),
   a. The period of time being reported on is not relevant.
   b. Special accrual and deferral procedures are used at interim dates even though such procedures are not allowed at year-end.
   c. The costs of unforeseen events (such as the settlement of litigation and extraordinary items) are allocated over the full year rather than being charged or credited to any particular quarter.
   d. Year-end bonuses would not be anticipated and accrued for interim reporting purposes.
   e. None of the above.

3. Under *APB Opinion No. 28*, which of the following statements concerning revenues is **false?**
   a. Companies having seasonal revenues must report such revenues in the interim period in which they are earned as opposed to allocating them over the full year.
   b. When receipts at an interim date precede the earnings process, the revenues must be deferred until the interim period in which the product is delivered or the service is rendered.
   c. If revenues to date are behind budgeted revenues and such difference is expected to be made up by the end of the annual period, the difference may be recognized as revenues in the interim period.
   d. The percentage-of-completion method for long-term construction-type contracts is acceptable for interim reporting with no modification from the procedures used at the end of the annual period.
   e. None of the above.

4. Under *APB Opinion No. 28*, which of the following statements concerning inventories is **false?**
   a. Complete physical inventories need not be taken at interim dates.
   b. A perpetual inventory system must be used to obtain the cost of goods sold during interim periods.
   c. Estimates must be made at interim dates for inventory shrinkage and obsolesence.
   d. Provisions for write-downs to market at interim dates should generally be made on the same basis as used at annual reporting dates.
   e. None of the above.

5. Under *APB Opinion No. 28*, which of the following statements concerning inventory pricing is correct?

    a.   No distinction is to be made between temporary and nontemporary declines in inventory market prices for interim reporting purposes.

    b.   If inventory losses from market declines are recognized at an interim date, any subsequent recoveries cannot be recognized.

    c.   Temporary declines in inventory market prices cannot be recognized at interim reporting dates.

    d.   An inventory loss from a market decline in the first quarter that is not expected to be recovered by the end of the year should be recognized as a loss proportionately in each of the first, second, third, and fourth quarters.

    e.   None of the above.

6. Under *APB Opinion No. 28*, which of the following statements concerning volume variances is correct?

    a.   Volume variances at interim dates that are planned and expected to be absorbed by the end of the annual period **may** be deferred at the interim date.

    b.   Volume variances at interim dates that are planned and expected to be absorbed by the end of the annual period **must** be deferred at the interim date.

    c.   Volume variances at interim dates that are planned and expected to be absorbed by the end of the annual period **may not** be deferred at the interim date.

    d.   For interim reporting purposes, no distinction is to be made between volume variances that are planned or unplanned.

    e.   None of the above.

7. Under *APB Opinion No. 28*, how is the cumulative effect of a change in the estimated income tax rate that occurs after the first interim reporting period to be reported?

    a.   On a prospective basis over the current and remaining interim periods.

    b.   In the first interim reporting period by restating the results of the first interim reporting period.

    c.   The effect may be deferred until the fourth quarter.

    d.   In the interim reporting period in which the change occurs.

    e.   None of the above.

Application Questions

8. Composit Company estimated its annual effective income tax rate to be 40% at the end of its first quarterly interim period for 19X1. At the end of the third quarter for 19X1, the company revised its estimated annual effective income tax rate to be 35%. Composit had pretax earnings of $100,000 for each of the first three quarters and expects pretax earnings for the fourth quarter to be $200,000. What amount should be reported for income tax expense in the third quarterly interim report?

    a. $25,000

    b. $30,000

    c. $35,000

    d. $40,000

    e.   None of the above.

9. Use the same information as in Question 8. What amount should be reported for income tax expense in the third quarterly interim report for the year to date (9 month) results?
   a. $105,000
   b. $110,000
   c. $115,000
   d. $120,000
   e. None of the above.

10. For interim financial reporting, which of the following items may be prorated over each of the quarters instead of being expensed in the quarter in which incurred or paid?

	Annual Audit Fees	Annual Major Repairs
a.	Yes	Yes
b.	Yes	No
c.	No	Yes
d.	No	No

11. For interim financial reporting, which of the following items may be prorated over each of the quarters instead of being expensed in the quarter in which incurred or paid?

	Property Taxes	Fine for Violation of Environmental Protection Rules
a.	Yes	Yes
b.	Yes	No
c.	No	Yes
d.	No	No

12. For interim financial reporting, which of the following items may be prorated over each of the quarters instead of being expensed in the quarter in which incurred or paid?

	Charitable Contributions	Severance Payments
a.	Yes	Yes
b.	No	No
c.	No	Yes
d.	Yes	No

13. For interim financial reporting, which of the following items may be prorated over each of the quarters instead of being expensed in the quarter in which incurred or paid?

	Loss on Early Extinguishment of Debt	Annual Fall Advertising Campaign
a.	Yes	Yes
b.	Yes	No
c.	No	Yes
d.	No	No

14. Under *APB Opinion No. 28*, interim financial reports are to include, as a minimum, which of the following items?
    a. A condensed income statement.
    b. Specified income statement items.
    c. A complete income statement.
    d. Comparative income statement items.
    e. None of the above.

15. Which of the following items is correct regarding interim financial reports issued by publicly owned companies?
    a. They must be reviewed by auditors before their release.
    b. They must be audited by auditors before their release.
    c. They must be reviewed by auditors if they are 10-Q quarterly reports being filed with the SEC (review must precede filing).
    d. They do not have to be reviewed or audited by auditors before their release.
    e. None of the above.

CHAPTER 19—SOLUTIONS

Completion Statements

1. discrete view
2. integral view
3. review procedures
4. discrete
5. integral
6. discrete
7. prospectively
8. retroactively

True-or-False Statements

1. False	11. False
2. True	12. True
3. True	13. True
4. True	14. True
5. False	15. False
6. False	16. True
7. False	17. True
8. True	18. False
9. True	19. True
10. False	20. False

Multiple-Choice Questions

1. e	9. a
2. b	10. a
3. c	11. b
4. b	12. d
5. e	13. c
6. a	14. b
7. d	15. d
8. a	

CHAPTER 20
SECURITIES AND EXCHANGE COMMISSION REPORTING

CHAPTER HIGHLIGHTS

1. State blue sky laws to regulate the purchase and sale of securities are supplemented in a major way by the Securities Act of 1933 and the Securities Exchange Act of 1934.

2. The 1933 Act applies to the **initial distribution** of securities to the public and is designed to require companies to provide full and fair disclosure of the character of securities sold to the public.

3. The 1934 Act applies to the **subsequent trading** in outstanding securities and its purpose is to provide for the regulation of securities exchanges and of over-the-counter markets.

4. The SEC is a **quasi-judicial agency** of the U.S. government that **administers** the 1933 Act, the 1934 Act, and several other acts.

5. The five commissioners of the SEC have the **statutory authority** to establish generally accepted accounting principles. (The commissioners rely on the Chief Accountant to furnish advice in this respect.)

6. Historically, the SEC has relied on the private sector organizations to establish GAAP. However, the SEC has not hesitated to **prohibit accounting practices** that it did not agree with.

7. A unique power of the SEC is that **it can order a company to revise their financial statements** if they do not agree with the accounting treatment.

8. The SEC is empowered to take **disciplinary actions against auditors** of publicly owned companies.

9. Accountants and auditors most often deal with Regulation S-X, which contains all of the **financial** disclosure requirements (including financial statements required) for all SEC filings.

10. All **nonfinancial** disclosure requirements are contained in Regulation S-K.

11. The **interpretations and practices** followed by certain departments of the SEC that are responsible for reviewing the disclosure requirements are contained in Staff Accounting Bulletins.

12. The 1933 Act is a unified piece of legislation dealing only with the sale of securities to the public.

13. Certain types of securities and securities transactions are **exempt from registration** under the 1933 Act (private offerings to sophisticated investors, strictly intrastate offerings, and small offerings handled as Regulation A offerings).

14. The most common "form" used under the 1933 Act is Form S-1.

15. Unlike the 1933 Act, the 1934 Act deals with several areas (A) registration of securities exchanges, (B) registration of securities on exchanges, (C) registration of over-the-counter securities, (D) filing of periodic and other reports, (E) proxy regulations, (F) antifraud and insider trading, and (G) regulation of brokers and dealers.

16. In filing periodic and other reports, companies commonly use (A) Form 10-K, annual report; (B) Form 10-Q, quarterly report; and (C) Form 8-K, current reports for material events.

COMPLETION STATEMENTS

1. State laws that regulate the purchase and sale of corporate securities are referred to as _____ .

2. The position within the SEC that has responsibility for all accounting and auditing matters in connection with the administration of the various acts is the _____ _____ .

3. Unlike the FASB, the SEC has _____ powers, whereby it can order companies to revise their financial statements if it does not concur with an accounting treatment.

4. Enumerations of the form and content of the information required to be included in registration statements and reports are called _____ .

5. Announcements pertaining to the various rules, regulations, and forms are called _____ .

6. Stocks and bonds are _____ .

7. A purchaser who purchases the stock of an issuer with a view toward distributing that stock to the public is called a(n) _____ .

8. In connection with the proposed sale of securities to the public, the name given to all the specified financial and nonfinancial information submitted in the appropriate form is called a(n) _____ .

9. In a proposed sale of securities to the public, that part of a registration statement that must be furnished to potential investors is called a(n) _____ .

10. The sale of securities to an institution or company that is considered to be a "sophisticated investor" is commonly referred to as a(n) _____ .

11. Securities not sold through a public offering are referred to as _____ securities.

12. A document empowering one person to vote for another is called a(n) _____ .

13. When soliciting proxies, information required to be furnished to the stockholders is contained in a(n) _____ .

14. Any person who has material nonpublic information is referred to as a(n) _____ .

TRUE-OR-FALSE STATEMENTS

1. T F The 1933 Act applies only to the initial distribution of securities to the public.

2. T F Registration under the 1933 Act refers only to the actual quantity of securities being registered—not the class of security being offered.

3. T F A company cannot become subject to the reporting requirements of the 1934 Act unless it has made a public offering under the 1933 Act.

4. T F If the SEC permits a registration statement to become effective under the 1933 Act, then the SEC has, in substance, warranted that the information therein is true and accurate.

5. T F Even though the SEC has the statutory authority to establish GAAP, the pronouncements of the FASB do not have to be approved by the SEC before their issuance.

6. T F The SEC has given the FASB the statutory authority to prescribe accounting policies.

7. T F The SEC has the power to order companies to revise their financial statements.

8. T F Regulation S-K deals with financial disclosure requirements.

9. T F Regulation S-X applies solely to the 1933 Act.

10. T F Regulation S-X specifies which "form" is to be used in SEC filings.

11. T F SEC "forms" are preprinted forms (similar to those used by taxing agencies) that must be filled out.

12. T F If the auditor of a publicly owned company resigns, voluntarily, this still must be reported to the SEC using Form 8-K.

13. T F In registering under the 1934 Act, a company does **not** register a quantity of securities.

14. T F If a privately owned company having 100,000 common shares outstanding registers the sale of 40,000 new common shares under the 1933 Act, then if the company is subject to the reporting requirements of the 1934 Act, the 40,000 new shares also must be registered under the 1934 Act.

15. T F The SEC has the power to institute criminal action against companies and auditors.

MULTIPLE-CHOICE QUESTIONS

1. The FASB reports to which of the following?
   a. The Chief Accountant of the SEC.
   b. The Division of Corporation Finance of the SEC.
   c. The SEC Commissioners.
   d. The General Accounting Office.
   e. None of the above.

2. In filings with the SEC, the form and content of the required financial statements to be included in the material being filed would be set forth in
   a. Staff Accounting Bulletins.
   b. Regulation S-K.
   c. Regulation S-X.
   d. The appropriate form being used.
   e. None of the above.

3. Which form is used to provide certain specified information and other materially important events to investors on a reasonably current basis?
   a. 10-K.
   b. 8-K.
   c. S-1.
   d. S-X.
   e. S-K.

4. A company that is subject to the reporting requirements of the 1934 Act will satisfy its annual reporting requirements using form
   a. S-1.
   b. 8-K.
   c. 10-K.
   d. S-X.
   e. S-K.

5. Companies that are subject to the reporting requirements of the 1934 Act will satisfy their quarterly reporting requirements using form:
   a. S-X.
   b. 8-K.
   c. 10-K.
   d. 10-Q.
   e. 8-Q.

6. A company that is issuing securities to the public for the first time for which there is no lawful exemption will register such securities with the SEC using form
   a. 1-A.
   b. S-1.
   c. 10-K.
   d. 8-K.
   e. S-X.

7. Conkle Company has 300,000 common shares outstanding and is a privately owned company. The company has just registered for sale 100,000 new shares of common stock. The company desires to have its common stock traded on the American Stock Exchange. How many shares must it register under the 1934 Act after it has registered the 100,000 new shares under the 1933 Act?
   a. 100,000 shares.
   b. 300,000 shares.
   c. 400,000 shares.
   d. None of the shares.

8. A company desiring permission for its common stock to be traded under the 1934 Act must file with the SEC a(n)
   a. Proxy statement.
   b. Offering circular.
   c. Prospectus.
   d. Registration statement.
   e. Financial reporting release.

9. A company soliciting its stockholders for the purposes of requesting from its stockholders permission to vote for them must prepare a
   a. Proxy statement.
   b. Registration statement.
   c. Financial reporting release.
   d. Prospectus.
   e. Form S-1.

10. Which of the following does **not** have to be reported to the SEC for publicly owned companies?
    a. The auditors resign.
    b. The auditors are fired—no accounting disagreements.
    c. The auditors inform the company that they do not intend to seek reappointment for the following year.
    d. The auditors are fired—most likely because of accounting disagreements.
    e. None of the above.

11. Which of the following items is **not** a provision of the 1934 Act?
    a. Registration of over-the-counter securities.
    b. Registration of securities exchanges.
    c. Filing of periodic and other reports.
    d. Proxy regulations.
    e. Antifraud and insider trading regulations.
    f. None of the above.

12. A publicly owned company and its auditors have a material disagreement over an accounting principle. After considerable discussion at high levels, the company agrees to report the item as proposed by the auditor. As a result of this agreement, the company would file with the SEC
    a. Form 8-K.
    b. Form S-1.
    c. Form 10-Q.
    d. Form 10-K.
    e. None of the above.

CHAPTER 20—SOLUTIONS

Completion Statements

1. blue sky laws
2. Chief Accountant
3. enforcement
4. forms
5. releases
6. securities
7. underwriter
8. registration statement
9. prospectus
10. private placement
11. restricted
12. proxy
13. proxy statement
14. insider

True-or-False Statements

1.	True	9.	False
2.	True	10.	False
3.	False	11.	False
4.	False	12.	True
5.	True	13.	True
6.	False	14.	False
7.	True	15.	False
8.	False		

Multiple-Choice Questions

1. e	7. d
2. c	8. d
3. b	9. a
4. c	10. e
5. d	11. f
6. b	12. e

CHAPTER 21

TROUBLED DEBT RESTRUCTURINGS, BANKRUPTCY REORGANIZATIONS, AND LIQUIDATIONS

CHAPTER HIGHLIGHTS

Bankruptcy Statutes

1. Under the bankruptcy statutes, a company is placed under the **protection of the bankruptcy court,** whereby creditors are prevented from taking legal action otherwise available to them.

2. The **bankruptcy statutes** apply to individuals, partnerships, corporations, and municipalities—excluded are insurance companies and certain financial institutions, such as banks and savings and loans, which are subject to alternative regulations.

3. A company can file for bankruptcy protection **voluntarily** or its creditors can file an **involuntary petition** if the debtor (A) is generally not paying its debts as they become due or (B) has appointed a custodian or given possession of its property to a custodian.

4. A special class of creditors created by the bankruptcy statutes is called "**creditors with priority.**" These creditors are given statutory priority over the claims of other **unsecured** creditors with regard to payment.

5. Creditors with priority include (A) administrative expenses related to the bankruptcy proceeding; (B) wages, salaries, and commissions earned within 90 days before the bankruptcy filing (up to $2,000 per employee); (C) employee benefit plan claims for contributions (with limitations); (D) deposits by individuals; and (E) taxes.

6. Chapter 7 of the bankruptcy statutes deals with **liquidation.**

7. Chapter 11 of the bankruptcy statutes deals with **reorganization,** whereby certain debts are forgiven and the company is able to get a "fresh start."

8. Filing for bankruptcy reorganization is a last resort short of liquidation. Most companies prefer to work out a troubled debt restructuring outside of the bankruptcy court, which can be done in far less time and avoids the stigma of having gone through bankruptcy proceedings.

Troubled Debt Restructurings

9. The accounting issues in troubled debt restructurings are (A) how to calculate whether any debt has been forgiven (includes whether or not interest should be imputed) and (B) how to report a forgiveness of debt.

10. *SFAS No. 15* does **not** take a current value approach. Instead, the total amount owed (the "carrying amount of the debt") is compared with the "total future cash payments" required to be made (no discounting to present value allowed).

11. If the carrying amount of the debt exceeds the total future cash payments, a **forgiveness of debt results, which must be reported as a gain** in the income statement (an extraordinary item if material). (Future income statements will report zero interest expense on this restructured debt up to the maturity date.)

12. If the total future cash payments exceed the carrying amount of the debt, then **the excess is reported as interest expense** between the restructuring date and the maturity date. In calculating the amount of interest expense each year, the "interest method" prescribed by *APB Opinion 21* is required to be used. (Future income statements often report unrealistically low interest expense until the maturity date of the debt.)

13. In most instances, *SFAS No. 15* does **not** apply to either quasi-reorganizations or formal bankruptcy reorganizations under Chapter 11 of the bankruptcy statutes.

Chapter 11 Bankruptcy Reorganizations

14. In a **Chapter 11 bankruptcy filing,** the debtor's management usually continues to control and operate the company while it develops a plan of reorganization. If the creditors approve of any plan of reorganization, certain debt is forgiven (formally referred to as a "discharge of indebtedness"). Certain debt, such as taxes and debt incurred under false pretenses, cannot be discharged under the bankruptcy statutes.

15. In **Chapter 11 bankruptcy reorganizations,** the accounting issues—determining how to calculate and report the forgiveness of debt—are the same as in troubled debt restructurings. However, the AICPA's *SOP 90-7*, which applies **exclusively** to bankruptcy reorganizations, applies—not *SFAS No. 15*.

16. The central idea of *SOP 90-7* is that the entity that emerges from Chapter 11 be deemed a **new entity** for which **fresh-start financial statements** should be prepared. **No beginning retained earnings or deficit is reported.** (A minority of entities emerging from Chapter 11 will not qualify for fresh-start accounting under *SOP 90-7*.)

17. Under *SOP 90-7*, comparative financial statements that straddle a confirmation date **cannot** be presented because it would be an inappropriate comparison of a **former entity** and a **new entity.**

18. Under *SOP 90-7*, any forgiveness of debt ("discharge of indebtedness") is (A) calculated using the **present values** of amounts to be paid determining using appropriate current interest rates and (B) reported as an **extraordinary item** in the

predecessor entity's final statement of operations.

19. Under *SOP 90-7,* all assets are restated to reflect their **fair value** at the date of reorganization. This is done by (A) determining the **"reorganization value"** of the entity—an amount that approximates what a willing buyer would pay for the assets of the emerging entity immediately after the restructuring, (B) allocating the reorganization value to the entity's tangible and intangible assets, and (C) reporting any unallocated value as "reorganization value in excess of amounts allocable to identifiable assets" **(goodwill).**

20. Under *SOP 90-7,* the **"old entity"** (prior to the confirmation date) is to (A) report bankruptcy related losses and expenses in **a separate "reorganization items" category** in its statement of operations and (B) report its liabilities **in specified categories** in any balance sheets issued (prepetition liabilities subject to compromise, prepetition liabilities not subject to compromise, and postpetition liabilities).

Chapter 7 Bankruptcy Liquidations

21. In a Chapter 7 filing (for liquidation), the court usually appoints a trustee to liquidate the company. Trustees have the power **to void fraudulent and preferential transfers** made by the debtor within certain specified periods preceding the filing date.

22. In a Chapter 7 filing, a special statement (called the **"statement of affairs"**) is prepared on a "quitting concern" basis. This statement provides information concerning how much money each class of creditors can expect to receive on liquidation of the company.

23. If the court or creditors desire information that relates the trustee's activity with the book balances existing when the trustee was appointed, then **a statement of realization and liquidation** (entirely a historical statement) can be prepared.

COMPLETION STATEMENTS

Bankruptcy Law

1. The two kinds of petitions that may be filed with the bankruptcy courts are _____ _____ and _____ .

2. A special class of creditors created by the bankruptcy statutes is called _____ _____ .

3. The forgiveness of debt or the granting of other concessions by a lender outside of the bankruptcy courts is called a(n) _____ .

4. In determining whether a forgiveness of debt has resulted in a troubled debt restructuring, the carrying amount of the debt is compared with the _____ _____ .

5. A conceptual issue in calculating the amount of forgiveness of debt in a troubled debt restructuring is whether or not interest should be _____ .

6. Two theoretical ways how a forgiveness of debt in a troubled debt restructuring may be viewed as are a(n) _____ and a(n) _____ _____ .

7. Chapter 11 of the bankruptcy statutes deals with _____ .

8. Chapter 7 of the bankruptcy statutes deals with _____ .

9. The day-to-day activities of a company are controlled and operated by _____ _____ in a bankruptcy reorganizations and by _____ _____ in bankruptcy liquidations.

Chapter 11 Bankruptcy Reorganizations

10. In a bankruptcy reorganization, the debtor or its creditors will file a _____ _____ .

11. In a bankruptcy reorganization, a(n) _____ does **not** occur unless the court has approved the plan of reorganization.

12. The power granted to bankruptcy appointed trustees to undo fraudulent and preferential transfers by debtors are called _____ powers.

13. Under *SOP 90-7*, the entity that emerges from a Chapter 11 bankruptcy reorganization is a(n) _____ entity for which _____ _____ financial statements should be prepared.

14. Under *SOP 90-7*, an entity emerging from a Chapter 11 bankruptcy reorganization does not report any beginning _____ or _____ _____ .

15. Under *SOP 90-7*, comparative financial statements that straddle a confirmation date cannot be presented because it would be an inappropriate comparison of a(n) _____ entity and a(n) _____ entity.

16. Under *SOP 90-7*, forgiveness of debt is reported as a(n) _____ _____ .

17. Under *SOP 90-7*, forgiveness of debt is calculated using the _____ _____ of amounts to be paid using _____ .

Chapter 7 Bankruptcy Liquidations

18. In a bankruptcy liquidation, a financial statement prepared on a quitting concern basis is called the _____ .

19. In a liquidation filing, if the court desires information that relates the activity of the trustee with the book balances existing when the trustee was appointed, then a financial statement called the _____ is prepared.

TRUE-OR-FALSE STATEMENTS

Bankruptcy Law

1. T F A municipality **cannot** be forced into bankruptcy proceedings involuntarily by its creditors.

2. T F Savings and loans can be forced into bankruptcy proceedings involuntarily by its creditors or depositors.

3. T F The subject of the bankruptcy proceeding is formally referred to as the bankrupt.

4. T F Chapter 7 of the bankruptcy statutes deals with liquidations.

5. T F An eligible corporation may be involuntarily forced into bankruptcy proceedings under Chapter 7 or Chapter 11 of the bankruptcy statutes.

6. T F To file an involuntary petition for bankruptcy proceedings, a majority of creditors must sign the petition.

7. T F Creditors with priority are given statutory priority over the claims of all other creditors with regard to payment.

8. T F As to the priority of "creditors with priority," the highest priority is that of administrative expenses.

Troubled Debt Restructurings

9. T F A major disadvantage of a troubled debt restructuring versus a bankruptcy reorganization is that interest stops accruing only in bankruptcy reorganizations.

10. T F Under *SFAS No. 15*, the carrying value of the debt is compared with the present value of the total future payments in calculating whether a forgiveness of debt has resulted.

11. T F Under *SFAS No. 15*, a forgiveness of debt is never reported as a capital contribution—it must be reported in the income statement.

12. T F *SFAS No. 15* does not apply to most bankruptcy reorganizations.

13. T F If a company reports forgiveness of debt in a troubled debt restructuring, then it will **not** report interest expense in future periods on the restructured debt.

14. T F *SFAS No. 15* applies to both debtors and creditors.

Chapter 11 Bankruptcy Reorganizations

15. T F In a Chapter 11 bankruptcy proceeding, it is customary to have management control and operate the company's day-to-day activities.

16. T F Taxes owed to federal or other governmental units are **not** discharged in bankruptcy reorganizations.

17. T F For a plan of reorganization to be accepted by a class of creditors, at least two-thirds in dollar amount and in number of creditors must vote in favor of the plan.

18. T F Under *SOP 90-7*, a forgiveness of debt for an entity emerging from Chapter 11 bankruptcy proceedings must be reported as an extraordinary item.

19. T F Under *SOP 90-7*, a forgiveness of debt for an entity emerging from Chapter 11 bankruptcy proceedings is calculated by comparing carrying values to the total estimated future payments.

20. T F Under *SOP 90-7*, a forgiveness of debt for an entity emerging from Chapter 11 bankruptcy proceedings may be calculated using present value procedures or the methodology of *SFAS No. 15*.

21. T F Under *SOP 90-7*, comparative financial statements that straddle the confirmation date can be presented only if certain disclosures are made.

22. T F Under *SOP 90-7*, an entity emerging from a Chapter 11 bankruptcy reorganization proceeding can report a positive retained earnings but **not** a negative retained earnings (accumulated deficit).

23. T F Under *SOP 90-7*, an entity emerging from a Chapter 11 bankruptcy reorganization proceeding need not present its debt in any special categories in its balance sheet.

24. T F Under *SOP 90-7*, an entity emerging from a Chapter 11 bankruptcy reorganization proceeding must value its assets at their fair values.

25. T F Under *SOP 90-7*, an entity emerging from a Chapter 11 bankruptcy reorganization proceeding **cannot** report goodwill.

Chapter 7 Bankruptcy Liquidations

26. T F In a liquidation through the bankruptcy court, the appointment of a trustee is common but **not** done in most cases.

27. T F The "statement of affairs" is a statement of realization and liquidation in a different format (to please the bankruptcy court).

28. T F The statement of realization and liquidation is a proforma statement.

MULTIPLE-CHOICE QUESTIONS

Bankruptcy Law

1. The bankruptcy statutes do **not** apply to which of the following entities?
    a. Railroads.
    b. Municipalities.
    c. Partnerships.
    d. Insurance companies.
    e. None of the above.

2. Which of the following conditions is **not** necessary for an involuntary bankruptcy petition to be filed?
    a. The debtor's assets are less than its liabilities.
    b. The debtor is not paying its debts as they become due.
    c. A custodian was appointed to take possession of the debtor's property.
    d. The debtor has liabilities of $5,000 or more.
    e. None of the above.

3. Which of the following items is **not** classified as a "creditor with priority." (Disregard limitations.)
    a. Federal, state, and local income taxes.
    b. Wages, salaries, and commissions.
    c. Bankruptcy lawyer legal fees.
    d. Expenses incurred by creditors in recovering concealed assets.
    e. None of the above.

4. Which of the following conditions must exist for an involuntary bankruptcy petition to be filed?
    a. The majority of creditors must sign the petition.
    b. Unsecured creditors must be owed at least $5,000.
    c. There must be three or more creditors.
    d. There must be twelve or more creditors.
    e. None of the above.

Troubled Debt Restructurings

5. For purposes of determining if a gain on restructuring of debt exists,
    a. The total future cash payments are calculated at their present value.
    b. The total future cash payments are to include amounts that are contingently payable.
    c. The carrying value of the debt is to exclude any interest payable.
    d. The total future cash payments are to include amounts that are contingently payable only if the contingency is probable.
    e. None of the above.

6. In a troubled debt restructuring in which the total cash payments specified in the new terms exceed the carrying amount of the debt,
    a. The excess must be reported as interest expense in future periods.
    b. The excess is reported as an extraordinary loss, if material.
    c. The excess is charged against the restructured debt liability account.

    d.   The excess is netted against any gain on the restructuring.

    e.   None of the above.

7. In a troubled debt restructuring in which the carrying amount of the debt exceeds the total cash payments specified in the new terms,

    a.   The excess is reported as an adjustment to interest expense in future periods using the "interest method" prescribed by *APB Opinion No. 21*.

    b.   The excess is credited to a restructured liability account.

    c.   A gain on restructuring will be reported in the income statement.

    d.   The carrying amount of the debt would be calculated by imputing interest.

    e.   None of the above.

8. Cashlow Company has just completed a troubled debt restructuring involving its 10% debenture bonds payable that have (A) a face value of $5,000,000, (B) unamortized bond discount of $200,000, and (C) accrued interest of $700,000. In addition, $60,000 of deferred debt issuance costs pertain to this debt. The "carrying amount of the debt" under *SFAS No. 15* is

    a. $4,740,000
    b. $4,800,000
    c. $5,000,000
    d. $5,440,000
    e. $5,500,000
    f. $5,640,000
    g. $5,700,000

9. Cashless Company has just completed a troubled debt restructuring involving certain debt that has a "carrying amount" of $2,000,000, as defined in *SFAS No. 15*. In the negotiations with the lender, the company calculated (A) the total fair value of the consideration to be given as being $1,600,000, (B) the present value of the total fair value of the consideration to be given as being $1,300,000, and (C) the total future payments as being $1,900,000 without interest payments and $2,200,000 with interest payments. The gain on restructuring to be reported under *SFAS No. 15* is

    a. $-0-
    b. $100,000
    c. $200,000
    d. $400,000
    e. $700,000

10. Cali Company owes a total of $1,000,000 ($900,000 principal and $100,000 interest) to a financial institution that has agreed to the following:

    (1)   The $100,000 accrued interest is cancelled.

    (2)   The due date of the $900,000 principal is extended to 2 years from now.

    (3)   The interest rate for the following 2 years is 5% (a 5% reduction from the old rate).

    (4)   If earnings exceed certain specified levels over the next 2 years, the interest rate for the 2 years reverts to 10%. (The probability of this occurring is very low.)

What is the gain on restructuring of the debt?

    a. $-0-
    b. $10,000
    c. $80,000
    d. $100,000
    e. $200,000

Chapter 11 Bankruptcy Reorganizations

11. Under *SOP 90-7*, a company currently in Chapter 11 bankruptcy reorganization proceedings would report bankruptcy related costs as

    a.   An extraordinary item.
    b.   A direct charge to equity.
    c.   Part of general and administrative expenses.
    d.   A separate line item in the income statement.
    e.   None of the above.

12. Under *SOP 90-7*, which is **not** one of the debt categories that a company currently in Chapter 11 bankruptcy reorganization proceedings would use in its balance sheet?

    a.   Prepetition liabilities subject to compromise.
    b.   Prepetition liabilities not subject to compromise.
    c.   Postpetition liabilities subject to compromise.
    d.   Postpetition liabilities not subject to compromise.
    e.   None of the above.

13. Use the information in Question 12, but assume the entity has recently emerged from Chapter 11 bankruptcy proceedings and is preparing a balance sheet 30 days later. Also, disregard the word "not."

14. An entity that has just emerged from a Chapter 11 bankruptcy reorganization proceeding and is applying *SOP 90-7*, will

    a.   Usually report a much larger forgiveness of debt than if it had a troubled debt restructuring for which *SFAS No. 15* would be applicable.
    b.   Never report goodwill.
    c.   Eliminate any balance in Additional Paid-in Capital.
    d.   Report its liabilities using prescribed categories.
    e.   None of the above.

15. Under *SOP 90-7*, an entity that has just emerged from a Chapter 11 bankruptcy reorganization proceeding would **not** report which of the following accounts?

    a.   Goodwill.
    b.   Accumulated Deficit.
    c.   Accumulated Depreciation.
    d.   Additional Paid-in Capital.
    e.   None of the above.

16. Under *SOP 90-7*, an entity emerging from a Chapter 11 bankruptcy reorganization proceeding would report in which of the following manners?

Procedures for Valuing Debt	Manner of Reporting Forgiveness of Debt
a. Present values	Extraordinary item
b. Present values	Direct credit to equity
c. Book values	Extraordinary item
d. Lesser of total future payments or book values	Extraordinary item
e. None of the above.	

17. Use the same information as in Question 9, except that the situation is a Chapter 11 bankruptcy reorganization. The amount of forgiveness of debt to be reported is

    a. $-0-
    b. $100,000
    c. $200,000
    d. $400,000
    e. $700,000

CHAPTER 21—SOLUTIONS

Completion Statements

Bankruptcy Law

1. voluntary, involuntary
2. creditors with priority
3. troubled debt restructuring
4. total future cash payments
5. imputed
6. nonoperating gain, capital contribution
7. reorganizations
8. liquidations
9. management, trustees

Chapter 11 Bankruptcy Reorganizations

10. plan of reorganization
11. discharge of indebtedness
12. avoidance
13. new, fresh-start
14. retained earnings, accumulated deficit
15. new, former
16. extraordinary item
17. present value, current interest rates

Chapter 7 Bankruptcy Liquidations

18. statement of affairs
19. statement of realization and liquidation

True-or-False Statements

Bankruptcy Law

1. True	5. True
2. False	6. False
3. False	7. False
4. True	8. True

Troubled Debt Restructurings

9. True	12. True
10. False	13. True
11. True	14. False

Chapter 11 Bankruptcy Reorganizations

15. True	21. False
16. True	22. False
17. False	23. True
18. True	24. True
19. False	25. False
20. False	

Chapter 7 Bankruptcy Liquidations

26. False
27. False
28. False

Multiple-Choice Questions

Bankruptcy Law

1. d	3. e
2. a	4. e

Troubled Debt Restructurings

5. b	8. d
6. a	9. a
7. c	10. a

Chapter 11 Bankruptcy Reorganizations

11. d	15. b
12. c, d	16. a
13. e	17. e
14. a	

CHAPTER 22

GOVERNMENTAL ACCOUNTING: BASIC PRINCIPLES AND THE GENERAL FUND

CHAPTER HIGHLIGHTS

1. The Governmental Accounting Standards Board establishes accounting principles for state and local governmental units.

2. If the accounting treatment of a transaction or event is not specified in a GASB pronouncement, and the FASB has dealt with the topic, the FASB pronouncement applies.

3. GAAFR (published by the Government Finance Officers Association) neither prescribes nor authoritatively interprets GAAP for governmental units—it merely **provides detailed guidance** for applying governmental GAAP.

4. Much like consolidated financial statements in the private sector give readers a summary overview of financial position and results of operations, **"general purpose financial statements"** do likewise for state and local governmental units.

5. For governmental funds, the measurement base is the **flow of resources**—this is *not* an income statement-type measurement.

6. Governmental operations may be classified into three broad categories: governmental, proprietary, and fiduciary.

7. A **fund** is a fiscal and accounting entity with a self-balancing set of accounts.

8. The difference between a fund's assets and liabilities is called the **fund equity.**

9. Governmental and fiduciary type funds use the account Fund Balance to keep track of the fund equity. For proprietary funds, the accounts Contributed Capital and Retained Earnings are used to keep track of the fund equity.

10. When **conflicts exist** between legal provisions and financial reporting on a GAAP basis, governmental units **must report on a GAAP basis** and demonstrate legal compliance by providing additional schedules, narrative explanations, or possibly a separate legal-basis report.

11. Proprietary funds (Enterprise Funds and Internal Service Funds) and one type of fiduciary fund (Nonexpendable Trust Funds) have the objective of profit measurement or capital maintenance; accordingly, the **accrual basis** is used for these funds.

12. All governmental funds (General Fund, Special Revenue Funds, Capital Projects Funds, and Debt Service Funds) and two kinds of fiduciary funds (Expendable Trust Funds and Agency Funds) use the **modified accrual basis.**

13. Under the **modified accrual basis, revenues** are recognized in the period in which they become "available" and "measurable." Available means collectible within the current period or soon enough thereafter to be used to pay liabilities of the current period.

14. Under the **modified accrual basis, expenditures** are recognized in the period in which the liability is incurred (with one exception for interest on general long-term debt).

15. **When restrictions exist** such that a portion of the fund equity of a governmental fund is earmarked for a specific purpose, the restriction is presented as **a reservation of the Fund Balance account.**

16. Interfund transactions fall into one of four categories: (A) loans and advances, (B) quasi-external transactions, (C) residual equity transfers, and (D) operating transfers.

17. Interfund borrowings of **one year or less** are called **loans,** whereas interfund borrowings for **longer periods** are called **advances.**

18. **Quasi-external transactions** are transactions in which one fund provides a service to another fund—a service that would be provided by an outside private company if not provided internally. The fund providing the service reports **revenues;** the fund receiving the service reports **expenditures** (or expenses if a proprietary fund).

19. **Residual equity transfers** are nonrecurring or nonroutine transfers of equity between funds made in connection with the formation, expansion, contraction, or discontinuance of a fund. Such transfers are reported as direct additions to or subtractions from the beginning of year fund equity accounts.

20. **Operating transfers** are made in connection with the normal operations of the recipient fund.

21. If an interfund transfer cannot be classified as a loan or advance, a quasi-external transaction, or a residual equity transfer, then, **by default,** it is deemed to be an operating transfer.

22. The "Other Financing Sources and Uses" section of the statement of revenues, expenditures, and changes in fund balance used is used to report (A) bond proceeds, (B) operating transfers in, (C) operating transfers out, (D) proceeds from sale of General Fixed Assets, and (E) proceeds from capital leases—no other types of transactions are reportable in this section of the operating statement.

23. "General Purpose Financial Statements" consist of five specific financial statements in which the presentations are made on a **combined** basis for the purpose of presenting an overview of financial position and results of operations.

24. In addition to General Purpose Financial Statements, governmental units also provide **"combining"** financial statements and **individual** fund and individual account group-statements. (These statements must follow the **identical format** of the more significant combined financial statements.)

25. **General long-term debt** is the liability of the governmental unit as a whole and not that of any specific fund. Such debt is accounted for in the General Long-term Debt Account Group (a self-balancing set of accounts that is not a fund).

26. Fixed assets that are not required to be accounted in a specific fund are called **General Fixed Assets.** Such assets are accounted for in the General Fixed Assets Account Group.

27. **Depreciation expense is not reported** in the operating statement of governmental funds and expendable trust funds.

28. The **statutory authorization** for spending an estimated amount during a coming year is called an **appropriation.**

29. **Annual budgets** for the General Fund and Special Revenue Funds are always recorded in the general ledger for control purposes. (For Capital Projects Funds and Debt Service Funds, this is done only if it serves a useful purpose.)

30. To prevent spending more than has been authorized, the amounts for purchase orders and contracts entered into are recorded in the general ledger as **encumbrances.** Such entries have no effect on reported operations.

31. The preferred method of **accounting for inventories of supplies** is the "consumption method," whereby the acquisition of inventory is treated as the **conversion of resources** and the use of inventory is treated as an **outflow of resources.**

32. In the operating statement of a governmental fund, **revenues are classified by source. Expenditures are classified by character** (current, capital outlay, or debt service) **and function** (such as public safety, sanitation, health, welfare).

COMPLETION STATEMENTS

1. For state and local governmental units, the organization currently responsible for establishing accounting principles is the _____ .

2. A guide book used widely by state and local governmental units and published by the Government Finance Officers Association is called _____ .

3. In governmental accounting, the current measurement base is the flow of _____ _____ .

4. The outflow of resources is collectively referred to as _____ .

5. The accounting for certain operations separately from other operations is known as _____ .

6. The three broad classes of funds used in government are _____ , _____ , and _____ .

7. For governmental funds, the _____ basis of accounting is used.

8. For proprietary funds, the _____ basis of accounting is used.

9. For governmental funds, the operating statement is called a statement of _____ _____ .

10. The fund equity of a governmental fund is kept track of in a general ledger account called _____ .

11. Interfund transactions fall into one of the following four categories: _____ _____ , _____ , _____ , and _____ .

12. A type of interfund transaction in which one fund provides a service to another fund is called a(n) _____ .

13. Transfers of equity between funds made in connection with the formation, expansion, contraction, or discontinuance of a fund are called _____ .

14. Transfers made between funds in connection with the normal operations of the recipient fund are called _____ .

15. For governmental funds, the third major category in the operating statement other than revenues and expenditures is called _____ .

16. The five specific financial statements that are designed to present an overview of financial position and operations are called _____ .

17. The statutory authorization for spending an estimated amount during the year is referred to as a(n) _____ .

18. When a fund liability is incurred, _____ are recognized.

19. A commitment to spend by issuing purchase orders or signing contracts is called a(n) _____ .

20. Recording annual budgets in the general ledger as a control mechanism is called _____ .

TRUE-OR-FALSE STATEMENTS

1. T F   The Governmental Accounting Standards Board's codification of existing governmental GAAP is set forth in GAAFR.

2. T F   The accounting treatment for an item is not dealt with in a GASB pronouncement. If the treatment of the item is dealt with in a FASB pronouncement, governmental units must follow the FASB pronouncement.

3. T F   The pronouncements of the GFOA are another source of governmental GAAP.

4. T F   In governmental accounting, the statement of revenues, expenditures, and changes in fund balance is comparable to an income statement incorporating changes in retained earnings as used in the private sector.

5. T F   In the statement of revenues, expenditures, and changes in fund balance, expenditures is the broad term used to describe the current costs of providing services.

6. T F   The measurement base for governmental funds is the flow of resources.

7. T F   Education, public safety, the judicial system, and social services are examples of services that are accounted for in proprietary funds.

8. T F   A fund is a fiscal and accounting entity, but not a legal entity.

9. T F   When a conflict exists between legal provisions and GAAP financial reporting, the financial statements are prepared on the GAAP basis, with accompanying schedules and explanations addressing legal compliance responsibilities—not vice-versa.

10. T F   Concerning the recognition of revenues under the modified accrual basis, "measurable" means that a revenue source is collectible within the current period or soon enough thereafter to be used to pay liabilities of the current period.

11. T F   For modified accrual basis funds, expenditures are recognized in the period in which the fund liability is incurred.

12. T F   In a quasi-external transaction, one fund reports a revenue and the other fund reports either an expenditure or an expense.

13. T F   A unique feature of residual equity transfers is that they are nonrecurring or nonroutine.

14. T F   An interfund transfer made for the purpose of expanding the capital of a specific fund is an example of an operating transfer.

15. T F   Operating transfers are made in connection with the normal operations of the recipient fund—not the disbursing fund.

16. T F   In the operating statement of proprietary funds, operating transfers are classified under "other financing sources and uses."

17. T F   Transfers from the General Fund to a Debt Service Fund to enable principle payments to be made on General Long-term Debt is an example of an operating transfer.

18. T F   In the operating statement of governmental funds, proceeds from the sale of general fixed assets cannot be reported in the "other financing sources and uses" category.

19. T F   It is rare for the General Fund to report the receipt of bond proceeds in its operating statement.

20. T F   Combining financial statements and individual fund statements are required to follow the **identical** format of the combined financial statements.

21. T F   The General Fixed Assets Account Group is **not** a separate fund.

22. T F   The accrual basis of accounting encompasses the recording of depreciation.

23. T F   The statutory authorization for spending an estimated amount during the year is called an appropriation.

24. T F   In recording the annual budget, the account BUDGETARY FUND BALANCE may be recorded as either a debit or a credit.

25. T F   In recording the annual budget, the account APPROPRIATIONS—OPERATING TRANSFERS OUT would always be recorded as a credit.

26. T F   The budgetary account ENCUMBRANCES may be thought of as a "liability-to-be" account.

27. T F   For the General Fund, the annual budget is **always** reversed at year-end.

28. T F   Under the consumption method, the acquisition of inventory is viewed as the use of resources.

29. T F   Governmental units usually do **not** honor purchase orders outstanding at year-end.

30. T F   Closing out the budgetary accounts pertaining to outstanding purchase orders at year-end signifies that the purchase orders will **not** be honored in the coming fiscal year.

MULTIPLE-CHOICE QUESTIONS

Conceptual Questions

1. The latest edition (1988) of *Governmental Accounting, Auditing and Financial Reporting* (GAAFR)

   a.   Authoritatively interprets GAAP for governmental units.
   b.   Prescribes GAAP for governmental units.
   c.   Codifies GAAP for governmental units.
   d.   Is solely an audit guide designed for outside auditors.
   e.   None of the above.

2. In the operating statement of the General Fund,

   a.   Inflows of resources are compared with outflows of resources.
   b.   Revenues are compared with expenses.
   c.   Cash inflows are compared with cash outflows.
   d.   Revenues are compared with the costs of providing services.
   e.   None of the above.

3. Governmental operations can be classified into categories, one of which is **not**

   a.   Fiduciary.
   b.   Budgetary.
   c.   Governmental.
   d.   Proprietary.
   e.   None of the above.

4. The objective of achieving interperiod equity is attained by

   a.   The use of the modified accrual basis of accounting.
   b.   Measuring the inflow and outflow of resources.
   c.   Presenting a statement of revenues, expenditures, and changes in fund balance.
   d.   Presenting general purpose financial statements.
   e.   None of the above.

5. The account Contributed Capital would appear in which of the following fund types?

	Governmental Funds	Proprietary Funds
a.	Yes	Yes
b.	No	No
c.	No	Yes
d.	Yes	No

6. Which of the following funds are classified as governmental funds?

	Debt Service Funds	Internal Service Funds
a.	Yes	Yes
b.	No	No
c.	No	Yes
d.	Yes	No

7. Under the modified accrual basis of accounting, revenues are recognized
   a. When the liability for the related expenditures is accrued.
   b. In the period in which the economic event giving rise to the revenues occurs.
   c. When the revenues have been earned.
   d. When it has been determined that they are collectible.
   e. None of the above.

8. Under the modified accrual basis of accounting, expenditures (other than the exceptions) are recognized
   a. When the related revenue is recognized.
   b. When the liability is measurable and resources are available so that payment can be made in the current period or within sixty days after year-end.
   c. When the liability is incurred.
   d. When the liability is susceptible to accrual.
   e. None of the above.

9. Which of the following accounts is **not** a budgetary account?
   a. Appropriations.
   b. Encumbrances.
   c. Fund balance.
   d. Estimated revenues.
   e. None of the above.

Application Questions

10. Which of the following accounts is always credited when the budget is recorded for the General Fund?
    a. Estimated Revenues.
    b. Budgetary Fund Balance.
    c. Fund Balance Reserved for Encumbrances.
    d. Appropriations—Operating Transfers In.
    e. None of the above.

11. Which of the following accounts is debited when the budget for the General Fund is reversed at year-end?
    a. Encumbrances.
    b. Estimated Revenues.
    c. Fund Balance Reserved for Encumbrances.
    d. Appropriations—Operating Transfers In.
    e. None of the above.

12. When supplies accounted for under the "consumption method" are received, which account would be debited?
    a. Inventory.
    b. Expenditures.
    c. Fund Balance Reserved for Encumbrances.
    d. Encumbrances.
    e. None of the above.

13. The Appropriations account is **always** debited when
   a. Contracts are entered into.
   b. Supplies are ordered.
   c. The budget is reversed at year-end.
   d. The nonbudgetary accounts are closed out at year-end.
   e. None of the above.

14. Which of the following accounts is debited at year-end to close it out?
   a. Fund Balance.
   b. Encumbrances.
   c. Estimated Revenues.
   d. Appropriations—Residual Equity Transfer Out.
   e. None of the above.

15. Which of the following accounts is debited at year-end when a governmental unit determines that it will not be able to collect as much property taxes as initially estimated?
   a. Deferred Revenues.
   b. Revenues.
   c. Expenditures.
   d. Fund Balance.
   e. None of the above.

16. Which of the following accounts is credited at year-end when a governmental unit determines that collections of property taxes will be significantly delayed?
   a. Estimated Revenues.
   b. Revenues.
   c. Deferred Revenues.
   d. Encumbrances.
   e. None of the above.

17. Which of the following accounts in the General Fund is debited when an unanticipated cost overrun occurs in a city library expansion project and cash is disbursed from the General Fund to pay for the overrun?
   a. Other Financing Sources—Operating Transfers Out.
   b. Residual Equity Transfer Out.
   c. Expenditures.
   d. Due to Capital Projects Fund.
   e. None of the above.

18. Which of the following accounts is credited in the General Fund when equipment accounted for in the General Fixed Asset Account Group is sold at **below** its initial cost?
   a. Equipment.
   b. Other Financing Sources—Proceeds from Sale of Equipment.
   c. Revenues.
   d. Residual Equity Transfer In.
   e. None of the above.

CHAPTER 22—SOLUTIONS

Completion Statements

1. Governmental Accounting Standards Board
2. *Governmental Accounting, Auditing, and Financial Reporting*
3. resources
4. expenditures
5. fund accounting
6. governmental, proprietary, fiduciary
7. modified accrual
8. accrual
9. revenues, expenditures, and changes in fund balance
10. fund balance
11. loans and advances, quasi-external transactions, residual equity transfers, and operating transfers
12. quasi-external transaction
13. residual equity transfers
14. operating transfers
15. other financing sources and uses
16. combined financial statements
17. appropriation
18. expenditures
19. encumbrance
20. budgetary accounting

True-or-False Statements

1. False
2. True
3. False
4. False
5. False
6. True
7. False
8. True
9. True
10. False
11. True
12. True
13. True
14. False
15. True
16. False
17. True
18. False
19. True
20. True
21. True
22. False
23. True
24. True
25. True
26. False
27. True
28. False
29. False
30. False

Multiple-Choice Questions

1. e
2. a
3. b
4. e
5. c
10. e
11. e
12. a
13. c
14. d

6.	d	15.	b
7.	e	16.	c
8.	c	17.	e
9.	c	18.	b

CHAPTER 23

GOVERNMENTAL ACCOUNTING: SPECIAL PURPOSE FUNDS AND ACCOUNT GROUPS

CHAPTER HIGHLIGHTS

1. **Special Revenue Funds** account for the proceeds of specific revenue sources (other than for capital projects and expendable trusts) **that are legally restricted to expenditure for specified purposes.** Typically, Special Revenue Funds obtain most of their revenues from specific taxes or nontax sources not directly related to services provided. For accounting purposes, they are **a clone of the General Fund.**

2. **Capital Projects Funds** account for the proceeds of financial resources that are to be used for the **acquisition or construction of major capital facilities** (other than those financed by proprietary funds and Trust Funds). At the completion of the project, the cost of the facility is recorded as a fixed asset in the General Fixed Asset Account Group. (Capitalization is optional for public domain or "infrastructure" fixed assets.)

3. The **General Fixed Assets Account Group** accounts for a governmental unit's fixed assets that are **not** accounted for in an Enterprise Fund, an Internal Service Fund, or a Trust Fund. This group of accounts is **not** a fund, but rather a self-balancing group of accounts. **Accumulated depreciation** may be reflected for general fixed assets in the General Fixed Assets Account Group (an optional treatment); however, **depreciation expense is never reported in the operating statements of the four governmental funds.**

4. **Debt Service Funds** are created for long-term debt that is initially recorded as a liability in the General Long-term Debt Account Group. Debt Service Funds account for the **matured portion** of such long-term debt as well as any payment of principal and interest. The only unusual feature of this fund is that **interest is not reflected as a liability until the date it is due and payable.**

5. The **General Long-term Debt Account Group** accounts for debt that (A) has a maturity date of more than one year at the time of issuance and (B) is not properly shown in proprietary funds or Trust Funds. **At the maturity date,** the debt is transferred to a Debt Service Fund; accordingly, this account group includes the portion of long-term debt that is due and payable in the coming fiscal year.

6. **Special Assessments** made against properties that directly benefit from improvements (sidewalks, street lighting) are usually accounted for in Debt Service Funds, inasmuch as monies collected from the special assessments are used to service special assessment bonds having governmental backing that are issued to finance the improvements (which debt is recorded in the General Long-term Debt Account Group). However, **if the governmental unit is not obligated in any manner whatsoever in the event of default,** then only collection activity (cash receipts) is recorded in an Agency Fund. Regardless of whether the governmental unit obligated in some manner, **all construction activity** related to the improvements is accounted for in a Capital Projects Fund.

7. **Internal Service Funds and Enterprise Funds** (proprietary funds) are accounted for in a manner that parallels that of commercial businesses. Internal Service Funds provide services to departments within a governmental unit—never to outside unaffiliated customers. Enterprise Funds provide services primarily to the general public.

8. **Agency Funds** (a fiduciary type of fund) act as conduits for the transfer of money. Assets always equal liabilities (thus there is no fund equity).

9. **Trust Funds** (a fiduciary type of fund) involve investing and using money in accordance with stipulated provisions of trust indenture agreements or statutes. **Nonexpendable Trust Funds** (the principal must be preserved intact) and **Pension Trusts** are accounted for in essentially the same manner as proprietary funds. **Expendable Trust Funds** are accounted for in essentially the same manner as governmental funds.

10. The **annual financial report** for governmental units is called "The Comprehensive Annual Financial Report." Financial statements therein are presented using a "reporting pyramid" concept in which financial information is presented at four levels, each of which provides more detailed information than the previous level. Level 1 presents **combined financial statements** (the overview section) that are called the "general purpose financial statements."

COMPLETION STATEMENTS

1. A type of fund in which the fund assets equal fund liabilities is a(n) _____ _____ .

2. The proceeds of specific revenue sources (other than expendable trusts or for major capital projects) that are legally restricted to expenditure for specified purposes are accounted for in a(n) _____ .

3. The proceeds from a bond offering relating to the construction of a library are recorded in a(n) _____ .

4. General long-term debt that has matured is accounted for in a(n) _____ _____ .

5. Money disbursed by the General Fund to pay for a cost overrun in a Capital Projects Fund would be classified as a(n) _____ .

6. Roads, bridges, streets, sidewalks, and similar assets that are immovable and of value only to the governmental unit are called _____ or _____ fixed assets.

7. Bonds that bear the full faith of the governmental unit for which repayment is **not** required to be from the operations of an Enterprise Fund are called _____ _____ .

8. Special assessment debt for which the government is obligated in some manner is recorded as a liability in _____ .

9. Special assessment debt for which the government is **not** obligated in any manner is recorded as a liability in _____ .

10. Trust funds may be classified as being either _____ or _____ .

11. In the balance sheet of an Enterprise Fund, assets that have limitations as to use are classified as _____ .

12. Level 1 of the "financial reporting pyramid" consists of _____ financial statements.

13. Level 2 of the "financial reporting pyramid" consists of _____ financial statements.

14. Level 3 of the "financial reporting pyramid" consists of _____ statements.

TRUE-OR-FALSE STATEMENTS

1. T F The accounting for Special Revenue Funds is no different than the accounting for the General Fund.

2. T F If the activity of a governmental operation recovers less than half of its operating costs from user charges, the activity **must** be accounted for in a Special Revenue Fund.

3. T F The acquisition of a multi-million dollar computer system (hardware and software) for traffic control would **not** require any entries in a Capital Projects Fund.

4. T F The construction of major capital facilities in a Capital Projects Funds results in the facilities being reported as assets in the Capital Projects Fund only until the construction of the assets is completed.

5. T F If a bond issue for the construction of a library is issued at a premium and the premium is required to be set aside for debt service, the Capital Projects Fund would still report the premium as an inflow in its operating statement.

6. T   F   At the completion of a capital project, some remaining cash is transferred to the appropriate Debt Service Fund. This would be reported in both funds as a residual equity transfer.

7. T   F   All improvements constructed through Capital Projects Funds eventually are recorded in the General Fixed Assets Account Group.

8. T   F   There is no such thing as a Special Assessment Fund.

9. T   F   **All** general obligation bonds are accounted for in the General Long-term Debt Account Group.

10. T   F   Debt Service Funds make both principal and interest payments on general long-term debt.

11. T   F   Interest is **never** reflected as a liability in Debt Service Funds until the date it is due and payable.

12. T   F   Debt Service Funds obtain all of their cash as a result of operating transfers from the General Fund.

13. T   F   Debt ceases to be accounted for in the General Long-term Account Group when its maturity date is no more than one year later.

14. T   F   All construction activity financed by special assessment bonds is accounted for in Capital Projects Funds regardless of whether the government is obligated in some manner on the special assessment bonds.

15. T   F   Special assessment debt for which the government is **not** obligated in any manner is reported as a liability in an Agency Fund.

16. T   F   Nonexpendable Trust Funds prepare the same financial statements as used for proprietary funds.

17. T   F   A statement of cash flows is prepared for Agency Funds.

18. T   F   A Debt Service Fund can record its annual budget in the general ledger using budgetary accounting.

19. T   F   If a governmental unit has no more than one fund for each type of special purpose fund, combined financial statements need **not** be prepared.

20. T   F   Expendable trust funds use the accrual basis of accounting.

MULTIPLE-CHOICE QUESTIONS

Conceptual Questions

1. Special Revenue Funds are conceptually the opposite of which type of fund?
    a. Internal Service Funds.
    b. Enterprise Funds.

    c. Expendable Trust Funds.
    d. Capital Projects Funds.
    e. None of the above.

2. The decision to build a new city hall to be financed through the issuance of general obligation bonds will **not** eventually result in entries in which of the following funds or account groups?
    a. Capital Projects Fund.
    b. Debt Service Fund.
    c. General Fixed Assets Account Group.
    d. General Long-term Debt Account Group.
    e. None of the above.

3. State gasoline sales taxes to be used for highway improvements would be accounted for in which type of fund?
    a. Special Revenue Fund.
    b. Special Assessment Fund.
    c. Capital Projects Fund.
    d. Internal Service Fund.
    e. None of the above.

4. Which of the following fund types does **not** report fixed assets in its financial statements?
    a. Enterprise Funds.
    b. Expendable Trust Funds.
    c. Internal Service Funds.
    d. Nonexpendable Trust Funds.
    e. None of the above.

5. The account Special Assessment Receivables—Current could appear in which type of fund?
    a. Agency Funds.
    b. Capital Projects Funds.
    c. Debt Service Funds.
    d. Special Revenue Funds.
    e. None of the above.

6. Which of the following accounts could appear in an Agency Fund as a result of the issuance of special assessment bonds for which the government is **not** obligated in some manner?

	Deferred Revenues	Special Assessment Receivables—Current
a.	Yes	Yes
b.	Yes	No
c.	No	Yes
d.	No	No

Application Questions

7. The capitalization of a newly constructed civic center in the General Fixed Assets Account Group would result in which of the following entries?
   a. Debit Investment in General Fixed Assets.
   b. Credit Expenditures.
   c. Credit Other Financing Uses.
   d. Credit Fund Balance.
   e. None of the above.

8. Which of the following accounts is reported as a debit balance in the combined balance sheet that is one of the "general purpose financial statements"?

	Amount Available in Debt Service Fund	Investment in General Fixed Assets
a.	Yes	Yes
b.	No	No
c.	Yes	No
d.	No	Yes

9. Which of the following fund types would **not** be reported in the combined statement of revenues, expenses, and changes in retained earnings/fund balances (the fourth of the five general purpose financial statements)?
   a. Enterprise Funds.
   b. Expendable Trust Funds.
   c. Internal Service Funds.
   d. Pension Trust Funds.
   e. None of the above.

10. Which of the following funds would **never** be reported in the combined statement of revenues, expenditures, and changes in fund balances—budget and actual (the third of the five general purpose financial statements)?
   a. Debt Service Fund.
   b. Internal Service Fund.
   c. General Fund.
   d. Special Revenue Fund.
   e. None of the above.

11. Which of the following fund types would **not** be included in the combined statement of revenues, expenditures, and changes in fund balances (the second of the five general purpose financial statements)?
   a. Special Revenue Funds.
   b. Debt Service Funds.
   c. General Funds.
   d. Agency Funds.
   e. None of the above.

12. Which of the following fund types would **never** be used as the result of the issuance of special assessment bonds?

    a.   Agency Funds.
    b.   Capital Projects Funds.
    c.   Debt Service Funds.
    d.   Special Revenue Funds.
    e.   None of the above.

CHAPTER 23—SOLUTIONS

Completion Statements

1. Agency Fund
2. Special Revenue Fund
3. Capital Projects Fund
4. Debt Service Fund
5. operating transfer
6. public domain, infrastructure
7. general obligation bonds
8. General Long-term Debt Account group
9. none of the funds or account groups
10. expendable, nonexpendable
11. restricted assets
12. combined
13. combining
14. individual fund and account group

True-or-False Statements

1. True	11. True
2. False	12. False
3. True	13. False
4. False	14. True
5. True	15. False
6. True	16. True
7. False	17. False
8. True	18. True
9. False	19. False
10. True	20. False

Multiple-Choice Questions

1. b	7. e
2. e	8. b
3. a	9. b
4. b	10. b
5. c	11. d
6. d	12. d

CHAPTER 24
ACCOUNTING FOR NONPROFIT ORGANIZATIONS

CHAPTER HIGHLIGHTS

Introductory Material

1. The objective of nonprofit organizations is to provide various types of services to their membership or to society as a whole. Often, the fees charged to the users of their services are less than the expenditures incurred to provide the services (with the shortage having to be made up from other governmental units or from donations by individuals and businesses).

2. The traditional **matching concept** used to determine net income does not apply to many nonprofit organizations as it does to business enterprises. Amounts are not expended to generate resource inflows. Instead, resource inflows are obtained in order to provide services.

3. The reporting practices contained in the **audit guides** are deemed to constitute generally accepted accounting principles for the entities covered.

4. **Externally imposed spending restrictions** provide the rationale for fund accounting and reporting.

5. Some nonprofit organizations do not use fund accounting. This is appropriate when there are no externally imposed spending restrictions or the external donor(s) will accept a simple "appropriation" of Fund Balance disclosing the restriction.

6. When a funds structure is used, the separation into various funds is made by using (A) funds in support of current operations, (B) funds with resources in support of fixed assets, and (C) funds for providing accountability for fiduciary responsibilities.

7. **The accrual basis of accounting** is used for all nonprofit organizations for external financial reporting purposes.

Colleges and Universities

1. Colleges and universities account for current operations using a Current Unrestricted Fund and a Current Restricted Fund.

2. Colleges and universities present (A) balance sheets (layered by fund); (B) a statement of current funds revenues, expenditures, and other changes (a flow of re-

sources statement—not an income statement); and (C) a statement of changes in fund balances for all funds.

3. The Plant Funds Group used by colleges and universities includes (A) the amount already expended for capital facilities (the Investment in Plant Fund), (B) amounts set aside for future capital expenditure (the Unexpended Plant Fund and the Renewal and Replacement Fund), and (C) amounts set aside for servicing debt (the Retirement of Indebtedness Fund).

4. Indebtedness incurred to finance plant acquisition and construction is shown as a liability of the Investment in Plant Fund—but not until the proceeds are spent.

5. Private colleges and universities must reflect depreciation of long-lived assets in their general purpose external financial statements.

6. Restricted contributions are initially credited to the Fund Balance account of the Current Restricted Fund. When the restrictions are met or lapse (generally by spending the money in accordance with the stipulations), revenues are reported in the Current Restricted Fund. (For this fund, revenues always equal expenditures.)

7. Pledges are recorded as receivables, net of allowances for uncollectibles, when received, with the net amount being reported as revenues. If the pledge has installments covering more than one year, then the revenue is prorated between years.

8. The monetary value of donated services should be recognized as gift revenues (with an offsetting debit to expenditures) by colleges and universities. (Usually only colleges and universities operated by religious groups have donated services.)

Health Care Providers

1. Fund accounting and reporting is optional.

2. If fund accounting is used, current operations are accounted for in a General Fund.

3. The distinguishing feature of items accounted for outside the General Fund is that they are donor restricted as to use.

4. The General Fund accounts for both the investment in plant and long-term debt.

5. Health care providers present (A) balance sheets for all funds (the format may be either combined, also called "aggregated," or layered, also called "disaggregated"); (B) a statement of revenues and expenses (of General Funds only); (C) a statement of changes in fund balances (for all funds); and (D) a statement of cash flows (of General Funds only).

6. The statement of revenues and expenses includes depreciation expense. Accordingly, this statement presents the results of operations. Thus, the financial reporting for health care providers is most like commercial accounting.

7. A major issue concerning the presentation of items in the statement of revenues and expenses is whether an item should be classified as "operating" or "nonoperating."

8. Revenues, expenses, gains, and losses arising from activities that constitute the ongoing major or central operations of the entity are classified as "operating."

9. Gains and losses from transactions that are peripheral or incidental to the providing of health care services as well as gains and losses from events stemming from the environment that may be largely beyond the control of the entity and its management are classified as "nonoperating."

10. For many hospitals, the "Nonoperating Gains and Losses" section of the statement of revenues and expenses includes (A) unrestricted gifts and bequests, (B) income on investments of endowment funds (if not restricted as to use), (C) income on investments whose use is limited (these investments are classified as such and shown in a special category in the balance sheet), and (D) income on other investments accounted for in the General Fund. Bear in mind that for some entities, some of these items may be classified as part of revenues ("operations"). For example, a hospital that needs an annual major fund-raiser to sustain normal operations would classify contributions in the revenues section—not in the nonoperating gains and losses section.

11. **Bad debts** are required to be reported as **expenses** in the statement of revenues and expenses—not as an adjustment to patient service revenues.

12. Patient service revenues are reported **net of contractual adjustments,** such as discounts given to third-party payors.

13. The **value of health care services provided on a charity care** basis (free of charge) is **not** expected to result in cash inflows. Accordingly, the value of charity care provided does **not** qualify for recognition as receivables or revenues in the financial statements.

14. The entity's **policy for providing charity care** must be disclosed in the notes to the financial statements, along with the **level of charity care provided,** as measured based on the provider's rates, costs, units of service, or other statistics.

Voluntary Health and Welfare Organizations (VHWOs)

1. Fund accounting (although not mandatory) is used by most VHWOs as a means of showing the extent to which restrictions have been placed on certain assets by donors, by law, or by other external authorities, which prohibit their use directly or currently for operating purposes.

2. Current operations are accounted for in the Current Unrestricted Fund and the Current Restricted Fund.

3. Fixed assets and related long-term debt are both accounted for in a Land, Building, and Equipment Fund.

4. VHWOs present (A) a balance sheet for all funds (layered format usually); (B) a statement of support, revenues, and expenses, and changes in fund balances (in combining format, that is, a separate column for each fund with a combined total column); and (C) a statement of functional expenses (expenses of all funds).

5. The statement of support, revenues, and expenses, and changes in fund balances includes depreciation expense (as does the statement of functional expenses), which is shown in the column for the Land, Building, and Equipment Fund. Accordingly, this statement—on a combined basis—presents results of operations.

6. The distinguishing feature of the statement of support, revenues and expenses, and changes in fund balances is that it has a broad category called "public support" (often referred to as "outside money") that precedes revenues (often referred to as "inside money") and expenses. Contributions is usually the major item in this category.

7. Restricted contributions as to purpose are reported as support upon receipt of the contribution (which may be when a pledge is made). If a portion of a pledge received during the period are specified by the donor for use in future periods, such portions should be recorded as a deferred credit in the balance sheet at year-end. (The reporting of restricted contributions as support upon receipt is markedly different than the recognition criteria used for colleges and universities and providers of health care services, both of which initially credit Fund Balance and then recognize such items in the operating statement (as revenues) upon incurrence of an expenditure.)

Certain Nonprofit Organizations (CNOs)

1. Fund accounting and reporting is optional.

2. If fund accounting is used, a typical funds structure would be similar to voluntary health and welfare organizations; that is, it would have (A) a Current Unrestricted Fund and a Current Restricted Fund, (B) a Plant Fund (Land, Buildings, and Equipment), and (C) Endowment Funds and possibly Loan and Annuity Funds.

3. CNOs present (A) a balance sheet; (B) a statement of activities that displays support (if any), revenues, expenses, capital additions (such as investment income), and changes in the fund balances entity's capital; and (C) a statement of changes in financial position (a statement of cash flows may be used instead). For item (B), a separate statement of changes in fund balances/entity's capital is presented if the beginning and ending fund balances/entity's capital is not included in the statement of activities.

4. The statement of activities includes depreciation expense. Accordingly, this statement reflects results of operations. (Depreciation need not be provided on landmarks, monuments, cathedrals, or historical treasures.)

5. Restricted contributions are not recognized as revenue until the expenditure of the restricted funds. Unexpended amounts are credited to a deferred revenue account—not a Fund Balance account.

6. The audit guide for CNOs is not applicable to those type of entities that operate essentially as commercial businesses for the direct economic benefit of its members or stockholders (such as pension plans, mutual banks, mutual insurance companies, trusts, and farm cooperatives).

COMPLETION STATEMENTS

1. An accounting entity established for the purpose of accounting for resources to be used for specific activities or objectives in accordance with special regulations is called a(n) _____ .

2. The assets, liabilities, fund balances, and changes in the fund balances of any non-profit organization may be classified into six basic self-balancing fund groups, which are (A) _____ , (B) _____ , (C) _____ , (D) _____ , (E) _____ , and (F) _____ .

3. For nonprofit organizations **other than health care providers,** the name given to the two types of funds used in support of current operations are (A) _____ and (B) _____ . For health care providers, these two funds are called (A) _____ and (B) _____ .

4. Funds with resources in support of fixed asset renewal, replacement, and expansion are called _____ .

5. The four types of funds used to provide accountability for fiduciary responsibilities are (A) _____ , (B) _____ , (C) _____ , and (D) _____ .

6. Funds received and held by an organization as fiscal agent for others are accounted for in _____ funds.

7. Funds established for the purpose of lending money to students, faculty, and staff are called _____ funds.

8. Cash or other property donated to a nonprofit organization with the stipulation that the principal is nonexpendable are accounted for in _____ funds.

9. A group of funds of similar character (for example, all of a nonprofit organization's endowment funds) is referred to as a(n) _____ .

10. Funds for which use is restricted by outside agencies or persons as contrasted with funds over which the organization has complete control and discretion are called _____ funds.

11. The governing board of an organization, rather than a donor or other outside agency, has the right to retain and invest or spend the principal of funds that are called _____ funds. They also are called _____ funds.

12. A promise to make a contribution to an organization in the amount and form stipulated is called a(n) _____ .

13. The Plant Funds Group of a university would consist of which four types of funds
(A) _____ , (B) _____ ,
(C) _____ , and (D) _____ .

14. The equivalent of an Agency Fund (used by universities and hospitals) for voluntary health and welfare organizations is a(n) _____ fund.

15. In the operating statement of a voluntary health and welfare organization, donations, gifts, grants, and bequests are all reported under the broad category called
_____ .

TRUE-OR-FALSE STATEMENTS

Colleges and Universities

1. T F For colleges and universities, fund accounting is **optional** under the applicable audit guide.

2. T F Colleges and universities would not have any of their funds called General Fund.

3. T F For **state** colleges and universities, the modified accrual basis (as used by state and local governmental units) is required.

4. T F For colleges and universities, a statement of current funds revenues, expenses, and other changes is reported.

5. T F For colleges and universities, a statement of current funds revenues, expenditures, and other changes is reported.

6. T F For colleges and universities, a statement of cash flows is reported.

7. T F For colleges and universities, pledges are recognized as revenues on the cash basis.

8. T F For colleges and universities, an unrestricted pledge covering three years of giving would result in reporting pledge revenue in each of the three years.

9. T F For colleges and universities, GAAP reporting requires depreciation to be recorded only for private colleges and universities—not state colleges and universities.

10. T F For colleges and universities, the applicable audit guide permits investments to be valued in the balance sheet at market value, even if above cost.

Health Care Providers

1. T F The audit and accounting guide, *Audits of Providers of Health Care Services*, is applicable to both profit and nonprofit health care entities, including hospitals of governmental units.

2. T F Nonprofit health care providers report operations using a statement of revenues and expenses of general funds.

3. T F Nonprofit health care providers use a statement of cash flows in lieu of a statement of changes in fund balances.

4. T F For health care providers, fund accounting is optional.

5. T F For health care providers that use fund accounting, a Current Funds Group is used instead of a General Fund.

6. T F Health care providers account for plant and equipment in the General Funds—not in a Plant Funds Group.

7. T F Health care providers that use fund accounting use Special Purpose Funds—not the Current Restricted Funds subgroup.

8. T F For health care providers, investment income is required to be reported as a nonoperating item.

9. T F For health care providers, only the current installment of a multiyear pledge is accrued as a receivable.

10. T F For health care providers, investments in marketable equity securities must be valued at the lower of cost or market.

11. T F For health care providers, investments in marketable debt securities must be valued at the lower of amortized cost or market whether or not there is an intent to hold the securities to maturity.

12. T F For health care providers, depreciation is reported in the operating statement, even if the entity is a nonprofit organization.

Voluntary Health and Welfare Organizations (VHWOs)

1. T F VHWOs report on the cash basis of accounting.

2. T F VHWOs report a statement of cash flows.

3. T F The primary operating statement of VHWOs is the statement of functional expenses.

4. T F VHWOs are required to report aggregated (combined) balance sheets instead of disaggregated (layered) balance sheets.

5. T F For VHWOs, pledges that relate to future periods cannot be reported in the operating statement until the applicable future period(s).

6. T F For VHWOs, a statement of support, revenues and expenditures, and changes in fund balances is reported.

7. T F For VHWOs, depreciation is reported in the operating statement.

8. T F VHWOs recognize contributions that are restricted as to purpose as support in the operating statement immediately upon receipt.

9. T F For VHWOs, the value of donated services is recognized as both public support and expense only under certain circumstances.

10. T F For VHWOs, investments may be valued at market value, even if above cost.

Certain Nonprofit Organizations (CNOs)

1. T F For CNOs, the operating statement may be called the "statement of activities."

2. T F For CNOs, the operating statement reports expenses—not expenditures.

3. T F For CNOs, it is inappropriate to use the Retained Earnings account in the equity section of the balance sheet, even though the remaining portion of the balance sheet has the same format as that used for commercial businesses.

4. T F For CNOs, fund accounting is required under the applicable audit guide, regardless of the nature of the entity.

5. T F For CNOs, depreciation expense is usually **not** reported in the operating statement.

6. T F For CNOs, the equity section could be described using the terminology Fund Balance.

7. T F For CNOs, certain fixed assets (such as landmarks, monuments, and historical treasures) are **not** depreciated.

8. T F For CNOs, donated services may **not** be reflected in the financial statements.

9. T F For CNOs, pledges **cannot** be accrued and reported as receivables.

10. T F For CNOs, marketable equity securities and marketable debt securities that are not expected to be held to maturity are accounted for in an identical manner.

MULTIPLE-CHOICE QUESTIONS

Colleges and Universities—Conceptual Questions

1. For colleges and universities, which of the following funds is **not** used to provide accountability for fiduciary responsibility?
    a. Agency Funds.
    b. Annuity and Life Income Funds.
    c. Loan Funds.
    d. Current Restricted Funds.
    e. None of the above.

2. Which of the following is **not** one of the plant funds for colleges and universities?

    a.   Investment in Plant.

    b.   Unexpended Plant Funds.

    c.   Renewals and Replace Funds.

    d.   Retirement of Indebtedness Funds.

    e.   None of the above.

3. Which of the following funds is **not** one of the endowment and similar funds used for colleges and universities?

    a.   Endowment Funds.

    b.   Term Endowment Funds.

    c.   Specific Purpose Funds.

    d.   Quasi-Endowment Funds.

    e.   None of the above.

4. Which of the following financial statements is used by colleges and universities?

    a.   Statement of Changes in Fund Balances (all funds).

    b.   Statement of Revenues, Expenditures, and Other Changes (all funds).

    c.   Statement of Cash Flows.

    d.   Statement of Activities.

    e.   None of the above.

5. Which of the following financial statements is used by colleges and universities?

    a.   Statement of Revenues and Expenses and Changes in Fund Balance.

    b.   Statement of Current Funds Revenues, Expenditures, and Other Changes.

    c.   Statement of Current Funds Revenues, Expenses, and Other Changes.

    d.   Statement of Current Funds Revenues and Expenses.

    e.   None of the above.

6. The fund balance of a college's Current Restricted Fund increased during the year. This would be reflected in the statement of current funds revenues, expenditures, and other changes by which of the following manners?

    a.   Reporting revenues at amounts greater than amounts reported for expenditures and mandatory transfers.

    b.   Reporting the difference as the separate line item "Excess of restricted receipts over transfers to revenues."

    c.   Reporting the difference as the separate line item "Excess of transfers to revenues over restricted receipts."

    d.   Reporting the difference as the separate line item "Mandatory transfers."

    e.   None of the above.

7. Which of the following items would be reported as a revenue in the Current Funds of a university?

	Unrestricted Gifts	Restricted Gifts that Have Been Expended	Restricted Gifts That Have Not Been Expended
a.	Yes	No	No
b.	Yes	Yes	Yes
c.	Yes	Yes	No
d.	Yes	No	Yes
e.	No	Yes	No

Colleges and Universities—Application Questions

8. The following receipts were among those recorded by Ultra University during its fiscal year ended August 31, 19X3:

    Unrestricted Gifts Received:
        Expended $500,000
        Unexpended $200,000
    Restricted Gifts Received:
        Expended .... $ 70,000
        Unexpended .... $ 30,000

    During the fiscal year ended August 31, 19X3, the university also expended $14,000 under the stipulations that accompanied a restricted gift that was received in the prior fiscal year. How much should be reported for revenues in the Unrestricted Current Fund for the fiscal year ended August 31, 19X3?

    a. $200,000
    b. $500,000
    c. $700,000
    d. $770,000
    e. $784,000

9. Use the same information as in Question 8. How much should be reported as revenues in the Restricted Current Fund for the fiscal year ended August 31, 19X3?

    a. $30,000
    b. $70,000
    c. $84,000
    d. $114,000
    e. None of the above.

10. For the fiscal year ended August 31, 19X5, Candida College's records reflect the following information:

    Tuition assessments (gross—all students) $3,000,000
    Scholarships granted 400,000
    Class cancellations 100,000
    Tuition remissions granted to faculty
        members' families 40,000

    What amount should be reported for revenues in the Current Funds?

    a. $2,460,000
    b. $2,500,000
    c. $2,600,000
    d. $2,900,000
    e. $2,960,000
    f. $3,000,000

11. Use the same information in Question 10. To what extent would any of the above items result in the reporting of expenditures in the Current Funds?

    a. $-0-
    b. $40,000
    c. $100,000

    d. $140,000
    e. $440,000
    f. $540,000

12. Cobbler College is sponsored by a religious group. Volunteers from this religious group regularly contribute their services to Cobbler and are paid only nominal amounts to reimburse them for their commuting costs. During 19X1, $18,000 was paid to these volunteers. The gross value of services performed by these volunteers, determined by comparisons to lay-equivalent salaries, amounted to $600,000. What amount should be reported for expenditures in 19X1 for these volunteers' services?

    a. $-0-
    b. $18,000
    c. $600,000
    d. $618,000
    e. None of the above.

Health Care Providers—Conceptual Questions

1. For nonprofit health care providers and governmental hospitals, which of the following financial statements is **not** used?

    a. A statement of revenues and expenditures of general funds.
    b. A statement of changes in fund balances.
    c. A statement of cash flows of general funds.
    d. A balance sheet.
    e. None of the above.

2. For nonprofit health care providers and governmental hospitals, which of the following funds would **not** be used?

    a. General Funds.
    b. Specific Purpose Funds.
    c. Current Restricted Funds.
    d. Plant Replacement and Expansion Funds.
    e. None of the above.

3. Where would health care providers account for the following items?

	Investment in Plant	Long-term Debt
a.	Plant Funds Group	Plant Funds Group
b.	General Funds	General Funds
c.	General Funds	Plant Funds Group
d.	Plant Funds Group	General Funds

4. Which of the following categories would appear in the operating statement of health care providers?

    a. Nonoperating gains and losses.
    b. Expenditures and mandatory transfers.
    c. Public support.
    d. Other transfers and additions.
    e. None of the above.

5. For health care providers, which of the following statements is **not** correct?

    a. Balance sheets may be presented in a disaggregated manner (layered).

b. Balance sheets may be presented in an aggregated (combined) manner.

c. The statement of revenues and expenses may be expanded to show the changes in the fund balance for the year.

d. Investment income is required to be reported as a nonoperating item.

e. None of the above.

6. Which of the following is **not** one of the conditions for reporting the estimated value of donated services to a health care provider?

a. If the donated services were not available, the services would be performed by salaried personnel.

b. The entity has a clearly measurable basis for the amount to be recorded.

c. The services are significant and form an integral part of the efforts of the entity.

d. The entity controls the employment and duties of the service donors just as if the donors were employees.

e. None of the above.

7. For a health care provider, unrestricted gifts and bequests received during the year would be

a. Reported as a gift in a specific purpose fund.

b. Credited directly to the Fund Balance account.

c. Reported as an Other Revenue in the revenues section.

d. Reported as an Unrestricted Gift and Bequest in the nonoperating gains and losses section.

e. None of the above.

8. For a health care provider, the receipt of gifts and bequests that can be used only for plant expansion would be

a. Credited directly to the Fund Balance account in the General Fund.

b. Credited directly to the Fund Balance account in a donor-restricted fund.

c. Reported as a Gift in the nonoperating gains and losses section of the applicable donor-restricted fund.

d. Reported as a transfer in the statement of changes in fund balances for the year.

e. None of the above.

Health Care Providers—Application Questions

9. Harperville Hospital's board of directors designated that $500,000 of General Fund cash be set aside for matching gifts and bequests solicited for a hospital wing expansion. During the year in which this board action occurred, the hospital received $400,000 of gifts and bequests to be used only for the expansion project. No monies were spent during the year. How much would be reported at the end of the year in the balance sheet for each of the following funds?

	General Funds	Plant Expansion Fund
a.	$-0-	$900,000
b.	$900,000	$-0-
c.	$500,000	$400,000
d.	$-0-	$400,000
e.	$500,000	$-0-

10. During 19X2, $600,000 cash in a Plant Expansion Fund of a hospital was expended on a building project at the capital facility. An additional $200,000 that had been designated by the hospital's Board of Directors to be set aside for the expansion project was also expended. For 19X2, how much would be reported in the statement of revenues and expenses for General Fund for each of the following items?

	Capital Expenditures	Nonoperating Gains— Gifts and Bequests
a.	$600,000	$200,000
b.	$600,000	$-0-
c.	$800,000	$-0-
d.	$800,000	$200,000
e.	$-0-	$-0-

11. Use the same information as in Question 10. How should the $600,000 have been accounted for and expended?

    a. The $600,000 should be expended in the Plant Expansion Fund, resulting in a capital asset that is then transferred to the General Fund.
    b. The $600,000 should be expended in the Plant Expansion Fund, resulting in a capital asset that is then transferred to an Investment in Plant Fund.
    c. The $600,000 should be transferred to the General Fund, with the transfer being reported in the statement of changes in fund balances for both of the funds.
    d. The $600,000 should be transferred to the General Fund, with the transfer being reported in only the statement of cash flows for the General Fund.
    e. None of the above.

12. Hye Hospital is able to fulfill its basic function of providing health care services only by receiving significant annual contributions, which it solicits each year in an annual fund-raising drive. Hoe Hospital is able to fulfill its basic function of providing health care services without receiving significant annual contributions, although it occasionally receives some contributions. How should these contributions be reported in the statement of revenues and expenses?

	Hye Hospital	Hoe Hospital
a.	Nonoperating Gains	Revenues
b.	Revenues	Nonoperating Gains
c.	Revenues	Revenues
d.	Nonoperating Gains	Nonoperating Gains

13. In 19X1, Hoe Hospital began operations and had (under its established rate structure) billings of $7,000,000, of which $5,400,000 was collected by year-end. At year-end, a $100,000 allowance for uncollectible accounts was deemed appropriate. In addition, during 19X1 Hoe performed charity services on numerous patients who could not afford any payments. Based on normal billing rates, the value of this charity was $1,000,000; these patients were **not** billed. Also in 19X1, $300,000 of discounts were given to third-party payors. What amount should Hoe report for Net Patient Service Revenues for 19X1?

    a. $5,400,000   f. $7,000,000
    b. $6,400,000   g. $7,600,000
    c. $6,600,000   h. $7,700,000

        d. $6,700,000   i. $7,900,000
        e. $6,900,000   j. $8,000,000

14. Use the same information as in Question 13. What amount would Hoe record in its general ledger as Gross Patient Service Revenues?
    a. $8,000,000
    b. $7,900,000
    c. $7,700,000
    d. $7,600,000
    e. $7,000,000
    f. $6,700,000

15. Use the same information as in Question 13. What amount would Hoe report in the Expenses section of the statement of revenues and expenses for 19X1?
    a. $-0-   f. $1,100,000
    b. $100,000   g. $1,300,000
    c. $300,000   h. $1,400,000
    d. $400,000
    e. $1,000,000

16. Use the same information as in Question 13. What amount would Hoe report in the Nonoperating Gains and Losses section of the statement of revenues and expenses for 19X1?
    a. $-0-   f. $1,100,000
    b. $100,000   g. $1,300,000
    c. $300,000   h. $1,400,000
    d. $400,000
    e. $1,000,000

Voluntary Health and Welfare Organizations (VHWOs)— Conceptual Questions

1. For VHWOs, which of the following financial statements is **not** used?
    a. Balance sheet.
    b. Statement of revenues and expenses, and changes in fund balances.
    c. Statement of support, revenues, and expenses, and changes in fund balances.
    d. Statement of functional expenses.
    e. None of the above.

2. Fixed assets of VHWOs are reported in which fund?
    a. General Funds.
    b. Current Unrestricted Funds.
    c. Current Restricted Funds.
    d. Plant Funds Group.
    e. Land, Building, and Equipment Fund.

3. How are pledges that relate to a future period reported for VHWOs?
    a. As a deferred revenue in the liability section of the balance sheet of the unrestricted current funds.
    b. As a deferred revenue in the liability section of the balance sheet of the restricted current funds.
    c. Not reported in any fund because it should not be accrued as a receivable.

d. As a contribution in the public support section of the statement of revenues and expenses, and changes in fund balance in the year in which the pledge is made.

e. None of the above.

4. For VHWOs, when are pledges recognized as revenues?

	Unrestricted Pledges	Restricted Pledges (as to purpose)
a.	When made.	When made.
b.	When collection is made.	When collection is made.
c.	When made.	When collection is made.
d.	When collection is made.	When the related expenditure is made.
e.	When made.	When the related expenditure is made.

5. For VHWOs that have fixed assets, in which fund is depreciation expense reported?

a. Current Funds—Unrestricted.

b. Current Funds—Restricted.

c. Land, Building, and Equipment Fund.

d. Endowment Funds.

e. Depreciation expense is not reported in any of the funds.

6. Vola Foundation is a VHWO that is funded by contributions from the general public. During 19X2, unrestricted pledges of $300,000 were received, of which it was estimated that 10% would be uncollectible. By the end of 19X2, cash collections totaled $210,000, and it was expected that only $50,000 would be collected in the future. Donors did **not** specify any periods during which the donations were to be used. What amount should Vola include under public support in 19X2 for contributions?

a. $210,000

b. $260,000

c. $270,000

d. $300,000

e. None of the above.

7. Vita Foundation is a VHWO that is funded by contributions from the general public. During 19X1, Vita sold some office equipment for $6,000 cash. The equipment's cost was $27,000, and its book value was $2,000. The gain was properly recorded. In connection with this sale, what other entry must Vita record?

	Debit	Credit
a.	Fund balance—reserved	Fund balance—unreserved
b.	Fund balance—unreserved	Fund balance—reserved
c.	Fund balance—unexpended	Fund balance—expended
d.	Fund balance—expended	Fund balance—unexpended
e.	None of the above.	

8. Use the same information as in Question 7. What is the amount of the debit and credit entry made in Question 7?

a. $2,000

b. $4,000

c. $6,000

    d. $25,000

    e. $27,000

9. Veda Foundation is a VHWO that is funded by contributions from the general public. During 19X1, a new computer was purchased at a cost of $18,000. Because the Land, Building, and Equipment Fund had no liquid assets, it was necessary to use cash in the unrestricted current fund. How will this transaction be reported in the 19X1 financial statements?

    a. As an expenditure in the operating statement for the Unrestricted Current Fund.

    b. As an expenditure in the operating statement for the Land, Building, and Equipment Fund.

    c. As an adjustment to the fund balance in the "Other changes in fund balance" section of the statement of support, revenue and expenses, and changes in fund balance—a decrease for the unrestricted current fund and an increase for the Land, Building, and Equipment Fund.

    d. As an investing activity outflow in the statement of cash flows.

    e. None of the above.

Certain Nonprofit Organizations (CNOs)—Conceptual Questions

1. For CNOs, which of the following descriptions would **not** be used?

    a. Retained earnings.

    b. Cumulative excess of revenues over expenses.

    c. Fund balance.

    d. Entity capital.

    e. Membership equity.

2. For CNOs, which of the following methods of accounting is used?

    a. Accrual basis.

    b. Cash basis.

    c. Modified accrual basis.

    d. Accrual basis for some funds and modified accrual basis for other funds.

    e. None of the above.

3. For CNOs, which of the following statements is correct?

    a. Recording depreciation expense is optional.

    b. Recording depreciation expense is prohibited.

    c. The value of donated services may not be recognized in the financial statements.

    d. The ability and intention to hold marketable debt securities to maturity is to be disregarded in how to account for them.

    e. None of the above.

4. For CNOs, which of the following statements is correct?

    a. The audit guide specifies a funds structure.

    b. For an organization that uses a Land, Building, and Equipment Fund, depreciation expense is reported as an expense in the statement of support, revenues, and expenses of that fund—not in the statement of support, revenues, and expenses of a current fund.

c. An employer-employee relationship need not exist between the organization and its volunteers in order to recognize the value of donated services in the financial statements.

d. Restricted income from investments of current restricted funds should be reported as a deferred amount in the statement of support, revenues, and expenses of the restricted fund.

e. None of the above.

Certain Nonprofit Organizations—Application Questions

5. Fifo Foundation, a research organization supported by contributions from the general public, reported the following costs in its schedule of functional expenses for the year ended December 31, 19X4:

Fund raising $400,000
General and administrative 200,000
Research 900,000

What amount should be reported for program services for 19X4?

   a. $200,000
   b. $400,000
   c. $600,000
   d. $900,000
   e. $1,100,000
   f. $1,500,000

6. The following expenditures were among those incurred by a nonprofit botanical society during 19X8:

Printing of annual report .... $ 5,000
Unsolicited merchandise sent to encourage
   contributions $10,000

What amount should be classified as fund-raising costs in the society's activity statement for 19X8?

   a. $-0-
   b. $5,000
   c. $10,000
   d. $15,000

7. In May 1988, Lois Lifo donated $500,000 to her church, with the stipulation that the income generated from this gift be paid to Lois during her lifetime. The conditions of this donation are that, after Lois dies, the principal can be used by the church for any purpose voted on by the church elders. The church invested the $500,000 and had earned $24,000 of interest by December 31, 19X8, and this amount was remitted to Lois. In the church's December 31, 19X8, financial statements, how should this be reported?

   a. $24,000 should be reported under support and revenue in the activity statement.

   b. $500,000 should be reported under support and revenue in the activity statement.

   c. $524,000 should be reported under support and revenue in the activity statement.

   d. $500,000 should be reported as deferred support in the balance sheet.

e. The gift and its terms should be disclosed only in notes to the financial statements.

8. Sunn City has a nonprofit Center for Performing Arts organization. In 19X1, it received a legally enforceable $30,000 pledge from a donor who specified that the amount pledged be used in 19X3. The donor paid the pledge in cash in 19X2. How should the pledge be accounted for in the financial statements?

   a. A $30,000 deferred credit in the balance sheet at the end of 19X1, and as support in 19X2 in the amount of $30,000.

   b. A $30,000 deferred credit in the balance sheet at the end of 19X1 and 19X2, and as support in 19X3 in the amount of $30,000.

   c. Support in 19X1 in the amount of $30,000.

   d. Support in 19X2 in the amount of $30,000, and no deferred credit in the balance sheet at the end of 19X1.

   e. Support in the amount of $10,000 for 19X1, 19X2, and 19X3, and as a deferred credit for $20,000 in the balance sheet at the end of 19X1 and $10,000 at the end of 19X2.

9. Use the same information in Question 8, except that the pledge is **not** legally enforceable. How should the pledge be accounted for in the financial statements?

   a. Support in 19X1 in the amount of $30,000.

   b. Support in 19X2 in the amount of $30,000, and no deferred credit in the balance sheet at the end of 19X1.

   c. Support in 19X3 in the amount of $30,000, and no deferred credit in the balance sheet at the end of 19X1 and a deferred credit in the balance sheet at the end of 19X2 for $30,000.

   d. Support in 19X3 in the amount of $30,000, and no deferred credit in the balance sheet at the end of 19X1 and 19X2.

   e. A $30,000 deferred credit in the balance sheet at the end of 19X1, and as support in 19X2 for $30,000.

CHAPTER 24—SOLUTIONS

Completion Statements

1. fund
2. current funds, plant funds, endowment and similar funds, agency funds, annuity and life income funds, loan funds
3. current unrestricted funds, current restricted funds, general fund, specific purpose funds
4. plant funds
5. endowment and similar funds, agency funds, annuity and life income funds, loan funds
6. agency
7. loan
8. endowment
9. fund group
10. restricted funds
11. quasi-endowment, designated
12. pledge

13. unexpended plant funds, renewal and replacement funds, retirement of indebtedness funds, investment in plant fund
14. custodian fund
15. support

True-or-False Statements

Colleges and Universities

1. False	6. False
2. True	7. False
3. False	8. True
4. False	9. True
5. True	10. True

Health Care Providers

1. True	7. True
2. True	8. False
3. False	9. False
4. True	10. True
5. False	11. False
6. True	12. True

Voluntary Health and Welfare Organizations

1. False	6. False
2. False	7. True
3. False	8. True
4. False	9. True
5. True	10. True

Certain Nonprofit Organizations

1. True	6. True
2. True	7. True
3. True	8. False
4. False	9. False
5. False	10. True

Multiple-Choice Questions

Colleges and Universities

1. d	7. c
2. e	8. c
3. c	9. c
4. a	10. d
5. b	11. e
6. b	12. c

Health Care Providers

1.	a	9.	c
2.	c	10.	e
3.	b	11.	c
4.	a	12.	b
5.	d	13.	d
6.	e	14.	e
7.	d	15.	b
8.	b	16.	a

Voluntary Health and Welfare Organizations

1.	b	6.	b
2.	e	7.	d
3.	a	8.	a
4.	a	9.	c
5.	c		

Certain Nonprofit Organizations

1.	a	6.	c
2.	a	7.	d
3.	e	8.	b
4.	b	9.	c
5.	d		

CHAPTER 25

ACCOUNTING FOR PRIVATE NONPROFIT ORGANIZATIONS: NEW FASB STANDARDS ON CONTRIBUTIONS AND FINANCIAL STATEMENTS

CHAPTER HIGHLIGHTS

General Matters

1. The new FASB standards apply to all **private** NPOs.

2. The new FASB standards supersede those provisions of the AICPA audit guides that **conflict** with the new standards.

3. The new FASB standards become effective for **fiscal years beginning after December 15, 1994,** except for NPOs having less than $5 million in total assets and less than $1 million in annual sales. These smaller NPOs have an additional year before having to comply.

4. **Public** NPOs are not affected in any way by the new FASB standards. The AICPA audit guides still apply to these NPOs in their entirety until the GASB issues a pronouncement(s) to the contrary.

5. The new FASB standards impact certain NPOs more than other NPOs.

6. The new FASB standards will require more extensive disclosures in the notes to the financial statements.

Contributions

7. The major change is that all four types of NPOs are to report almost all unrestricted and restricted contributions (including contributions that establish endowments) as contributions **in the revenues and gains category of the statement of activities when received.**

8. A **contribution** is an **unconditional** (no strings attached) **transfer** of cash or other assets in a voluntary, nonreciprocal transfer by a person or entity acting other than as an owner of the NPO.

9. **Unconditional promises,** which may be **oral or written,** to give cash or other assets in the future fall within the definition of an unconditional transfer. Accordingly, such contributions give rise to "Contributions Receivable" in the balance sheet.

10. To **recognize unconditional promises** in the financial statements, **sufficient evidence** in the form of verifiable documentation that a promise was made must exist.

11. **Conditional promises to give** are conceptually the opposite of unconditional promises to give and therefore are **not** contributions as defined in *SFAS No. 116.*

12. **Conditional promises to give** depend on the occurrence of a **specified future and uncertain event** that must occur to bind the promisor and thus transform the promise from conditional to unconditional status.

13. A **conditional promise to give** may be deemed unconditional if the possibility that the specified future event will **not occur** is **remote** (same as a high probability existing that it will occur).

14. If assets have been received and the retention and use of such assets is **conditional upon a future event,** the offsetting credit is to a Refundable Advance account (a liability) until the conditional event occurs.

15. The **exceptions** to recognizing contributions of monetary and nonmonetary assets **when received** are (A) the item in point 14 and (B) collection items (mentioned later).

16. Contributions of monetary and nonmonetary assets are valued at the **fair value** of the assets received.

17. **Determining the fair value** may require (A) obtaining quoted market prices, (B) using independent appraisals, or (C) using other appropriate methods.

18. **Present value procedures** are appropriate for estimated future cash flows for unconditional promises to give that are expected to be collected over a period **longer than one year.**

19. When present value procedures are used, the subsequent recognition of the **interest element** is reported as **contribution income—not** as interest income.

20. **Contributions of services** are recognized as revenues when received **only if** (A) **nonfinancial** assets are created or enhanced or (B) **specialized skills** are provided by individuals possessing those skills.

21. For contributed services, **disclosures must be made** of (A) a description of the nature and extent, (B) the amounts recognized as revenues, and (C) the programs or activities in which the services were used.

22. Recognizable contributed services are usually recorded at the **fair value** of the services contributed. For recognizable contributed services that create or enhance **nonfinancial assets,** however, the fair value of the asset or asset enhancement may be recognized instead.

23. **Collection items** (contributed works of art, historical treasures, and similar assets received) **need not** be recognized in the financial statements if three conditions—pertaining to use, care, and use of proceeds upon sale—are satisfied. **Selective capitalization** is prohibited.

24. Contributions must be reported in the statement of activities **by category:** unrestricted, temporarily restricted, or permanently restricted.

25. **Donor-restricted contributions** whose conditions are **fulfilled in the same period** in which the contribution is recognized **may** be reported in the unrestricted category if the entity (A) consistently follows this policy and (B) discloses this policy.

26. Contributions that create **endowments** (principal is invested in perpetuity) are **permanently restricted contributions.**

27. **Income earned on endowments** can be reported in any of the three net asset categories, as appropriate based on donor stipulations.

28. Contributed assets that are restricted as to either (A) **purpose** or (B) **time period,** are classified as **temporarily restricted assets.**

29. **Contributed fixed assets** are classified based on either (A) **donor stipulations** or (B) the NPO's **accounting policy** in the absence of donor stipulations.

30. In the **absence of donor stipulations** concerning a contributed fixed asset, the NPO **must establish an accounting policy** as to whether a time restriction exists. If yes, the fixed asset is classified as restricted (temporarily or permanently, as appropriate). If no, the fixed asset is classified as unrestricted when the fixed asset is **placed in service.**

31. **Restrictions on long-lived assets** classified as temporarily restricted (that have been placed in service) **expire over the estimated useful lives of the assets.** This expiration is recognized in the statement of activities **as a separate line item** (a reclassification that shows a decrease in the temporarily restricted category and an increase in the unrestricted category.

Financial Statements

32. *SFAS No. 117* specifies (A) **what financial statements** are to be presented and (B) **what specific information,** as a minimum, is to be shown in those statements.

33. *SFAS No. 117* requires for the NPO as a whole (A) a statement of **financial position,** (B) a statement of **activities,** and (C) a statement of **cash flows.** VHWOs must also report—in a separate statement—expenses **by natural classification** in a matrix format.

34. Unlike the AICPA audit guides, which are fairly prescriptive, *SFAS No. 117* imposes no more stringent reporting standards than those that exist for commercial for-profit entities.

35. Thus, a NPO has the **option** to present an **intermediate measure of "operating income"**—providing it is done in a statement that also reports the change in unrestricted net assets (equity) for the period.

36. To provide information on **financial flexibility,** *SFAS No. 117* requires classifications of an entity's **net assets (equity)** based on (A) whether donor-imposed restrictions exist and (B) the type of donor-imposed restrictions. The three classes are (A) **unrestricted,** (B) **temporarily restricted,** and (C) **permanently restricted.**

37. The statement of financial position is to focus on the NPO as a whole and show amounts for the NPO's **total assets, total liabilities,** and **total net assets (equity).** The net assets (equity) section is to show the total amount **for each class of net assets.**

38. **Information about liquidity** may be shown in any of several ways.

39. Disclosures about the nature and amount of donor-imposed restrictions must be made.

40. The term **"fund balance"** is **not** used in the statements prescribed by *SFAS No. 117.*

41. The **statement of activities** is to show **revenues, gains, and other support by category** (unrestricted, temporarily restricted, and permanently restricted).

42. **Expirations of restrictions** are to be reported separately in the statement of activities.

43. All **expenses** are to be shown in the unrestricted category.

44. The statement of activities is to show for the organization as a whole the amount of the **change in each classification of net assets.**

45. **Gross amounts** must be reported for revenues and expenses (including special events), with limited exceptions.

46. If fund accounting is used for **internal record keeping purposes,** it will be necessary to prepare some form of "aggregating worksheet" to arrive at amounts to be presented in the financial statements issued for external reporting purposes.

COMPLETION STATEMENTS

Contributions

1. Contributions are _____ transfers of cash or other assets.

2. A transfer in which value is not received or given in exchange is a(n) _____ _____ .

3. A promise to give is a contribution if the promise is _____ _____ .

4. In general, contributions are recognized _____ .

5. A(n) _____ promise to give is not a contribution.

6. Contributions of monetary and nonmonetary assets are valued at their _____ _____ .

7. Three ways to determine the fair value of a contribution are (A) _____ _____ , (B) _____ , and (C) _____ _____ .

8. Contributed services are recognized if they (A) create or enhance _____ _____ or (B) require _____ .

9. In general, contributed services are measured at the _____ _____ of the services received. However, recognizable contributed services that create or enhance nonfinancial assets may be recognized instead at the fair value of the _____ .

10. Contributed works of art, historical treasures, and similar assets are called _____ _____ .

11. Assets in item 10 may not be _____ capitalized.

12. The three categories in which contributions are to be reported are _____ _____ , _____ , and _____ _____ .

13. Contributions that create _____ are permanently restricted contributions.

14. Term endowments would be classified as _____ contributions.

15. Promises with future payment dates would usually be classified as _____ _____ contributions.

16. Contributions of fixed assets would usually be classified as either _____ _____ or _____ depending on _____ or the NPO's _____ _____ in the absence of _____ .

17. Restrictions on long-lived assets classified as temporarily restricted net assets _____ over the life of the assets.

Financial Statements

18. Under *SFAS No. 117*, private NPOs must issue financial statements that focus on the NPO as a(n) _____ .

19. Under *SFAS No. 117*, private NPOs must classify their net assets (equity) based on (A) whether _____ exist and (B) the type of _____ _____ .

20. Under *SFAS No. 117*, private NPOs must show in their statement of financial position amounts for the NPO's _____ , _____ _____ , and _____ .

21. Under *SFAS No. 117*, private NPOs must show three classes of net assets (equity in their statement of financial position: (A) _____ , (B) _____ , and (C) _____ .

22. The unrestricted net asset category in the statement of financial position could be subdivided between (A) _____ net assets and (B) _____ net assets.

23. Under *SFAS No. 117*, revenues, gains, and other support must be reported by _____ in the statement of activities.

24. Under *SFAS No. 117*, all expenses are shown in the _____ _____ category in the statement of activities.

25. Under *SFAS No. 117*, expirations of restrictions are reported _____ _____ in the statement of activities.

26. VHWOs must also report expenses by _____ classification in a separate financial statement using a(n) _____ format.

27. In general, revenues and expenses are reported at their _____ _____ amounts.

28. The statement of activities may be in _____ format or in _____ format.

29. For each category of net assets, the statement of activities must show for the NPO as a whole the amount of _____ .

30. The statement of cash flows may be prepared using the _____ _____ method (the preferred method) or the _____ _____ method.

31. *SFAS No. 117* _____ the use of fund accounting for internal record-keeping purposes.

TRUE-OR-FALSE STATEMENTS

Contributions

1. T F Under *SFAS No. 116*, the definition of contributions does **not** include **conditional promises to give.**

2. T F Under *SFAS No. 116*, the definition of contributions includes both **reciprocal** and **nonreciprocal** transfers.

3. T F Under *SFAS No. 116*, **unconditional promises to give** must be **in writing** to qualify as a recognizable contribution.

4. T F Under *SFAS No. 116*, **unconditional promises to give** are recognized in the financial statements **when received**—not when collected.

5. T F Under *SFAS No. 116*, a communication that is **unclear** as to whether it constitutes an **unconditional promise to give** is deemed an unconditional promise **if it is legally enforceable.**

6. T F Under *SFAS No. 116*, **conditional promises to give** are considered unconditional if the probability that the specified future event will occur is **remote.**

7. T F Under *SFAS No. 116*, assets that have been received and that can be retained and used **only if a conditional future event occurs** are classified in the asset section as Refundable Advances.

8. T F Under *SFAS No. 116*, contributions that create **endowments** are always reported in the statement of activities—**never** as direct adjustments to equity.

9. T F Under *SFAS No. 116*, contributions are recognized **when received,** with limited exceptions.

10. T F Under *SFAS No. 116*, contributions received are measured at their **fair value.**

11. T F Under *SFAS No. 116*, contributions received must be measured at the **present value of estimated future cash flows.**

12. T F Under *SFAS No. 116*, the **interest element** in a present value measurement is subsequently recognized as **contribution income—not** interest income.

13. T F Under *SFAS No. 116*, **contributed services** are recognized **only if** they create or enhance **nonfinancial assets.**

14. T F Under *SFAS No. 116*, the fair value of contributed services **received but not recognized** in the financial statements must be disclosed.

15. T F Under *SFAS No. 116*, repairs made to a building on a **volunteer basis** by a plumber would **not** be recognized in the financial statements.

16. T F   Under *SFAS No. 116*, **contributed services** are valued using the **minimum wage.**

17. T F   Under *SFAS No. 116*, contributed services that **create or enhance a non-financial asset** must be recorded at the fair value of the asset created or enhanced.

18. T F   Under *SFAS No. 116*, **collection items** need **not** be capitalized under certain circumstances.

19. T F   Under *SFAS No. 116*, **collection items** may be capitalized retroactively, prospectively, or selectively.

20. T F   Under *SFAS No. 116*, contributions that **create endowments** are classified as increasing **permanently restricted** net assets.

21. T F   Under *SFAS No. 116*, contributions that create term endowments are classified as increasing permanently restricted net assets.

22. T F   Under *SFAS No. 116*, **income earned on endowments** (other than term endowments) is reported as increasing **permanently restricted** net assets.

23. T F   Under *SFAS No. 116*, contributions that create **term endowments** are classified as increasing **temporarily restricted** net assets.

24. T F   Under *SFAS No. 116*, contributions with future payment dates **beyond one year** are **not** recognized in the financial statements.

25. T F   Under *SFAS No. 116*, contributions **with future payment dates** usually would be classified as increasing **temporarily restricted** net assets.

26. T F   Under *SFAS No. 116*, **contributions of fixed assets** are classified as increasing **unrestricted** net assets when the assets are **placed in service.**

27. T F   Under *SFAS No. 116*, **contributions of fixed assets** are classified as increasing **unrestricted** net assets when the assets are **placed in service** only in the absence of donor-imposed restrictions.

28. T F   Under *SFAS No. 116*, an **implied time restriction** on contributed fixed assets is assumed to exist in the absence of donor-imposed restrictions.

29. T F   Under *SFAS No. 116*, an NPO must establish an **accounting policy** as to whether or not an implied time restriction exists on contributed fixed assets only if no donor-imposed restrictions exist.

30. T F   Under *SFAS No. 116*, a **purpose restriction** is deemed to have expired when an expense has been incurred for that purpose.

Financial Statements

31. T F   Under *SFAS No. 117*, private NPOs must present financial statements that focus on the NPO as a whole.

32. T F Under *SFAS No. 117*, the statement of financial position must show total assets, total liabilities, and total net assets (equity).

33. T F Under *SFAS No. 117*, the statement of financial position must show total amounts for each classification of net assets.

34. T F Under *SFAS No. 117*, the statement of financial position may be in either the **classified format** (current/noncurrent categories) or the **unclassified format.**

35. T F Under *SFAS No. 117*, **"board-restricted" net assets** must be shown separately in the statement of financial position.

36. T F Under *SFAS No. 117*, an **intermediate measure of operations** cannot be shown in the statement of activities.

37. T F Under *SFAS No. 117*, the **"layered" format** is allowed in the statement of activities.

38. T F Under *SFAS No. 117*, **expirations of restrictions** must be reported separately in the statement of activities.

39. T F Under *SFAS No. 117*, **all expenses** are reported in the **unrestricted** category—even expenses incurred in satisfying donor-imposed restrictions.

40. T F Under *SFAS No. 117*, only VHWOs must show expenses by **function** in the statement of activities.

41. T F Under *SFAS No. 117*, revenues from **special events** that are ongoing and major activities are reported net of related expenses.

42. T F Under *SFAS No. 117*, **fund accounting** for internal record-keeping purposes is discouraged.

MULTIPLE-CHOICE QUESTIONS

Contributions

1. Under *SFAS No. 116*, **donor-restricted** contributions are recognized in the financial statements
   a. When collected.
   b. When received.
   c. When the restrictions expire.
   d. When the conditions stipulated by the donor are fulfilled.
   e. None of the above.

2. Under *SFAS No. 116*, which of the following contributions are **not** recognized in the statement of activities?
   a. Contributions that create endowments.
   b. Contributions that create temporary endowments.

    c.   Contributions of fixed assets.

    d.   Contributions of services that enhance nonfinancial assets.

    e.   None of the above.

3. Under *SFAS No. 116*, the fair value of a contribution **cannot** be determined by using

    a.   Market quotations.

    b.   Appraisals.

    c.   Present value calculations of expected future cash flows.

    d.   Hours donated times the standard billing rate per hour.

    e.   None of the above.

4. Under *SFAS No. 116*, which of the following contributed services are **not** recognized in the financial statements?

    a.   Contributed services that enhance nonfinancial assets.

    b.   Contributed services that create nonfinancial assets.

    c.   Contributed services that are performed by persons having specialized skills.

    d.   Contributed services performed by persons not having specialized skills.

    e.   None of the above.

5. Under *SFAS No. 116*, contributions are reported in the statement of activities using all of the following categories **except**

    a.   Board-restricted.

    b.   Permanently restricted.

    c.   Temporarily restricted.

    d.   Unrestricted.

    e.   None of the above.

Financial Statements

6. Under *SFAS No. 117*, which of the following categories of net assets is **not** required to be shown in the statement of financial position?

    a.   Permanently restricted

    b.   Temporarily restricted

    c.   Board-restricted

    d.   Unrestricted

    e.   None of the above.

7. Under *SFAS No. 117*, which of the following statements **is false** concerning the statement of financial position?

    a.   Assets and liabilities may be presented in a layered format (by fund).

    b.   Assets and liabilities may be presented using a classified format.

    c.   Assets and liabilities may be presented using an unclassified format, sequenced by liquidity.

    d.   The difference between total assets and liabilities can be described as equity instead of net assets.

    e.   None of the above.

8. Under *SFAS No. 117,* VWHOs must present

    a. A separate statement showing expenses by both function and natural classification.
    b. A separate statement showing expenses by function.
    c. A separate statement showing expenses by natural classification.
    d. Expenses by natural classification in the statement of activities.
    e. None of the above.

CHAPTER 25—SOLUTIONS

Completion Statements

Contributions

1. unconditional
2. nonreciprocal
3. unconditional
4. when received
5. conditional
6. fair value
7. market quotations, appraisals, present value calculations
8. nonfinancial assets, specialized skills
9. fair value, asset or asset enhancement
10. collection items
11. selectively
12. unrestricted, temporarily restricted, permanently restricted
13. endowments
14. temporarily restricted
15. temporarily restricted
16. temporarily restricted, unrestricted, donor-imposed stipulations, accounting policy, donor-imposed stipulations
17. expire

Financial Statements

18. whole
19. donor-imposed restrictions, donor-imposed restrictions
20. total assets, total liabilities, total net assets (equity)
21. unrestricted, temporarily restricted, permanently restricted
22. board-designated, unrestricted
23. category
24. unrestricted
25. separately
26. natural, matrix
27. gross
28. columnar, layered
29. change
30. direct, indirect
31. permits

True-or-False Statements

Contributions

1. True	16. False
2. False	17. False
3. False	18. True
4. True	19. False
5. True	20. True
6. False	21. False
7. False	22. False
8. True	23. True
9. True	24. False
10. True	25. True
11. False	26. False
12. True	27. False
13. False	28. False
14. False	29. True
15. False	30. True

Financial Statements

31. True	37. True
32. True	38. True
33. True	39. True
34. True	40. False
35. False	41. False
36. False	42. False

Multiple-Choice Questions

Contributions

1. b
2. e
3. e
4. d
5. a

Financial Statements

6. c
7. a
8. a

CHAPTER 26
PARTNERSHIPS: FORMATION AND OPERATION

CHAPTER HIGHLIGHTS

1. A **partnership** is an association of two or more persons (individuals, corporations, or other partnerships) who are co-owners of a business and who share profits and losses in an agreed-upon manner.

2. In **general partnerships,** all partners have **unlimited liability** to partnership creditors if the partnership is unable to pay the creditors. Thus, **the creditors can go after the personal assets** of the partners.

3. In **limited** partnerships, certain partners have **limited liability** (usually equal to the capital invested) to partnership creditors if the partnership is unable to pay the creditors. Thus, **the creditors have no recourse against personal assets** of these partners. (In limited partnerships, there must be at least one general partner.)

4. The **major advantage** of the partnership form of organization is the **ease of formation.**

5. The **major disadvantages** of the partnership form of organization are (A) the unlimited liability (for general partnerships) and (B) the difficulty in disposing of the partnership interest (generally more a problem for limited partners).

6. Partnerships are entities that have to **report the taxable income of the partners,** but the partnerships themselves do not pay income tax.

7. Each of the 50 states has laws governing partnerships, with most of the states having adopted the **Uniform Partnership Act** or a variation thereof.

8. The **partnership agreement** is merely a written expression of what the partners have agreed to. One of the most important provisions is the manner of sharing profits and losses, which may be in any manner the partners choose.

9. The business of a partnership should always be accounted for separately from the personal transactions of the partners.

10. Partnerships (unlike public corporations) do not have to follow generally accepted accounting principles, and they often do not.

11. The focus in accounting for partnerships is that of **achieving equity** (fairness) among the partners.

12. A partner's **drawing account** is a contra capital account.

13. When a partnership is formed, assets contributed to the partnership should be **recorded at their current values**—not historical cost to the individual partners. Likewise for liabilities assumed by the partnership.

14. Appendix C Question: Each partner must keep track of his or her individual **tax basis** in the partnership (done outside the partnership general ledger) so that a determination can be made of the taxable gain or loss when the partnership interest (a capital asset) is disposed of.

15. Appendix C Question: Profits increase tax basis; losses decrease tax basis. Contributions increase tax basis; distributions (withdrawals) decrease basis. An increase in partnership liabilities is treated as an increase in tax basis (shared in the profit and loss ratio); the opposite is true for a decrease in liabilities.

COMPLETION STATEMENTS

1. Partnerships in which each partner is personally liable to the partnership's creditors if partnership assets are insufficient to pay such creditors are called _____ _____ partnerships.

2. Partnerships in which certain partners are **not** personally liable to the partnership creditors if partnership assets are insufficient to pay partnership creditors are called _____ partnerships.

3. Professional businesses that have incorporated are called _____ .

4. An account used to charge current-year withdrawals by partners is called the _____ _____ account.

5. For income tax purposes, a partner's interest in a partnership is referred to as that partner's _____ .

6. When a partnership is formed, equity dictates that assets contributed into the partnership be recorded at their _____ .

7. The fundamental objective in all of partnership accounting is that of achieving _____ among the partners.

TRUE-OR-FALSE STATEMENTS

1. T   F   A corporation **cannot** be a partner.

2. T   F   Accounting firms **cannot** operate as professional corporations.

3. T   F   Forming a partnership is easier than forming a corporation.

4. T F In general partnerships, **all** partners have unlimited liability.

5. T F By using the partnership form of organization, the "double taxation" of earnings is avoided.

6. T F Partnerships do **not** pay income taxes.

7. T F A partner's drawing account is a contra capital account.

8. T F In recording the initial capital contributions in the general ledger, assets are recorded at their adjusted basis.

9. T F In dividing profits and losses, the use of an "order of priority provision" makes sense only if the partners agree not to use a residual sharing ratio in the event profits do **not** exceed the total of the salary allowances and the imputed interest on capital balances.

10. T F It is unsound to allocate profits and losses solely on the basis of capital balances.

11. T F The Uniform Partnership Agreement states that partners who act in the partnership interest are entitled to remuneration.

12. T F Appendix C Question: A decrease in partnership liabilities results in a **decrease** to the tax basis of the partners.

13. T F Appendix C Question: The tax laws are **not** structured around a partner's equity as recorded in the partnership general ledger.

14. T F Appendix C Question: A partner's tax basis **cannot** be determined by using the amounts recorded in the general ledger capital accounts.

MULTIPLE-CHOICE QUESTIONS

Conceptual Questions

1. The partnership form of organization is
    a. A legal entity.
    b. A taxable entity.
    c. A legal entity and a taxable entity.
    d. Closer to being a corporation than a sole proprietorship.
    e. None of the above.

2. The professional corporation form of organization is
    a. Neither a legal entity nor a taxable entity.
    b. A legal entity but not a taxable entity.
    c. A taxable entity but not a legal entity.
    d. A taxable entity and a legal entity.
    e. None of the above.

3. When a partnership is formed, equity dictates that assets and liabilities contributed to the partnership be recorded at their
   a. Historical cost.
   b. Current values.
   c. Adjusted tax basis.
   d. Book values.
   e. None of the above.

4. A unique feature of general partnerships compared with public corporations is that
   a. They do **not** have to file income tax returns.
   b. They are **not** governed by state laws.
   c. They must keep their books on the tax basis.
   d. They have complete latitude in deciding whether to follow generally accepted accounting principles.
   e. None of the above.

5. Under the Uniform Partnership Act,
   a. The cash basis of accounting must be used.
   b. Profits and losses must be divided equally among the partners.
   c. Interest must be imputed on capital if the capital balances are not maintained equally.
   d. Generally accepted accounting principles must be followed.
   e. None of the above.

6. Appendix C Question: For income tax reporting purposes, which of the following is **false?**
   a. Partnership profits decrease tax basis.
   b. The borrowing of money by a partnership increases the tax basis of each of the partners.
   c. Partnership cash distributions to partners decrease tax basis.
   d. A partner's tax basis is usually different from the partner's general ledger capital balance.
   e. None of the above.

Application Questions

7. King and Queen formed a partnership on June 1, 19X1, and contributed the following assets:

	King	Queen
Cash..........	$100,000	$200,000
Land..........		(see below)

   The land has a current value of $500,000 and a historical cost to Queen of $400,000. Also, the land was subject to a mortgage of $50,000, which was assumed by the partnership. King and Queen share profits and losses in a 3:2 ratio, respectively. What should be the balance in Queen's capital account on June 1, 19X1?
   a. $550,000
   b. $650,000
   c. $670,000
   d. $700,000
   e. None of the above.

8. Appendix C Question: Use the same information as in Question 7. What is Queen's tax basis on June 1, 19X1?

    a. $520,000
    b. $570,000
    c. $620,000
    d. $670,000
    e. None of the above.

9. On January 1, 19X1, Dick and Jane formed a partnership with each contributing $100,000 cash. The partnership agreement provided that Dick would receive a salary allowance of $40,000 and that partnership profits and losses (computed after deducting Dick's salary allowance) would be shared equally. Additional information for the year ended December 31, 19X1, follows:

Cash drawings by Dick	$ 33,000
Partnership taxable income (before the salary allowance)	$100,000
Partnership net income (before the salary allowance)	$ 90,000
Partnership liabilities at year-end (a working capital bank loan obtained on December 20, 19X1)	$ 30,000

What is the capital balance of Dick as of December 31, 19X1?

    a. $132,000
    b. $137,000
    c. $165,000
    d. $170,000
    e. None of the above.

10. Appendix C Question: Use the same information as in Question 9. What is Dick's tax basis at December 31, 19X1?

    a. $132,000
    b. $137,000
    c. $145,000
    d. $152,000
    e. Nonc of the above.

CHAPTER 26—SOLUTIONS

Completion Statements

    1. general
    2. limited
    3. professional corporations
    4. drawings
    5. tax basis
    6. current values
    7. equity

True-or-False Statements

1. False	8. False
2. False	9. True
3. True	10. False
4. True	11. False
5. True	12. True
6. True	13. True
7. True	14. True

Multiple-Choice Questions

1. e
2. d
3. b
4. d
5. e
6. a
7. b ($200,000 + $500,000 − $50,000 = $650,000)
8. b ($200,000 + $400,000 − $30,000 = $570,000; the $30,000 amount is King's 60% share of the $50,000 mortgage.)
9. a ($100,000 + $40,000 + $25,000 − $33,000 = $132,000)
10. d ($100,000 + $40,000 + $30,000 − $33,000 + $15,000 = $152,000)

CHAPTER 27
PARTNERSHIPS: CHANGES IN OWNERSHIP

CHAPTER HIGHLIGHTS

1. The **purchase of an interest** from one or more of a partnership's existing partners is a **personal transaction** between the incoming partner and the selling partner(s). The only entry required on the partnership's books is to **transfer** an amount from the selling partner's Capital account to the new partner's Capital account.

2. When changes in ownership occur, three methods are available **to minimize inequities** that would occur if no thought was given to undervalued assets or goodwill (A) the revaluing of assets/recording the goodwill method, (B) the special profit and loss sharing provision method, and (C) the bonus method.

3. If the agreed-upon **current values are erroneous** or if the agreed-upon **goodwill does not materialize,** only the special profit and loss sharing provision method will prevent an inequity to one or more of the partners.

4. The **bonus method** has the major advantage of not resulting in a departure from GAAP (as does the special profit and loss sharing provision method). Under this method, a portion of one or more partner's capital balance is transferred to one or more other partners (with the hope that the amount transferred will later be recouped from future profits).

5. The **revaluing of assets/recording the goodwill** method results in a departure from GAAP (in addition to adding an additional complexity in preparing the partnership tax return). Under this method, an incoming partner always gets credited to his or her capital account the full value of his or her asset investment.

6. Technically, **any change in ownership** legally **dissolves** the old partnership and results in the creation of a new partnership.

7. When a partner withdraws from a partnership, the partner is still **responsible for all partnership obligations existing at the time of the withdrawal** unless expressly released from this responsibility by partnership creditors.

8. A **major risk of joining an existing partnership** when a new partner agrees to become jointly responsible for all preexisting partnership debts is that there may be **unrecorded liabilities** (possibly from lawsuits).

9. When a partner withdraws from a partnership, the partner must determine whether he or she has a gain or loss for income tax reporting purposes.

10. The taxable gain or loss is determined by comparing the withdrawing partner's **proceeds** with his or her **tax basis.** The proceeds are the sum of cash received **plus** the share of existing partnership liabilities for which he or she is relieved of responsibility.

COMPLETION STATEMENTS

1. The combining of two independent partnerships is a(n) _____ .

2. When an incoming partner or the existing partner possesses an intangible element, the intangible element is called _____ .

3. The _____ method may be applied when the new partnership capital equals the sum of (A) the old partners' capital and (B) the new partner's asset investment (excluding goodwill).

4. The _____ method is applied when the new partnership capital is greater than the sum of (A) the old partners' capital and (B) the new partner's asset investment (excluding goodwill).

5. In a business combination in which the owners of both businesses continue as owners of the enlarged business, the business combination can be characterized as a(n) _____ .

6. Legally, a change in the ownership of a partnership is a(n) _____ _____ of the old partnership.

7. Both the bonus method and the goodwill method can result in an inequity to one or more partners if the goodwill assumed to exist does not _____ _____ .

8. Appendix Question: When a partner is admitted into a partnership, the amount of existing partnership liabilities for which the new partner becomes responsible is treated for income tax reporting purposes as an increase to the partner's _____ _____ .

9. Appendix Question: When a partner retires from a partnership, the amount of existing partnership liabilities for which the retiring partner is no longer responsible is treated for income tax reporting purposes as _____ .

10. Appendix Question: A gain or loss for income tax reporting purposes on a partner's disposal of a partnership interest is computed by comparing the partner's _____ _____ to his or her _____ .

TRUE-OR-FALSE STATEMENTS

1. T F The purchase of an interest from one or more of a partnership's existing partners is a personal transaction between the incoming partner and the selling partner(s) that does **not** require any entry on the partnership books.

2. T F The bonus method is used **only** when new partners are admitted—never when partners leave the partnership.

3. T F An important role for accountants when a change in ownership occurs in a partnership is to calculate the value of the goodwill.

4. T F Inequities can occur when the bonus method is used.

5. T F Inequities can occur when the "recording the goodwill" method is used.

6. T F Inequities can occur when the "special profit and loss sharing provision" method is used.

7. T F The bonus method can be used whether the new partner possesses goodwill or the existing partners possess goodwill.

8. T F If the value of the goodwill is not given when a new partner is admitted into a partnership, the bonus method is used.

9. T F When a partner withdraws from a partnership, the partner's gain or loss for tax reporting purposes is calculated by comparing the amount of cash received to the partner's tax basis.

10. T F When a partner withdraws from a partnership, the share of existing partnership liabilities for which he or she is relieved of responsibility is treated as a cash distribution to that partner for tax reporting purposes.

MULTIPLE-CHOICE QUESTIONS

Conceptual Questions

1. When a change in ownership occurs, which of the following methods does **not** depart from GAAP?
   a. The bonus method.
   b. The recording the goodwill method.
   c. The revaluing of assets method.
   d. None of the above.

2. When a change in ownership occurs, which of the following methods **does** depart from GAAP?
   a. The bonus method.
   b. The recording the goodwill method.
   c. The revaluing of assets method.
   d. Both the recording the goodwill method and the revaluing of assets method.
   e. None of the above.

3. A partner is withdrawing from a partnership. Which of the following methods is **least** likely to be used because it often is impractical?
    a. The bonus method.
    b. The recording the goodwill method.
    c. The special profit and loss sharing provision method.
    d. The revaluing of assets method.
    e. None of the above.

4. The existing partnership possesses goodwill and has undervalued assets. An incoming partner desires to have the full amount of his or her cash contribution credited to his or her capital account. Which method would **not** be used?
    a. The bonus method.
    b. The revaluing of assets method.
    c. The recording the goodwill method.
    d. The special profit and loss sharing provision method.
    e. None of the above.

5. An existing partnership appears to possess goodwill; however, the incoming partner thinks there is an extremely high risk that the presumed goodwill will not materialize. The incoming partner is best protected by using which of the following methods?
    a. The bonus method.
    b. The revaluing of assets method.
    c. The recording the goodwill method.
    d. The special profit and loss sharing provision method.
    e. None of the above.

6. Which of the following occurs when a person is admitted into a partnership that possesses goodwill and the bonus method is used?
    a. An entry is made solely within the capital accounts.
    b. The new partner receives a credit to his or her capital account that is **less than** his or her capital contribution.
    c. The new partner receives a credit to his or her capital account that is **more than** his or her capital contribution.
    d. The new partner receives a credit to his or her capital account **equal to** his or her capital contribution.
    e. None of the above.

7. Which of the following occurs when a person is admitted into a partnership that possesses goodwill and the recording the goodwill method is used?
    a. An entry is made solely within the capital accounts.
    b. The new partner receives a credit to his or her capital account that is **less than** his or her capital contribution.
    c. The new partner receives a credit to his or her capital account that is **more than** his or her capital contribution.
    d. The new partner receives a credit to his or her capital account **equal to** his or her capital contribution.
    e. None of the above.

Application Questions

8. Data for the partnership of Daye and Knight are as follows:

	Daye	Knight
Capital balances	$100,000	$200,000
Profit and loss sharing ratio	40%	60%

Rane is to be admitted into the partnership and is to have a 25% interest in capital and profits with a cash contribution of $140,000. Under the bonus method, what are the capital account balances of Daye, Knight, and Rane immediately after Rane's admission?

    a. $100,000, $200,000, and $140,000, respectively.
    b. $112,000, $218,000, and $110,000, respectively.
    c. $115,000, $215,000, and $110,000, respectively.
    d. $148,000, $272,000, and $140,000, respectively.
    e. None of the above.

9. Use the information in Question 8. Under the recording the goodwill method, what are the capital account balances of Daye, Knight, and Rane immediately after Rane's admission?

    a. $100,000, $200,000, and $140,000, respectively.
    b. $112,000, $218,000, and $110,000, respectively.
    c. $115,000, $215,000, and $110,000, respectively.
    d. $148,000, $272,000, and $140,000, respectively.
    e. None of the above.

10. Pace, Strider, and Walker are partners having capital balances of $300,000, $200,000, and $100,000, respectively. Their profit and loss sharing ratio is 5:3:2, respectively. Walker is withdrawing from the partnership. The partners agree that the partnership possesses goodwill of $120,000, which is **not** to be recorded on the partnership books. The partners agree that Walker may take some office equipment having a book value of $15,000 and a current value of $25,000. The total **cash payment** to Walker in full settlement of Walker's partnership interest is

    a. $99,000
    b. $101,000
    c. $109,000
    d. $111,000
    e. None of the above.

11. Use the information in Question 10 and determine the capital balance of Pace after the withdrawal of Walker.

    a. $283,750
    b. $285,000
    c. $288,750
    d. $290,000
    e. None of the above.

12. Use the information in Question 10 and determine the capital balance of Pace after the withdrawal of Walker assuming all of the goodwill is recorded.

    a. $315,000
    b. $320,000

c. $360,000
d. $365,000
e. None of the above.

CHAPTER 27—SOLUTIONS

Completion Statements

1. business combination
2. goodwill
3. bonus
4. recording the goodwill
5. pooling of interests
6. dissolution
7. materialize
8. tax basis
9. proceeds
10. proceeds, tax basis

True-or-False Statements

1. False
2. False
3. False
4. True
5. True

6. False
7. True
8. False
9. False
10. True

Multiple-Choice Questions

1. a
2. d
3. c
4. a
5. d
6. b
7. d
8. b ($100,000 + $200,000 + $140,000 = $440,000; $440,000 × 25% = $110,000; $140,000 – $110,000 = $30,000 bonus to Daye and Knight, shared $12,000 (40%) and $18,000 (60%))
9. d ($140,000 ÷ 25% = $560,000; $560,000 – $440,000 = $120,000 of goodwill to be shared between Daye and Knight 40% and 60%, respectively.)
10. b ($100,000 + $2,000 share of undervalued office equipment + $24,000 share of goodwill = $126,000; $126,000 – $25,000 = $101,000)
11. d ($300,000 + $5,000 share of undervalued office equipment – $15,000 share of bonus given to Walker for goodwill = $290,000)
12. d ($300,000 + $60,000 share of goodwill + $5,000 share of under-valued office equipment = $365,000)

CHAPTER 28

PARTNERSHIPS: LIQUIDATIONS

CHAPTER HIGHLIGHTS

1. **Gains and losses incurred on the realization of assets** are allocated among the partners **in the profit and loss sharing ratio,** unless agreed to otherwise by the partners.

2. If a partner's Capital account is **not** sufficient to absorb his or her share of the losses incurred in liquidation, and such partner is unable to eliminate the deficit either by additional cash contribution or by setoff, the deficit is **allocated to the remaining partners** who have positive Capital balances.

3. A partner who has to absorb some or all of the capital deficit of another partner has **legal recourse** against that partner.

4. If profits and losses are shared in the ratio of the capital balances, none of the partners will ever have a deficit balance **until the losses incurred in liquidation exceed the total capital of the partnership.**

5. Sharing profits and losses **in the ratio of the capital balances** is one of the **most important safeguards** used in partnership agreements.

6. Under the **rule of setoff,** a deficit balance in a partner's capital account can be eliminated to the extent that such partner has a loan **to** the partnership.

7. Activity that occurs during the liquidation process can be portrayed in a **statement of realization and liquidation** (a historical statement).

8. Under the court procedure of **marshalling of assets,** partnership creditors have first priority as to partnership assets, and personal creditors of an insolvent partner have first priority as to the personal assets of that partner.

9. In a liquidation **under Chapter 7 of the bankruptcy statutes,** the marshalling of assets procedure is modified such that partnership creditors **share on a pro rata basis** with personal creditors of an insolvent partner in the distribution of the personal assets of that partner.

10. In installment liquidations, no cash distributions are made to partners **until creditors have been paid in full** (also true for lump-sum liquidations).

11. In installment liquidations, the amount to be distributed to each partner at any point in time can be determined by preparing either **schedules of safe payments** at each cash distribution date or a **cash distribution plan** at the beginning of the liquidation process.

12. Using either schedules of safe payments or a cash distribution plan results in the distribution of cash to partners in a manner that **brings the capital balances into the profit and loss sharing ratio.**

13. Conceptually, the first cash distribution to partners in an installment liquidation goes to that partner **who has the highest loss absorption potential.**

14. The loss absorption potential of each partner can be calculated by **dividing the capital balance by the profit and loss sharing percentage of that partner.** If a partner has a loan to the partnership, the loan should be added to the capital balance in making the calculation.

COMPLETION STATEMENTS

1. The termination of a partnership's business activities is known as _____ _____ .

2. The two kinds of liquidations are _____ and _____ _____ .

3. The subtraction of a partner's deficit balance in his or her Capital account from the balance of any loan outstanding to the partnership is done under the _____ _____ .

4. A legal doctrine whereby a partnership's creditors are given first claim on partnership assets, and personal creditors of an insolvent partner are given first claim on that partner's personal assets is the _____ .

5. An entirely historical statement that reflects only the actual transactions that have occurred during the liquidation process is called a(n) _____ .

6. An analysis done at the beginning of the liquidation process that informs partners when they will receive cash in relation to the other partners is called a(n) _____ _____ .

7. In an installment liquidation in which cash is distributed to all of the partners, the distribution of the last dollar distributed will be in the ratio of the _____ _____ .

8. If in the first installment liquidation cash is distributed to only one partner, that partner must have the highest _____ .

9. In installment liquidations, the alternative to preparing a cash distribution plan at the beginning of the liquidation process is to prepare a(n) _____ at each installment liquidation date.

10. When a schedule of safe payments is made, it is necessary to make the _____

_____ .

TRUE-OR-FALSE STATEMENTS

1. T F A partnership can file for bankruptcy protection under Chapters 7 or 11 of the bankruptcy statutes.

2. T F In installment liquidations, as opposed to lump-sum liquidations, cash distributions may be made to partners before full payment is made to partnership creditors.

3. T F If the capital balances are maintained in the profit and loss sharing ratio, a partner will never have to absorb the capital deficit of any other partner.

4. T F If the capital balances are maintained in the profit and loss sharing ratio, a partner could still lose more than his or her capital balance.

5. T F In liquidation, a partner's loan to the partnership is effectively treated as part of that partner's capital.

6. T F The statement of realization and liquidation is a pro forma statement.

7. T F When a partnership has a loan to a partner that is not collectible, the most equitable treatment is to share the loss in the profit and loss sharing ratio.

8. T F When a partner has a loan outstanding to the partnership, the loan ranks on an equal level with other partnership liabilities under the Uniform Partnership Act.

9. T F Under the marshalling of assets procedure used by the courts, partnership creditors of an insolvent partner have first priority as to the personal assets of that partner.

10. T F Under the Bankruptcy Reform Act of 1978, partnership creditors share on a pro rata basis with personal creditors of an insolvent partner in the distribution of the personal assets of that partner.

11. T F In a lump-sum liquidation, it is unnecessary to prepare a schedule of safe payments.

12. T F The schedule of safe payments is always prepared at the beginning of the liquidation process.

13. T F Both the use of a cash distribution plan and the use of schedules of safe payments would result in the exact same distribution of cash to individual partners as to timing and amounts.

14. T F In an installment liquidation, cash is always distributed first to that partner having the highest capital balance.

15. T F It would not make any sense to prepare a schedule of safe payments when a partnership is insolvent.

MULTIPLE-CHOICE QUESTIONS

Conceptual Questions

1. To minimize potential inequities in the liquidation process, how should cash installments be distributed to partners?
   a. In the profit and loss sharing ratio.
   b. In the ratio of capital balances.
   c. Equally.
   d. First to the partner having the highest capital balance.
   e. None of the above.

2. Which of the following items would **not** be used or be applicable to a lump-sum liquidation?
   a. The marshalling of assets principle.
   b. The Bankruptcy Reform Act of 1978.
   c. The rule of setoff.
   d. A schedule of safe payments.
   e. None of the above.

3. Under the marshalling of assets procedure (and disregarding the Bankruptcy Reform Act of 1978), which of the following statements is **false?**
   a. Partnership creditors have first claim on partnership assets.
   b. Partnership creditors share on a pro rata basis with personal creditors of an insolvent partner in the distribution of the personal assets of such partner.
   c. Personal creditors of an insolvent partner have first priority as to the personal assets of such partner.
   d. Personal creditors of an insolvent partner and partnership creditors have priority over the claims of other partners who made up a capital deficit of an insolvent partner by making a contribution.
   e. None of the above.

4. Which of the following statements is correct under the rule of setoff?
   a. A partner's capital deficit can be eliminated to the extent that the partnership has a loan to that partner.
   b. Personal creditors of an insolvent partner have first claim as to the personal assets of that partner.
   c. If a partner is unable to make good his or her capital deficit, other partners who absorb the deficit have legal recourse against the insolvent partner.
   d. If cash is distributed to a partner who has a loan to the partnership and a positive capital balance, the cash distribution shall be applied in a manner that settles the partnership loan before any settlement of the partner's capital balance.
   e. None of the above.

5. In the first installment liquidation, cash was distributed only to one of the partners. Which of the following items must be true for this partner?

   a. He or she had the highest capital balance.
   b. He or she had the highest profit and loss sharing percentage.
   c. He or she had the highest loss absorption potential.
   d. He or she was the only partner having a loan outstanding to the partnership.
   e. None of the above.

6. What is the nature of the items listed below?

	Statement of Realization and Liquidation	Schedule of Safe Payments
a.	Historical	Point in time
b.	Point in time	Historical
c.	Point in time	Point in time
d.	Historical	Historical

Application Questions

7. The following condensed balance sheet is presented for the partnership of Banks, Robb, and Teller, who share profits and losses in the ratio of 4:3:2, respectively:

Cash	$ 20,000
Other assets	380,000
	$400,000
Liabilities	$148,000
Capital, Banks	60,000
Capital, Robb	122,000
Capital, Teller	70,000
	$400,000

   The partners decided to liquidate the partnership. The other assets are sold for $200,000. How should the available cash be distributed?

   a. Banks, -0-; Robb, $50,000; Teller, $22,000.
   b. Banks, -0-; Robb, $52,000; Teller, $20,000.
   c. Banks, $24,000; Robb, $24,000; Teller, $24,000.
   d. Banks, $32,000; Robb, $24,000; Teller, $16,000.
   e. None of the above.

8. Use the same information as in Question 7, except that Banks has a capital balance of $45,000 (instead of $60,000) and a loan to the partnership of $15,000.

   a. Banks, -0-; Robb, $50,000; Teller, $22,000.
   b. Banks, $15,000; Robb, $41,000; Teller, $16,000.
   c. Banks, $15,000; Robb, $42,500; Teller, $14,500.
   d. Banks, $15,000; Robb, $62,000; Teller, $30,000.
   e. None of the above.

9. Use the same information as in Question 7, except that the other assets of $380,000 include a $45,000 note receivable from Teller, who is personally insolvent. (Continue to assume that the remaining noncash assets were sold for $200,000.)

   a. Banks, -0-; Robb, $50,000; Teller, $22,000.
   b. Banks, -0-; Robb, $52,000; Teller, $20,000.
   c. Banks, -0-; Robb, $77,000; Teller, -0-.
   d. Banks, -0-; Robb, $72,000; Teller, -0-.
   e. None of the above.

10. The following condensed balance sheet is presented as of April 1, 19X1, for the partnership of Groopie, Loner, and Middler, who share profits and losses in the ratio of 4:3:1, respectively:

Cash	$ 50,000
Other assets	550,000
	$600,000
Liabilities	$214,000
Capital, Groopie	136,000
Capital, Loner	170,000
Capital, Middler	80,000
	$600,000

The partners decided to liquidate the partnership. On April 25, 19X1, the first cash sale of other assets with a carrying amount of $270,000 realized $230,000. Safe installment payments to the partners are to be made on this date. How should the available cash be distributed to the partners?

   a. Groopie, $22,000; Loner, $22,000; Middler, $22,000.
   b. Groopie, $140,000; Loner, $105,000; Middler, $35,000.
   c. Groopie, -0-; Loner, $32,000; Middler, $34,000.
   d. Groopie, -0-; Loner, $50,000; Middler, $40,000.
   e. None of the above.

CHAPTER 28—SOLUTIONS

Completion Statements

     1. liquidation
     2. lump-sum, installment
     3. rule of setoff
     4. marshall of assets procedure
     5. statement of realization and liquidation
     6. cash distribution plan
     7. capital balances
     8. loss absorption potential
     9. schedule of safe payments
    10. two worst-case assumptions

True-or-False Statements

1. True	9. False
2. False	10. True
3. False	11. True
4. True	12. False
5. True	13. True
6. False	14. False
7. False	15. True
8. False	

Multiple-Choice Questions

1. e
2. d
3. b
4. e
5. c
6. a
7. a (Allocate $180,000 loss to partners using 4:3:2 ratio; Allocate resulting $20,000 deficit of Banks to Robb and Teller in 3:2 ratio.)
8. a
9. d (Charge $45,000 uncollectible receivable to Teller's capital account; allocate $135,000 loss to partners using 4:3:2 ratio; allocate resulting $5,000 deficit of Teller to Robb inasmuch as Banks has a zero capital balance at this point.)
10. c (Allocate $40,000 loss to partners in 4:3:1 ratio; make worst-case assumption on remaining noncash assets of $280,000, allocating to partners in a 4:3:1 ratio; make second worst-case assumption on resulting $24,000 deficit of Groopie, allocating to Loner and Middler in a 3:1 ratio.)

CHAPTER 29
ESTATES AND TRUSTS

CHAPTER HIGHLIGHTS

1. Trusts that are created by a gift made in the will of a decedent are called **testamentary trusts.**

2. **Trustees** hold legal title to the property and administer the trust for the benefit of one or more other persons, who are called **beneficiaries.**

3. An **income beneficiary** is entitled to the income earned by the trust's assets, which are referred to as the **trust principal,** or **corpus.**

4. A **principal beneficiary** is entitled to the principal, or corpus, of the trust, which is distributed according to the terms of the trust agreement (usually at the specified termination date of the trust).

5. When the income and principal beneficiaries are **different persons,** a built-in clash of interests exists as to **who gets what.**

6. When the income and principal beneficiaries are the **same person(s),** a built-in clash of interests exists as to the **timing of distributions.**

7. Under the Revised Uniform Principal and Income Act (of 1962), the **rights of the income beneficiary begin at the date of death of the decedent** who created the trust.

8. The **interests of the income beneficiary** of the trust must be accounted for separately from the interests of the principal beneficiary of the trust **during the period of the estate administration,** as well as after the property is actually transferred to the trustee.

9. In determining **whether a transaction pertains to principal or income,** the determination is made by referring to (A) first, the trust agreement; (B) second, state law (which may be based on the Revised Uniform Principal and Income Act (of 1962); (C) third, case law; and (D) fourth, generally accepted accounting principles.

10. In determining **at the time of the person's death** the assets that are to be treated as part of the trust principal, the **accrual basis** is to be used (under the Revised Principal and Income Act).

11. **Probate** is the act by which the court determines if the will submitted to it meets the statutory requirements concerning wills. If the court so determines, then it issues a certificate or decree that enables the terms of the will to be carried out.

12. Under the **probate laws,** the affairs of decedents must be administered by fiduciaries who are **subject to the control of the state probate courts.**

13. A gift of **personal** property is called a **legacy;** a gift of **real** property is called a **devise.**

14. The **fiduciary of an estate** (the **executor** if named in the will, or the **administrator** if appointed by the probate court) (A) takes an inventory of the decedent's property, (B) pays estate liabilities, (C) prepares and files tax returns for the decedent and the decedent's estate.

15. **Accounting for trusts** is virtually identical to the accounting for estates, even though the nature of the transactions is substantially different.

16. For both estates and trusts, the interests of both the income beneficiary and the principal beneficiary can easily be **accounted for in a single general ledger using only one bank account** (that is separated into two general ledger accounts—one that pertains to principal and one that pertains to income).

17. Under the Revised Uniform Principal and Income Act (of 1962), **depreciation is mandatory,** and **unusual charges** against income **may be recouped from income** over a reasonable period of time.

18. Under the Revised Uniform Principal and Income Act (of 1962), **certain costs and expenses must be charged to principal** (costs of investing principal assets, costs of preparing property for rental or sale, taxes on gains allocated to principal, costs incurred to protect trust property). Certain other costs and expenses must be shared equally between principal and income (court costs, attorney fees, accounting fees, trustee's fees).

COMPLETION STATEMENTS

1. The making of plans for the orderly transfer of personal property upon death is known as _____ .

2. A person appointed by the court to administer the affairs of a decedent when no such person was named in the will is called a(n) _____ .

3. A person who is named in a decedent's will to serve as the personal representative of the decedent in administering the estate and who is appointed by the court to serve in that capacity is called a(n) _____ .

4. A gift of real property is referred to as a(n) _____ .

5. A gift of personal property is referred to as a(n) _____ .

6. A trust that is created during the life of a person is called a(n) _____ _____ .

7. A trust that comes into being upon the death of a person pursuant to provisions in the will of the decedent is called a(n) _____ trust.

8. That party to a trust who is entitled to the income earned on trust assets is called the _____ .

9. That party to a trust who is entitled to the principal or corpus of the trust is called the _____ .

10. That party to a trust who takes title to trust property and administers the property for the benefit of others is called the _____ .

11. The party to a trust agreement who created the trust is called the _____
_____ .

12. A term used to refer to having died with a will is _____ .

13. A term used to refer to having died without a will is _____ .

14. The recipient of personal property being distributed pursuant to a will is called a(n)
_____ .

15. For the most part, the basis used in accounting for estates and trusts is the _____
_____ basis.

16. The first reference source in determining whether an item pertains to trust income or trust principal is the _____ .

17. The second reference source in determining whether an item pertains to trust income or trust principal is _____ .

18. The burden of taxation for federal estate taxes falls on the _____ .

19. The burden of taxation for state inheritance taxes falls on each individual _____
_____ .

20. A term used to describe a transfer between spouses that is exempt from transfer taxes is called a(n) _____ .

21. The costs of investing and reinvesting principal assets are charged against _____
_____ .

TRUE-OR-FALSE STATEMENTS

1. T F The trustee is commonly referred to as a fiduciary.

2. T F The person creating the trust is called the trustor.

3. T F The income and principal beneficiary(s) may **not** be the same person(s).

4. T F A built-in conflict of interest does **not** exist when the income and principal beneficiary are the same person.

5. T F When the income and principal beneficiary(s) are **not** the same person(s), the built-in conflict of interests between the two classes revolves around the timing of distributions.

6. T F Trusts that are created by a gift made in the will of a decedent are called testamentary trusts.

7. T F State statutes pertaining to trusts must be followed even if the terms of the trust agreement conflict with such laws.

8. T F The rights of the income beneficiary under a testamentary trust commence at the time of the decedent's death—not at the time the property is actually distributed to the trustee.

9. T F For income tax reporting purposes, **both** estates and trusts are treated as taxable entities.

10. T F Conceptually, **both** estates and trusts are viewed as comprising two separate accounting entities—a "principal entity" and an "income entity."

11. T F In determining whether a transaction pertains to principal or income, generally accepted accounting principles are often the major point of reference.

12. T F When the treatment to be accorded an item is **not** clearly set forth in the trust agreement or state statutes, the determination of whether an item pertains to income or principal is made by the fiduciary—not the trust accountant.

13. T F When the income beneficiary and the principal beneficiary are **not** the same person, separate bank accounts must be maintained for cash pertaining to income and cash pertaining to principal.

14. T F In determining at the time of the person's death the assets that are to be treated as part of the trust principal, the Revised Uniform Principal and Income Act provides, in most respects, for the use of the accrual basis.

15. T F The income rights of the income beneficiary are established at the end of the estate administration using the accrual basis in most respects.

16. T F The probate courts deal only with cases in which a decedent has died testate (with a will).

17. T F In probate administration, the courts will appoint an executor if one is **not** named in the will.

18. T F In probate administration, the probate court does **not** take title to a decedent's property.

19. T F A gift of personal property is called a legacy.

20. T F Unlike state inheritance taxes, the federal estate tax is based on the right to give property.

21. T F Accounting for trusts parallels the accounting for estates.

22. T F The nature of the transactions for an estate are **not** much different from the nature of the transactions for a trust.

23. T F Under the Revised Uniform Principal and Income Act, depreciation is mandatory.

24. T F Under the Revised Uniform Principal and Income Act, extraordinary repairs are to be charged to principal—not to income.

25. T F Losses of any business in which principal is invested are charged to principal under the Revised Uniform Principal and Income Act.

MULTIPLE-CHOICE QUESTIONS

Conceptual Questions

1. Which of the following persons is a party to a trust agreement?

	Legatee	Executor
a.	Yes	Yes
b.	No	No
c.	Yes	No
d.	No	Yes

2. Which of the following parties takes title to the property that it administers?

	Trustee	Executor
a.	Yes	Yes
b.	No	No
c.	Yes	No
d.	No	Yes

3. Which kind of clash of interests exists when the income beneficiary and the principal beneficiary are **not** the same party?
   a. The timing of the distributions.
   b. Who pays the estate taxes.
   c. Who pays the cost of probate.
   d. Who gets what.
   e. None of the above.

4. In determining whether a transaction pertains to principal or income, which of the following is the **first** place to look?
   a. Case law.
   b. Generally accepted accounting principles.
   c. State law.

d. The trust agreement.
e. The Revised Uniform Principal and Income Act.

5. Testamentary trusts are deemed to be created at the
   a. Conclusion of probate proceedings.
   b. Time the trustor signs the trust agreement.
   c. Time of the trustor's death.
   d. Time the trustee takes possession of the property.
   e. None of the above.

6. Which of the following transactions would **not** result in either an increase **or** a decrease in the trust principal?
   a. Gains on disposition of principal assets.
   b. Losses on disposition of principal assets.
   c. Distribution of gifts.
   d. Payment of funeral expenses.
   e. None of the above.

7. Under the Revised Uniform Principal and Income Act (of 1962), which of the following is correct?
   a. Extraordinary repairs paid out of principal may be recouped from income through depreciation charges.
   b. Depreciation is optional.
   c. The costs of preparing property for rental or sale are charged against income.
   d. Costs incurred in making capital improvements paid out of principal may **not** be recouped from income through depreciation charges.
   e. None of the above.

Application Questions

8. Depreciation expense was recorded on trust assets, as provided for under the Revised Uniform and Principal Act (of 1962). Which of the following debits and credits would **not** be made or eventually result from this action?

	Principal Entity	Income Entity
a.	Debit Cash.	Credit Cash.
b.	Debit Depreciation Expense.	Credit Accumulated Depreciation.
c.	Credit Accumulated Depreciation.	Debit Depreciation Expense.
d.	Debit Due from Income.	Credit Due to Principal.
e.	None of the above.	

9. Major unexpected repairs were paid out of trust principal. These repairs should benefit the next 5 years, counting the current year. Which of the following debits and credits would **not** be made or eventually result from this action assuming recoupment may be made from the income beneficiary?

	Principal Entity	Income Entity
a.	Debit Major Repairs.	Credit Accumulated Repairs Amortization.
b.	Credit Major Repairs.	Debit Repairs Expense.
c.	Debit Due from Income.	Credit Due to Principal.
d.	Debit Cash.	Credit Cash.

CHAPTER 29—SOLUTIONS

Completion Statements

1. estate planning
2. administrator
3. executor
4. devise
5. legacy
6. inter vivos
7. testamentary
8. income beneficiary
9. remainderman or principal beneficiary
10. trustee
11. trustor
12. testate
13. intestate
14. legatee
15. cash
16. trust agreement
17. state trust laws
18. estate
19. heir
20. marital deduction
21. principal

True-or-False Statements

1. True
2. True
3. False
4. False
5. False
6. True
7. False
8. True
9. True
10. True
11. False
12. True
13. False
14. True
15. False
16. False
17. False
18. True
19. True
20. True
21. True
22. False
23. True
24. False
25. True

Multiple-Choice Questions

1. b
2. c
3. d
4. d
5. c
6. e
7. a
8. b
9. a